SUCCESSFUL

ENTREPRENEURIAL

MANAGEMENT

HOW TO CREATE
PERSONAL
AND
BUSINESS ADVANTAGE

Century Communications

JOHN BUTLER

Published by: Century Communications,
                         3 Newlands Business Park, Naas Road,
                         Dublin 22, Ireland.
                         Telephone: 353-1-4595950
                         Fax: 353-1-4595949
                         E-mail: butlerj@century-management.ie

Author: John Butler

Edited by: Michael Freeman MCB

Design and Origination: Treadstone International Ltd.

Printed by: Colour Book

Ordering Information: This book is available through most good
                         bookshops, or direct from the publisher at
                         special quantity discount rates when purchased
                         in bulk by organisations, associations, libraries,
                         or businesses.

ISBN: ISBN 1 903106 00 1

CONTENTS

THIS BOOK IS DEDICATED TO
MY BEST FRIEND, LOVING WIFE, AND BUSINESS PARTNER IMELDA
FOR HER STEADFAST SUPPORT AND INSPIRATION
MY FANTASTIC DAUGHTER MICHELLE WHOSE YOUTHFUL WISDOM
HELPED ME AT CRITICAL POINTS OF RESEARCH AND DEVELOPMENT
AND
MY FANTASTIC DAUGHTER MARIA WHO BOTH ENCOURAGED AND
CHALLENGED ME CONTINUOUSLY TO GET PUBLISHED.

ACKNOWLEDGEMENTS

The influences of more than 100,000 people are packed into this book. They have contributed directly or indirectly to my own development and that of my team. My own thoughts have been influenced by thousands of entrepreneurs and professional managers with whom I have worked over the last ten years, which was one of the most dramatic periods in business history.

This book is a synthesis and a consolidation of the best ideas, techniques and strategies that I have learned and practised throughout my career. I have had some of the best teachers in the world – the men and women who are at the coal-face of business every day. I thank them all.

I thank in particular:

- The thousands of entrepreneurs and business owners, and executives and professional managers who put their faith in me as their mentor, coach and adviser. Their experiences have shaped my experiences. As a result, I have become a translator and a disseminator of *their* wisdom to thousands of other people on the journey of life and business development.

- Wonderful thinkers, writers and speakers including Ken Blanchard, Stephen Covey, Peter Drucker, Daniel Goleman, Michael Hammer, Rosabeth Moss Kanter, Tom Peters, Peter Senge and Ken Shelton. Through their books and seminars, these people have given me a deep insight into the best ideas and techniques in the world today.

- The outstanding professionals around the world who continuously help me in numerous ways to formulate my thoughts and ideas. They include: Frank and Claudia Scheelen in Germany, Sune and Sophia Gellberg in Sweden, Tony Quiterio Paulo in Portugal, Alain Dolbeau, Patrice Fabert, Marc Levitt and Claude Arheix in France, Adi Eber in Austria, Max Muller, and Henk Kalkman in Holland, Fanny Jonmundsdottir in Iceland, and Ritva Serkamo, Jari Sarasvuo and Fredrik Shauman in Finland, Janes Hudovernik in Slovenia and Trevor Pons in England.

- Thom and Bev Shields in New Zealand, Bill Natsumi in Japan, Robert and Mavis Yu in Taiwan and Martin Westcott in South Africa.

- Ib Moller and Paul Fergus and their great team in Canada.

- Cam and Christina Fraser, Victor Risling, Don Klassen, Steve and Diane Muntean, Voss and Robin Graham, Cliff Hurst, David Pemberton and a host of professional consultants throughout the United States of America.

- Bill, Dave and Karen Bonnstetter at TTI International in Arizona for the fantastic partnership we are developing. I thank Bill, in particular, for his advice, insights and brilliant research on the subject of personality.

- My personal assistant Louise Sheeran who painstakingly typed the words for this book many times. I thank Linda Ronan who prepared early drafts and Denise Byrne, Peggy Redmond, Sandra Doble, Bridget Hayden, Martina Moran and Bernie Fagan, for their back-up.

- Michael Freeman, my editor and publishing director, whose expertise contributed greatly to the production of this book. He played a huge role in the preparation of the manuscript. His ability to make words work and develop concepts is superb.

- Dick and Liz Molloy in Galway, David and Christine Smyth in Waterford, Billy and Noelle O'Connor in Cork, Kevin and Marie Fahey in Athlone, Bart and Iris McEnroe in Cavan, Padraig and Catriona Berry in Wicklow, and Kevin Davey, David Flood, Freddie O'Neill, Brian and Mary Richardson and Sheana O'Sullivan all in Dublin. I am privileged to work with this team of true professionals who inspire me constantly by their sheer grit and honest endeavours.

- Brian Tracy, who is my role model, for his special friendship. I thank Brian for believing in me. I thank him also for the many inspiring hours that we spent in Ireland, and at his home in San Diego discussing our common goals. His personal advice to me has been a major factor in my success. I will never forget his energy and professionalism during his three-day visit to the four corners of Ireland in May 1997 during which he packed in six seminars in five venues and addressed more than 3,000 managers.

- My wife Imelda who is my best friend and true-life partner. In addition to being a wonderful wife and mother, she is a dynamic business consultant. Working together, we are building one of the most successful consultancy practices in Europe today.

- My daughter, Maria, who kept challenging me to finish this book with the gutsy determination of a 15-year-old entrepreneurial teenager. Meanwhile, my elder daughter Michelle, helped me – unwittingly on many occasions – with her youthful wisdom at critical points while I was writing the many drafts of the manuscript.

Finally, I acknowledge the support of my mother and father, brothers and sisters and my extended family and friends. Their support and influence has had a major impact on my own development.

My family and friends are the best motivation that anyone could have for completing a work of this kind.

During the past ten years, I have been a personal adviser and mentor with several thousand business owners and entrepreneurs. I have spent countless hours looking into their eyes, listening to their stories, and questioning their motives and actions. While consulting and coaching with them, I found that 80% of the more successful ones had uncanny similarities in their story lines.

At first, they gave me a rag-bag of information with apparently no particular common elements that I could detect. Then Eureka!, I saw specific patterns of behaviour, mindsets and style for each of them. As this common feature became more apparent, I became more obsessed with unlocking the 'secret' of entrepreneurial success.

During this period, I was involved with numerous management and organisational development projects with thousands of professional managers who head up corporate teams and lead businesses and organisations. I discovered that some believe that management is something you are born with, or it is 'something you do to other people'. The majority try, often unsuccessfully, to practise management as a science and a skill. The elite few know that professional management is a mix of innate abilities, acquired competencies, and a mature mental mindset.

IF ONLY...

Facing each other across a room, the entrepreneur and the professional manager play an 'if only' game. The professional manager says: 'If only I could shake off the shackles of the bureaucratic corporate set-up, I would reach my enormous potential with relative ease. I want to take risks and have a go, but I am so restrained by the system that I am now in'. The entrepreneur says: 'If only I had the skills of the professional manager, I would plan, organise, lead and control my business activities with more discipline, and effectiveness, through a more streamlined management structure'.

I believe that half of the world's professional managers and executives would like to be entrepreneurs. I believe that half of all business owners and entrepreneurs wish that they could steal some of the professionalism of 'real' managers. My contention is that the entrepreneur and the professional manager have a lot to learn from each other. Both can do this by embracing the entrepreneurial management spirit, ethic and methodology.

The limitations that professional managers place on themselves are mental, psychological and real. But they are mostly mental. Their belief system is different from the entrepreneur. Their need for stability, structure and safety is the antithesis of everything in which the entrepreneur believes. They become conditioned to a certain way of doing things. Professional managers have twin challenges; one is to break out of their own mental comfort zone, and a second is to deal with their organisation's stranglehold.

In contrast, the pure entrepreneur has more mental freedom and is not as hemmed in by organisational constraints.

Few people understand what motivates the entrepreneur. Many people think that entrepreneurs are driven solely by money, by greed or by self-promotion. They cannot comprehend that entrepreneurs have a 'spiritual loneliness' which does not mean that they are loners or alone. They become spiritual prisoners to their focused pursuit of their life's passion. The lay person's view is that certain personality types would make better entrepreneurs. This is nonsense. The entrepreneurial passion even over-rides different personality types because the stronger emotion and drive always wins out. I believe it's an addictive opportunity for entrepreneurs to express their potential in a meaningful way.

FELLOW PRISONERS

All entrepreneurs have two primary frustrations. The first is to give explanation to these emotions and the second is to connect with somebody who truly understands what they're about. To add to their frustrations, entrepreneurs who meet other entrepreneurs have difficulty verbalising this predicament. However, they can see it, sense it and even feel it in a fellow entrepreneur. They are prisoners of their own entrepreneurial journey.

To meet a like-minded person who clearly understands the inner quest of the entrepreneur is rare. The real struggle in this regard for the entrepreneur is to connect with somebody who understands these emotions and mentalities.

The entrepreneur has been given a dictionary definition of: 'one who organises and directs a business undertaking, assuming the risk for the sake of the profit'. These elements of personal risk and the profit motive differentiate entrepreneurs from the corporate professional managers and executives who perform their duties in return for a salary.

CHANGE IS SCARY

Because of this difference, it is not surprising that for generations entrepreneurs and professional managers have approached their work with different mind-sets. Such different approaches were acceptable in the past. Today, certainty is replaced by choice. Choice is scary. Change is scary. If we combine the original, raw, entrepreneurial spirit with solid and structured professional management skills we achieve a new synergy which I call entrepreneurial management. This new dynamic is critical to handling choice and change and creating personal and business advantage in the 21st century.

Professional managers and entrepreneurs throughout the world face conflicting demands and expectations, constraints and opportunities. The new world is full of paradoxes which are directly related to professional management development and the entrepreneurial movement. Entrepreneurs are in more demand than ever. And we seem to be entering a new era in which most members of the labour force will be offered some form of self- employment during their work career. The evidence of this move to self-employment is everywhere. It is evidenced in contracting, outsourcing, value-adding partnerships, telecottaging and small-office-home-office (SOHO) entrepreneurs.

Management and work performance competencies are being measured as never before. Different formulas of employeeship are replacing the traditional 'job for life'! An Economic and Social Research Institute (ESRI) survey shows that 7% of the workforce are part-timers and that this figure is rising fast. Some 45% of the 65,000 jobs in the retail sector are filled by part-timers and this figure is set to increase to 75% early in the 21st century. Developments in new technology and telecommunications are giving individuals freedoms that they only dreamed about. There is no escaping it. Adjustments to a new world of individualism will dominate our lives in the foreseeable future.

A FRESH APPROACH

The business world will need professional managers who have the required skills, know-how and attitudes to manage that adjustment successfully. Professional management methods have developed from the Industrial Revolution over the past 200 years. Many struggling business organisations are using traditional management methods. They wonder why their businesses are struggling. Because of the accelerated pace of change in today's business and social worlds there is a need as never before for a fresh approach. This book presents a fresh approach.

The purpose of this book is to challenge your thinking and to call you into action to embrace and blend the mix of the disciplines of professional management and the entrepreneurial spirit to create personal and business advantage. Only you can bring your own flavour to this challenge. Ultimately, this is where your own entrepreneurial management opportunity lies.

Just as excellence, success and learning are journeys, and never destinations, so also is entrepreneurial management. It's the progressive development of your thinking, modus operandi and ultimately, your results.

Throughout this book, you will read about what is needed to develop the competencies necessary to become an entrepreneurial manager. You will recognise many of these competencies as traditional management practices. Their application, however, is all-important. If they are applied in the traditional way, they will have ordinary or average impact. If you apply them as an entrepreneurial manager, you will achieve extraordinary results.

Be careful that you don't interpret traditional management practices as wrong. In fact, few of the traditional management practices are wrong. Many managers resist new change initiatives by using old thinking frameworks and old experiences as their benchmark ('Once bitten, twice shy'). Their limited, linear thinking is preventing them from embracing old concepts that have been adapted in to a new form. Why does there have to be a right or wrong, yes or no, black or white answer? It is surely better to provide an *appropriate* answer that works.

THE TOOLS OF YOUR TRADE

Abraham Maslow, the godfather of motivational theorists, was watching his three-year-old grandson playing. The three-year-old was banging everything within reach with his new plastic toy hammer that he'd received for his third birthday. The wise old Maslow observed that, when the only tool you have is a hammer, everything looks like a nail! Similarly, when the tools that you have as an entrepreneur or as a manager are limited or under-utilised, their impact will be limited.

Many traditional management ideas are excellent in their own way. The reason they are under utilised has more often got to do with mental, even moral firepower (the entrepreneurial spirit!), than any other factor. There are very few really good new management skills and concepts that haven't been around for years. So, whether you are a professional manager or an entrepreneur, you should breathe new life into your activities with entrepreneurial management.

I am privileged to have worked with a number of people who fit the profile of the model entrepreneurial manager. Some are salaried executives who earn extraordinary bonuses because of the freedom and growth potential and risk they bring to professional management. Others are pure entrepreneurs who have matured and grown from being wild pioneers to learning and developing professional management skills.

Both realise that entepreneurialism and professional management can be brought together in a powerful synergy. How to achieve that synergy is shown in this book.

AN OPPORTUNITY TO CHANGE

More ...   Producers and business leaders want more sales, more profit, faster processes, more efficient systems, more productivity and more output.

Less ...   But they want to invest less time, less people, less money, less input to achieve it.

More ...   Consumers want more cars, better televisions, faster computers, more leisure time and more pleasure time customised to individual tastes.

Less ...   But they want them different, newer and at a cheaper price.

Customers have never in history had such a range of choices. Businesses have never had such a number of challenges. Central to the reconciliation of choice and challenge, and demand and supply, is change. Change provides opportunity.

Rapid change (accelerated change) is only a problem or a negative challenge if the mindset believes it to be so. Rapid change provides an almost infinite range of possibilities and opportunities to improve, grow, innovate, speed up, economise, simplify, differentiate, and much more.

Within the last ten years of the 20th century, business managers and leaders have had to adapt their thinking and approaches from the traditional thinking and approaches of the previous twenty years.

Sales to mass markets have had to change to sales to customised one-to-one markets. Meanwhile, distribution has changed from local to global, snail-mail (post) is being replaced by e-mail, brochures are being replaced by web pages on the Internet, shopping has been transformed to PC/TV shopping. Reality is being replaced by virtual reality with 3-D images of cars, clothes, furniture and jewellery with which you can interact on your PC/TV. You can have your cars or clothes fitted and customised to your preferred shapes and colours through holographic imagery, before ordering through e-mail or voice mail, (by speaking to your PC) from an automated warehouse at the far side of the world. Delivery will be to your door at a time convenient to you, at a price to fit your pocket, later that day or next day at the latest.

How about having a flat screen on each wall of your office? As you pass each flat screen, without stopping, your customised mentor talks to you, tells you what to eat today, how your heart rate is, where your partner is. She (your mentor) offers to order the shopping for you if you stop for ten seconds and check off a spoken list that she shows you from the flat screen on the wall, on the dashboard of your car, on your watch or from your mobile phone or smart-card sized notebook. If you don't want to stop, you can check it off as you walk by each flat screen, as you walk through the door, and you can sign off the list when you climb into your car, giving your pin number, before asking your mentor to get your travel agent for a flat screen talk face-to-face about your travel plans. Within twenty years, you may get rid of all the screens and see and thought-transfer your commands courtesy of a chip and screen that are connected to your brain and your eyes.

Meanwhile, cultures are changing almost with the speed of mood swings. Buy a car one day, tire of it the next ? Replace it with a similar car in a different colour next day or dispose of it altogether and don't worry about paying back the bank. There's always another bank. And life is for living today.

The 90's may have been called 'the decade of change'; the first decade of the 21st century will be 'the decade of instant response'. We had Man on the Moon in the 60's; less than 50 years later we'll want Man on Mars.

Millions of people around the world are in direct contact with each other through telecommunications such as the Internet, Intranet, Extranet, E-mail, Teleconferencing and global television. Man on Mars may be just another piece of computer software away.

The development of electronic communications and new technology allows intellectual capital and the flow of information to have more impact than the movement of goods. The microchip, which did not exist three decades ago, is helping people to achieve things beyond their wildest dreams.

The fastest rate of change in the history of mankind is here. It's happening in business, in society, in politics and in leisure. How to match the rate of change, how to cope with it, how to manage the many variables that are changing with change is the great challenge and great opportunity faced by business owners and executives all over the world for the 21st century.

THE CREATING BUSINESS ADVANTAGE MODEL™

PULL FACTORS

ENABLERS

COMPETENCIES
Define • Measure • Develop

PROCESSES
CIP • Analysis • BPM

SYSTEMS
Structures • Technologies

RESOURCES
Identify • Deploy • Optimise

PERSONAL
INTERPERSONAL
TEAM
ORGANISATION
CUSTOMERS

PUSH FACTORS

Ref. Page 107

Ref. Page 183

Your ability to integrate the dynamic systems within this book will ultimately determine the degree to which you will create personal and business advantage.

The CBA™ system integrates the best ideas and techniques of Entrepreneurial Management into one all-embracing system. This system gives you a panoramic view of all the elements and drivers required to help achieve your personal and business goals.

There are three stages in the operation of the CBA™ system. The first stage in all business development is human performance improvement. Ideally, the interaction between the personal (P), the interpersonal (I), the team (T), organisational (O) and customer (C) elements should be as smooth and rhythmic as possible – like the cogs in a well - oiled, finely tuned Swiss watch. The challenge at this stage is how to maximise human potential.

The second stage in creating personal and business advantage is to benchmark best practice competencies, understand business process management and structures, engage in systems thinking technologies, and deploy resources optimally. These are the essential infrastructures for the creation of personal and business advantage – the rail tracks upon which the fast moving train of enterprise runs.

The third stage of the CBA™ system is to engage in the exercises of Strategic Thinking and Strategic Planning to win the business game. The development of a total winning strategy is critical to entrepreneurial management success. Once the strategy team embraces this approach, much higher quality and sustainable planning emerges. Humans are much more emotional than analytical – especially with regard to their future history.

Getting inputs from a critical mass of people at different stages is central to developing a shared strategy that creates a sense of ownership and commitment. The Strategic Thinking and Planning (STP) model is a vehicle with which to achieve this.

I

MASTERING CHANGE:
21st century reality

Joe Smith was a hard working manager. He had been with the company for 15 years, and spent 12 of those as manager. His company is a classic success story of people, products, service and profits. He had contributed to that success. He knew his job inside out. He was loyal and willing. But something strange was happening that had not happened before in all of his 15 years in the company.

He worked ever harder, his productivity was up, but he found it more and more difficult to keep up with the increasing pace of events around him. His company and his industry were changing rapidly. He didn't understand how it could be so fast.

He felt overwhelmed by the enormity of changes. He was caught in a whirlwind. Like a lion in a cage, he was trapped. In reality, the world had moved on. But Joe was just working hard.

His managing director was struggling with how best to help Joe to cope with this new reality, and I asked him the zero-based question: 'Knowing what you now know about Joe Smith, would you still hire him?' The managing director answered with a definite 'Yes'.

Joe was one of many executives in similar circumstances in the company. But as part of a company-wide, root and branch, change strategy, I started working with Joe on defining, measuring and developing his core competencies. With the encouragement and support of his managing director, Joe embarked on a two-year development process. Over the first six months, he attended 18 days of specialised training to beef up his personal, professional and business acumen. He literally became a learning machine.

The ripple effect on his family life, his personal work performance, his team effectiveness and his relationship with his managing director was remarkable. Within 15 months, he was promoted with a 35% increase in salary. He has learned how to work smarter and not as hard. Joe has embraced personal and professional change, and literally transformed his life for the better.

DISARRAY AT ABC SERVICES

ABC Services have a staff of 75 people, a turnover of €18.5m and last year made a profit of €1.3m. An outsider's view of the business could suggest that 'everything is rosy'. Good finances, good product and customer base, good business location and site, a loyal staff. But ...

The rate of change outside the business was phenomenally greater than the rate of change inside the business. The managing director realised that the future was not so rosy. 'We must prepare for a fight. Or we must change. We must do something.' What to do was their worry. The managing director and his fellow executives felt that they knew the 'Whys' and 'Whats' of Change. The 'How' was the stumbling block. It was a mystery.

We conducted qualitative and quantitative surveys at every level in the company to establish where the real problem was coming from and to ensure that we didn't spend time and other resources trying to fix the 'wrong problem'.

I had intensive discussions on a one-to-one basis with the senior team, the middle managers and all the staff in focus groups. My colleagues surveyed customers and got a 28% response on critical service performance factors. We shadowed internal and external sales people and conducted a mystery shopping exercise to complete our world view. We found that there was a very unclear strategic direction, leadership was poor and there was no real driving force. There was simmering staff and customer dissatisfaction and the management was overworked and very stressed.

Within two years, this company transformed itself. After enormous personal investment in learning and development, we developed a five member management team, cut out enormous costs, developed profitable units, got everyone into a selling mode and implemented on-going product and process innovation.

The managing director led the changes and 80% of the staff bought into the changes over a six-month period. He proved that it is possible to change both the hard and the soft ways of the company. This was entrepreneurial management and change management in action.

I have worked closely with thousands of managers, entrepreneurs, and leaders in hundreds of businesses and organisations at all levels to help them cope with change. From this perspective, I have concluded that change gives you two options:

OPTION NUMBER ONE IS WAIT

Wait and see what happens. Maybe all this will pass. Perhaps it's just a fad. Wait for improvement in external factors such as adverse financial markets that contribute to change. Wait for them to improve. Pray for a miracle that external factors will have a positive effect on your personal, business or career situation. Study global trends and financial markets and hope that all boats will lift with a rising tide.

There will always be positive and negative global factors that will help or constrain your development. These factors are often conveniently used as excuses for failure to act. I can promise you that the outcome will be that if you wait, you'll wait forever.

An ordinary manager thinks that he will be swept to prosperity on some global improvement wave. He expects things to happen and problems to work out. He lives in hope.

OPTION NUMBER TWO IS ACT

Act. You know that you cannot change the wind, but you can adjust the sails. You can develop the philosophy and approach of entrepreneurial management. As an entrepreneurial manager you will work to control the factors within your control. You will work relentlessly to identify and maximise these factors and you will get as fit as possible to exploit them. You will set out to reposition yourself and you will re-deploy the current under-utilised capabilities within your organisation. This is your key to mastering change.

You, the entrepreneurial manager, can learn to maximise internal controllable resources, processes, systems and functions and therefore capitalise on the opportunities that accelerated change brings. You must be ever alert and always preparing. The converging forces driving change – technology, competition, and globalisation – won't go away. But, like the wind, they can be exploited and you can adjust the sails of your ship. That is why change is an opportunity that you must actively embrace.

TAKING CHARGE

Niccolo Machiavelli, father of the modern science of politics, said:

'There is nothing more difficult nor more doubtful of success, nor more dangerous to manage, than to initiate a new order of things.'

Change has always been difficult. But change itself has fundamentally changed. This book is about equipping you with a way of thinking and acting – taking charge of change – called entrepreneurial management. It assumes that you are, or want to be, an Entrepreneurial Manager.

In today's competitive world, you must embrace and manage change. As an Entrepreneurial Manager you must develop internal change strategies so that your organisation can match changes in the local and global marketplace.

By analysing and capitalising on the change process, by managing change strategically, and by understanding how to deploy key resources and competencies you, as an entrepreneurial manager, will be more likely to adapt and prosper in the fast changing business environment of the 21st century.

Ireland faces major challenges that inhibit its efforts to embrace change. Some of these challenges are:

COMPLACENT MANAGERS

Change before the 1990's was evolutionary. It was slow and material. Now it's revolutionary. It's rapid and wild.

Most managers in Ireland are ignorant of, or are complacent about, the impact of revolutionary world change on their business. 'Not knowing' and 'not being ready' are not good answers when you are in the middle of a revolution.

FICKLE CUSTOMERS

Stakeholders in business have relied too much on traditional measures of performance. Financial measures alone are limited measures of performance. Production measures are limited also. Measuring the cost of non-conformance is not enough. More inclusive measures are measures of customer service, staff morale, market share, effects of differentiation of products, and customer satisfaction.

There is a standardisation of products in most sectors today and virtually all products are of good quality. So what is your differentiating factor? What sets your product or service apart from the rest? How do you create business advantage?

Today's customer is discerning, fickle, moody and demanding of personalised attention. He/she measures the entire bundle of satisfactions from products and services and is prepared to switch custom to the company or shop that provides a better response, friendliness, a willingness to help and the intangible added-value.

BEGRUDGERY

Thomas J Watson, the founder of IBM, said the secret of success was to 'Double your failure rate'. More than 56% of new Irish businesses fail in their first five years. But how do most Irish people see failure in business? We need to understand that business failure is not the end but a learning step. We need to support enterprise by giving incentives to work hard and take risks. We need to change our thinking about people who make mistakes.

Professor J J Lee in his book *Ireland 1912-1985* described the destructive effects of begrudgery. In Ireland many would-be entrepreneurs have fallen victim to the begrudgery machine which goes into overdrive at the notion of setting up in business. It is time to move on from traditional envious thinking about progress, achievement and success. In sport, people in a community celebrate success and acknowledge failure. They should do likewise for business. They should give credit for initiative and risk.

STIFLING BUREAUCRACY

Bureaucratic structures are essential for order in certain large organisations and sectors such as the Public Service. Most public servants operate within the constraints of stifling bureaucratic structures. Many of them are depersonalised and institutionalised as a result. Without the support of the structure, they would be vulnerable and weak.

Rigid bureaucratic systems put brakes on progress. Businesses that have such structures should take them down and let in the light of flexible working, advanced creative thinking and the entrepreneurial spirit. Otherwise, the constraints of traditional thinking, old outmoded work systems and practices will limit their survival capacity when the shock of real change comes in the near future.

POLITICAL BIAS

Politicians create the local environment in which enterprise can thrive or die. But they are trapped in the quest for the purchase of votes in order to win the next general election. In contrast, business managers run the gauntlet of clientalism and the 'Parish-Pump Favours club' to purchase the attention of politicians for economic and social policies favourable to business development.

Politicians must be taught that the spirit of nationhood and statesmanship is similar to the entrepreneurial spirit. They must develop policies for a climate that will lessen obstacles and increase opportunities for business winners.

LABOUR PARADOX

Employers cannot find workers, yet there is high unemployment. The economy is booming, yet there is poverty. The incentive not to work outweighs the attraction of available jobs. There is a mismatch of skills to industry needs. It seems to be a succession of paradoxes. Successive Government policies of penalising hard workers, entrepreneurs and business initiatives while favouring laziness, has created this climate of lethargy. Entrepreneurs and business people in general must lobby politicians to change such a forbidding culture.

WE CAN DO IT

A remote island, a small open economy and a people with a history of rebellion and conflict would seem to be the opposite of the ideal conditions for growth and development. Ireland's phenomenal growth has taken place against a harsh background of civil war, famine and economic depression followed by a series of recessions. As we embrace the new millennium, Ireland's knowledge base, its work and business ethic, its developing infrastructure and its state-of-the-art telecommunications systems, together with its superior economic profile, are the envy of the world. We've proven that we can do it. Now let's show that we can do it many times more.

FIRST, CHANGE YOURSELF

The major forces of change such as technological developments, globalisation, new employment patterns, new organisational structures, and environmental issues are fast blowing old systems and old ways to smithereens. As much as 80% of all change initiatives struggle or fail to achieve their objectives. Change is destructive when it should be constructive. The major reason for this is that change itself is managed badly. Most managers don't know how to handle periods of change.

If you are to become a successful manager in the 21st century you must be an entrepreneurial manager who can adapt quickly to an economic shock such as a collapsed market, an oil crisis, a sudden percentage change in interest rates or more local challenges. You will need to learn new thinking skills, competencies and working relationships. You will need to prepare yourself for the situation that unfolds so that it becomes not a problem, but an opportunity,

In change-management initiatives in the past, the focus has been on *WHY* the change was necessary and on selling the concept of change to everyone in the organisation. Today, most managers know why. They know that the reasons range from new technologies and changing markets and competitors to economic factors and globalisation.

Most managers know WHAT changes are required. Most organisations have dabbled in customer care, ISO 9000 standards, Just-In-Time, Total Quality Management, World Class Manufacturing, Process Re-Design, empowerment, self-directed work teams and so on. The 'Whys' and the 'Whats' of change are much clearer now than they were a decade ago. The 'When', of course, is now.

As an entrepreneurial manager today you need to focus virtually all of your time on figuring out HOW to make the desired change. Most managers don't know how. Why is there so much cynicism about the application of what has been proven to be correct? Answer: the tools or the systems were correct, but the application (the 'How') was poor.

This book is a proven system of strategies and tactics on how to make the transition from being an ordinary manager to being an extra-ordinary manager – an entrepreneurial manager – who knows how and acts fast. At the core of this book is the principle: 'To change others and change organisations, first change yourself'.

When you embrace the concepts of change-management outlined in the forthcoming pages, apply them to yourself, then to other individuals, to your team or department or group, and ultimately to your whole organisation.

MOTIVATORS OF CHANGE

You are unlikely to embark on a change process unless you are being pushed into it – unless you are experiencing some form of pain, restlessness or dissatisfaction. On the other hand, you will need to be pulled towards improvement or some potential advantage.

MOTIVATORS OF CHANGE

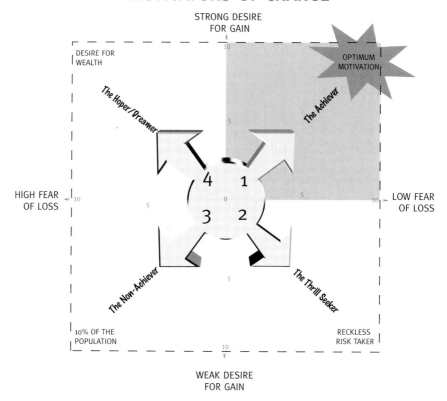

There are two primary motivators of change, whether it is personal change or business change. On the positive side, it is the desire for gain or improvement. On the negative side, it is the fear of loss. You can map yourself on the North-South desire for gain gradient and on the East-West fear of loss gradient to determine which quadrant you reside in right now. The motivated state (Quadrant 1) is obviously the best place to be.

Every individual and every organisation has two major motivators. On the negative side, it's the fear of loss (pain). On the positive side, it's the desire for gain. If these positive and negative factors are only of passive or academic interest to you, then significant personal or organisational change will probably not occur. Your job, as entrepreneurial manager, on the one hand is to increase the desire for improvement and on the other hand to reduce the potential for discomfort or loss. Both efforts require lots of influencing. It's a push and pull approach.

THREE STEPS TOWARDS CHANGE

Three bricklayers who worked side by side on a building site provide the classic story of the philosophy of entrepreneurial management. A passer-by asked the first bricklayer what he was doing. He replied: 'I'm laying some bricks.' The passer-by asked the same question of the second bricklayer, who replied: 'I'm building a wall'. In reply to the same question, the third bricklayer said: 'I'm building a cathedral'. Put all your initiatives into a total long-term solutions framework, not a short-term, quick fix framework. A cathedral is a far greater vision than a mere brick wall.

Most change initiatives fail to reach their objectives because of the initial failure to frame the big picture, to visualise the desired outcome and decide the many steps towards achieving that outcome. Just doing something is not enough. It's got to fit into the bigger picture. Every change initiative should be like a brick in building the cathedral, a step in creating the bigger strategic purpose. Here are three steps towards this process:

STEP 1 GET EARLY RESULTS

As an entrepreneurial manager you must first deliver early tangible results. This demonstrates to the nay-sayers that you are serious and that you are already working towards clearly defined goals. Small changes can demonstrate 'the new order of things'. Simple environmental improvements can work wonders and usually at low cost and effort. Just ask 'What could we do immediately to improve things around here?' Then get going. Do something. Do anything. Do it Now.

This is as important at a personal level as it is within your team. Everyone in the organisation must be made aware that a major change initiative is a long-term step by step process. Otherwise cynicism and scepticism will take over and these attitudes by themselves will kill most good initiatives. A changing mental framework helps this process. But you must persuade people, influence them, and sell it to them. Set specific goals.

The owner of one of my client companies did a total physical clean up of his business over one long Bank-holiday weekend to demonstrate his new, fresh approach. He painted his entire premises. He re-organised several of the offices. When reorganising his own office he realised that it was a better location for his customer services manager. To everyone's surprise he moved to a less glamorous office.

Visual and physical changes can demonstrate your resolve immediately. The key to starting a change process is attitude change. However, attitude change takes more time than physical/visual change and will have far more setbacks and many frustrations.

STEP 2 FOCUS ON IMPROVEMENT

Old performance systems can block progress. Most people have a natural resistance to changing old ways but it may be necessary to take the bull by the horns and slay some non-contributing 'sacred cows'. Regulations, policies or procedures may have been built into your system over time but now may be obsolete, too costly or unnecessary.

The gurus of Quality Improvement (Philip Crosby, W Edwards Deming, Joseph M Juran) state that the body of evidence proves that between 25% and 35% of a company's total sales revenues is wasted in doing things wrong, errors, re-works, mistakes, discounts, warranty claims, returns and many other indirect losses. This cost of doing things wrong is not recovered in most organisations and the potential for massively improving profits can be achieved by getting things right first time.

Joseph Juran, the great quality thinker of the 20th century, interviewed in Fortune Magazine (January 1999) said: 'The quality effort will occupy us for decades … it's a slow process. One of the limitations is cultural resistance … Invariably each industry says, "Our business is different". Within the industry each company says "we're different". And within each company managers are different … but with respect to quality the problems are identical'.

You are responsible for ensuring that your product or service conforms to requirements and that your staff commitment, expertise and your standards of performance are at a level of excellence. Deming said: '90% of all waste, errors, deficiencies and problems originate in the process'. Therefore, put measures, responsibility, psychology, and standards into your processes.

An executive in one of my client organisations which employs 700 people reduced his management structure from seven layers to four layers and set up small business units to give more localised authority to employees. All employees including managers were propelled into a small business environment almost overnight. What a shock! There was no more hiding from responsibilities. In a small business everyone is responsible.

Each employee faced two sets of challenges. One set was physical, structural and procedural. This set was relatively easy to overcome. The other set of challenges was emotional, mental and personal blockages. These challenges created a massive vacuum about who would 'take responsibility'. Moving to a new culture is not as easy as moving to a new building.

The management teams in another of my client organisations found it cost effective to subcontract all their deliveries rather than carry staff and transport costs. Another of my clients decided that it made economic sense to open on Saturdays and during lunch hours.

Yet another client said: 'Let's have a weekly communication meeting to sort out difficulties in a team context'. In order to gain credibility for yourself and the change process you may need to take out a few 'untouchables'.

When this happens everyone knows you are serious. We are all creatures of habit and we tend to slip back into old comfort zones quickly. Anticipate this danger.

When you implement the 'new order of things', keep the focus on encouragement and the future. When you take some initial steps most people will go along with the initiatives in the hope that in time it will 'go away'. Don't let it die. People need to be persuaded, communicated with and encouraged.

STEP 3 GET INVOLVEMENT

Stakeholder relationships are vital to your success. All your great ideas and initiatives will flounder if the people affected by your business decisions don't give you their support. As the world business climate changes, the rules of competitive business are being rewritten. The effect of this is to make people and relationships more than ever a key to sustainable success.

Only through deepened relationships with and trust for your key stakeholders will this be achieved. This will take time and must be scheduled in as key result areas. There are no short cuts to building relationships. There is a direct correlation between the amount of involvement you allow and the resultant level of commitment and overall outcome.

Tomorrow's company has an inclusive approach to its stakeholders. The better you know your stakeholders, the better you'll know how to influence them. You must create and shape your actions to bring each stakeholder on board. All stakeholder groups will have two questions: 'How will this affect me?' and 'What do I think of the people in charge and the change process proposed?'

Once you have embraced the change process, it is important to build bridges with a minimum of two to four influencers in each stakeholder category. Your overall approach is to include as many people as possible in your endeavours to change, improve and create a business advantage for your organisation.

THE BIG FIVE STAKEHOLDERS

There are five key stakeholders, each of whom requires a different approach:

1 CUSTOMERS

Your customers pay all the bills. So ask them for their perceptions of your organisation.

I recently conducted a Customer Research exercise for a company in which we asked 200 key customers how they perceived interactions and service performance with that company. The feedback was frightening. It revealed that my client was about to invest time and money in fixing the wrong problem.

It influenced how they set about making up lost ground in the marketplace and how they handled the transition from their current performance levels to their new desired state. It showed that there was a big gap between what the customers wanted improved and what the management team and staff felt the customers wanted.

The company felt they needed a more comprehensive range of product. The customers wanted a faster and friendlier response. Because of this feedback, the company halted the development of the product range and focused on solving the customers' real problems. Keeping current customers is hard work and it requires a well thought out strategy.

2 EMPLOYEES

Most change initiatives falter and fail or succeed and prosper with the attitudes of employees. Therefore your human relations skills are a critical success factor. How you handle the cocktail of beliefs, attitudes, values, conditions and personalities that make up the culture of your organisation is central to a successful change management initiative. Proper preparation and planning are essential if you are to get employees to co-operate with a major change initiative. Don't rush in where others have messed up.

You will not only need to consider how to bring individuals on board, but also how different groups and teams (eg production and sales) will interact.

I listened to a feedback session from 20 people in one department of an organisation. All agreed that the ISO 9000 standard they had achieved was 'just a fashion statement'. It looked good, but internally no one adhered to the standard. Furthermore, they argued that it blocked real improvement, was costly and made customers unhappy. When we conducted a Service Performance Analysis of the whole organisation and its customers we revealed that the causes of these problems were at a much deeper level – lack of meaningful involvement and lack of appreciation.

Your key to successful employee motivation towards change is good communications, systematic planning, honesty and integrity, 'empowerment' and, most importantly, gaining commitment and trust. Your role as an entrepreneurial manager is to create an environment where attitudes of self-employment among individual employees can prosper. What would *they* do? How would *they* deal with this problem if it was their own business?

Whilst most people know the solutions to their work problems, they have somehow allowed themselves to be conditioned into believing that they are limited and that they need the help of their managers to create a better work environment. It's called 'learned helplessness'. Most ordinary managers and business owners believe that empowerment means organisational chaos and a hand-over of control. It is an issue of trust, worthwhileness, and a host of other emotions.

As an entrepreneurial manager you realise that empowerment is one of the keys to managing change. You let go of your old habits and power-bases and set out to build an empowered workforce by taking the following action:

• You systematically build a strong case for change by showing how it will decrease costs, improve quality and service, and increase standards, profits and productivity. You ask employees for their opinion. You listen genuinely to their responses, document their feedback and work on the principle that there is a 1:1 ratio between the amount of involvement you get and the level of commitment.

• You lead by example so that it's obvious to everyone that you are serious about this change initiative. Many managers invest enormous resources in changing systems, structures and processes, but they continue to behave in the same old way themselves. There must not be a wide gap between what you say and what you do. You must, in fact, sell the change initiative over an extended period of time to demonstrate your personal commitment.

• You demonstrate that you, personally, have changed. You encourage other individuals and teams to sort out their own real and winnable issues. You institutionalise the change.

I have been a consultant adviser to the management of a traditional 100 year old company which was commercially successful and profitable. But the managing director realised that the winds of change were coming fast to his industry. New competitors from new industries were starting to supply his product better, faster and cheaper. We worked with him over two years through a total, integrated, organisation-wide change process. The change process succeeded.

I believe that the key reason for the change management success was the personal transformation of the managing director. He realised that the current state into which he had let his business develop (in terms of preparation for the future), was more a reflection of his own thinking and style than any other single factor. It was not the changing market, new technology or increased globalisation. It was the managing director.

He made a decision to change himself first. More importantly, he realised he needed to learn how to do this. He not only changed his thinking and management style, but his grooming and dress and his social and family life. In terms of change this is low risk and low cost but far more valuable in the long-term than investments in procedural areas.

Everyone watched his general transformation over about six months with attitudes ranging from admiration, to suspicion and ridicule. He himself started the personal, team and organisation process in his business. Now, it was much easier. He led by example.

Ralph Waldo Emerson said: 'Every organisation is the length and shadow of one man'. It was never more true than in this case. Despite numerous obstacles and challenges, when we initiated change throughout the organisation, there was minimal resistance.

3 SHAREHOLDERS/OWNERS

The concerns and fears of the employees often overshadow the interests of the Shareholders/Owners. Few within the organisation stop to ask: 'What do the Shareholders/Owners want?' 'What are their concerns and how will it affect them?' However, they are key stakeholders and they need to be continually informed. They should be included in the planning and ongoing development of any change management process. They generally operate at an executive level with the company.

An above average return on their high risk and their investment is a legitimate aspiration for them. Risk is not always understood. Or it is conveniently forgotten.

In one heart to heart 'let's all talk about how we feel' session, an employee challenged the members of the board of directors – the owners – about their plush cars and how they could reconcile this with cost-cutting efforts and wage restrictions. The reply by one director put everything in perspective for them. It demonstrated the need for and position of different stakeholders. He said in simple terms: ' The reason we set up this business was to get rich. Three of us mortgaged our homes and borrowed extensively to get it off the ground. If we had failed, it would have set us back for 20 years. That's a big risk. We make no apology therefore for reaping a reward as big as the risk we took. In other words, if the negative risk was 20 years, then the benefit risk is 20 years'.

This reply clarified the objectives of the company for that group honestly and directly. It also helped decide the calibre of staff members. Two key people left shortly afterwards but two others approached the board of directors and invested in the company. The jealousy factor simmered just under the surface for the two who left and undoubtedly affected their contribution. The goal 'to be rich' is surely a legitimate aspiration in a democracy and a capitalist economy. Riches, risk and change go hand in hand.

4 Suppliers and Other Business Partners

Suppliers, professional advisors and other business supporters of your organisation can be helpful in giving you a different perspective on change. They have their own experiences and they can help you in many ways.

I was involved in a change initiative where the company's firm of accountants was particularly helpful in obtaining benchmarks from a successful competitor. Tell your partners what you are doing, but above all explain Why. Different perspectives help clarify your thinking on change.

Your reasons Why are often more important than the more operational What. You should not assume that they would know or understand. They're not telepathic. So tell them.

5 The Community

Because of a higher awareness and concern for environmental and legal regulations, you consider and incorporate the implications of change for your local community. For bigger organisations, there may be national and international implications.

Communicate Consistently

As the entrepreneurial manager you become aware of Newton's Third Law which says: 'An object at rest tends to stay at rest until acted upon by external forces'. In other words, communicate consistently and honestly with all your stakeholders and keep the information flowing in various ways. Don't assume that they understand what's going on.

Use every communication method and channel to keep information about the change initiative flowing from senior management to your operational line employees, from operatives to management and back again.

These channels include:

- Verbal briefings of all kinds and the 'grapevine'. Regular 10 minute meetings are great.
- Progress charts, banners and posters.
- Newsletters and personalised letters.
- Celebration parties and learning lunches.
- Intranet and Internet.

You could set up a learning library where books, computer-based technology, audio and video materials are available on site or on loan to employees. This is an ideal way to educate people with the thinking and the practical skills to cope with change.

You need to give constant feedback. Always be on the lookout for channels of communication and methods of letting people in on things. A big demotivator is not being told what's going on.

MEASURE YOUR IMPROVEMENTS

Giving appropriate feedback on progress means measuring performance. Good performance measures should be linked to strategy, ensuring that you are sending signals that all can hear and respond to. It also shapes your culture. 'What gets measured, gets done'.

Here are five principles when considering how you measure change improvements:

1 RE-EVALUATE YOUR EXISTING MEASURES.

You may have become too comfortable with them. Replace them if necessary. Re-examine them. Introduce new measures. Can you do it better, faster, cheaper, easier? Ask the 'experts' who are closest to the job to come up with Areas for Improvement (AFIs). Then, really listen to their feedback.

2 MEASURE YOUR PROCESSES, NOT JUST YOUR RESULTS.

The results tell you there is a problem, not where it is. Process measurements tell you where. For every bad effect in your business, there is a cause. Most causes can be identified in the process stage. All work is a series of processes, some viable, some less viable. Positive outcomes (ends) are the consequence of using good processes (means). As the entrepreneurial manager you should concentrate on the means, the process. Let others concentrate on the final result. Get help if necessary.

Poor sales results can be traced back to some weaknesses in the critical success factors of selling. There are seven critical factors in selling as follows: Prospecting, Presenting, Closing, Handling Objections, Time and Territory Management, Product Knowledge, and Personal Competencies. Each of these needs to be measured to identify the weak link.

Unacceptably long time spans, for example, between ordering and delivery can be traced back through the accounts, administration and distribution channels.

Human relationships are a whole series of processes. For example, the process of building rapport between sales person and client can be greatly improved by asking the right questions and by actively listening and observing. Professional listening is a skill that very few managers understand yet it is vital to success. You must master this skill. If you nod your head, for example, it doubles the amount the person will say. If you suggest (rather than tell or insist) it is twice as likely to get appreciation. If you disagree, explain why.

3 MEASURE YOUR TEAMWORK.

Everyone works in a team. The smallest of enterprises is a team. There are several qualitative and quantitative ways to measure teamwork. Ideally, a comprehensive measure can be done once a year. The natural extension of personal control and responsibility is to maximise each individual's contribution in a team. Self-directed work teams, and rotating team leadership and responsibility have been successful in many industries around the world. When the team members are working well together, continuous change improvement strategies are most likely to make a big improvement. The leader has a massive influence on team performance. Now staff, colleagues, customers and boss can measure the key competencies of the leader.

4 THE RIPPLE EFFECT

Measure every resource, process, competency, and system within your organisation. Every element of your organisation has an implication on everything else. I call this the Ripple Effect. The cost of quality is massive in most businesses. 'Most unnecessary costs and wastage walk on two feet'. Consider implementing measures to reduce costs and improve quality on an ongoing basis rather than in times of crisis.

5 ESTABLISH A RANGE OF BENCHMARKS

Don't just have financial measures. Establish benchmarks against industry standards and against your competitors to compare costs, sales, quality, distribution and performance issues such as co-operation, responsiveness and complaints. What other ratios could you set in place to measure key result areas in your business? How your customers measure you 'is the ultimate measure'. How has your customer profile changed over the last three years? How will it change over the next three years? When did you last conduct a customer service performance analysis?

Your objective is to transform business performance by measuring and managing the drivers of business success. You must, however, link these measures to changes in your strategy and effectively make them part of your strategic management system. There are numerous challenges in getting buy-in throughout the organisation. These include aligning old and new measures, selecting infrastructures and other technologies, and dealing with information ownership and cultural issues.

MANAGE THE CHANGE PROCESS

As the entrepreneurial manager you gain a thorough understanding of the overall change process before launching any change initiatives. How do you change a square block of ice (your present condition) into the new form of a triangle (your desired state)?

You can use two methods to accomplish this task. The first method is the 'hammer approach' often used in times of crisis or as a last resort. In this approach, you use the hammer to smash the ice cube and force the pieces into the form of a triangle. The advantage of the 'hammer approach' is that it can be accomplished very quickly. However, more often than not, the result is not a smooth fit into the desired new state. This tends to lead to endless resistance, cynicism, and only token commitment and acceptance. With this approach, you tend to move bodies, not minds. Total buy-in includes physical buy-in (the hands to do the work), mental buy-in (the head to think about it) and cultural or emotional buy-in (the heart to value it).

You have a second option. Change the square ice cube into a triangle by de-freezing the ice cube and gradually guiding the liquid to the point where it can be re-frozen into the form of a triangle. This de-freezing, changing and re-freezing method takes longer, but usually results in a desired new structure shaped according to a plan and with the all-important buy-in by employees. You are more likely to win hands, heads and hearts with this process.

THE CHANGE PROCESS
UNFREEZE – CHANGE – REFREEZE

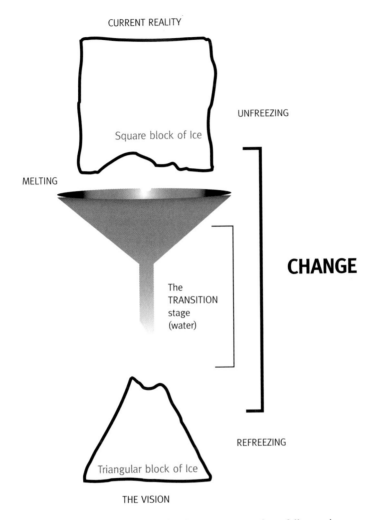

CURRENT REALITY

UNFREEZING

Square block of Ice

MELTING

CHANGE

The
TRANSITION
stage
(water)

REFREEZING

Triangular block of Ice

THE VISION

Successful change is achieved more easily when it is managed carefully, step by step, systematically over a period of time.

To change the shape of an ice-cube from a block shape to a triangular shape, you do not crush it with a hammer. You will achieve a much better effect if you place it over a funnel, unfreeze it by heating, reform it and then refreeze it.

Increased competition, technological advances, globalisation and ever shifting customer demands mean that only the most fluid and most responsive organisation will survive, prosper and embrace change as an opportunity.

Ref: Schein, E. (1951), 'The Mechanics of Change', in Bennis, W.G. et al, Interpersonal Dynamics, Dorsey Press and Kurt Lewin.

Your challenge is to bridge the gap between the undesirable old way of doing things (square ice cube) through the transition period (change) to the new culture and way of doing things (triangle ice cube). The ice cube model demonstrates the change process. How to make that transition is one of the biggest challenges for all entrepreneurial managers and organisations today.

Many organisations have employed 'ostrich management' methods. They put their heads in the sand and hope that change will go away. They inevitably realise that they have to use the 'hammer method' to instigate change. All too often it is too late.

CRISIS AND RECOVERY

The Chinese curse 'May you live in interesting times' has never been more relevant. Crisis or sudden change shocks employees, their families, the community as well as the stakeholders, suppliers and management. There is usually a long road from crisis to recovery.

Many organisations that suffer crises or have change forced on them follow a process of Shock, Anger, Rejection, Acceptance and Healing. It's called the SARAH process. When the realisation finally hits them, usually in the form of a crisis such as a major customer leaving them or a major competitor entering their market place, the degree to which they go through this process will determine whether they will survive or not. If they manage their journey through the process, they will be better able to cope with the long term effects of change.

The step by step SARAH process is as follows:

Shock – Individuals, teams and entire organisations get a bolt of reality. It's similar to a traumatic experience such as a major car accident.

A major client of mine lost a long-standing customer. The loss accounted for 50% of his business of the previous three years and virtually everyone in the company walked around in a daze for a month afterwards. Their first emotional response was immobilisation and shock. They thought: 'It couldn't happen to us'.

Anger – Individuals and teams in the organisation were annoyed and angry at the customer, the senior management and the sales department for not anticipating it. Blame! Blame! Blame! was their national anthem for two months afterwards. Fear of loss, redundancy, bankruptcy and all kinds of other concerns leaped into their minds. They had been in a nice comfort zone and were totally unprepared for this.

Rejection – Many individuals rejected – or resisted – this major trauma for the organisation by suggesting that the customer was too difficult to deal with anyway. Their attitude was that they could get another customer of this calibre and size. They reasoned that they could cut costs and reduce their expenditure to cope with the downturn. For some employees it was denial of reality. Some members of the sales/marketing team went 'gung-ho' into the marketplace in order to attract a new customer. They denied the reality that it could take 12 months to get a customer of this calibre. Depression levels increased … production levels decreased … stress increased … commitment decreased …

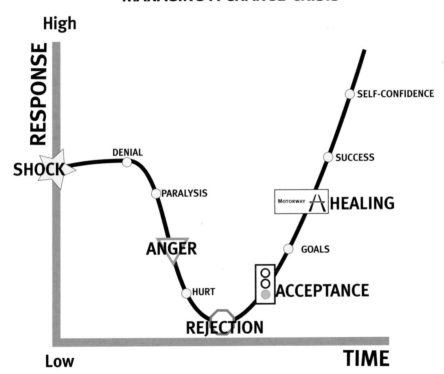

MANAGING A CHANGE CRISIS

A change process can be traumatic for a long time following the initial shock. You can lessen that trauma by understanding that change is a journey that takes time and may be hindered by many obstacles before you again achieve outstanding success and self-confidence. The SARAH – shock, anger, rejection, acceptance and healing – process is one way to 'travel' through a traumatic period of change or a crisis.

Acceptance – Gradually, everyone started to accept reality. This would have serious repercussions for their business. There would be redundancies. There would have to be major rapid hammer-like changes within the organisation. For years, this organisation had major resistance from the unions and the workforce to certain change initiatives. This time, the whole organisation was transformed within six months. It was Do or Die. They chose Do.

Healing – Humans have an amazing capacity to regenerate and recover from dramatic events. So do organisations. Very quickly this organisation started to heal itself and accept the inevitable. Healing and hope go hand in hand. More importantly, a new sense of purpose and focus emerged from almost everyone within the organisation. Within six months they had captured two new customers which restored about 35% of their old business. More importantly, they have implemented many of the concepts in this book and have embraced learning and ongoing development as essential to their long-term success. They are now preparing for future shocks. Ongoing change is an accepted norm rather than a dreaded disaster.

Your role is to handle change related stress to achieve a successful outcome. Follow the SARAH process. Many managers abandon change initiatives because they interpret resistance as immovable obstacles rather than as emotional, even natural, responses. If they knew that anger and negative resistance is often the storm before the calm, then they would wait out the storm for success.

LEADERS AND CHAMPIONS

Two types of players are essential for the team charged with the successful transformation of the organisation during a change process. The key player on the team is the Change Leader who sponsors and legitimises the entire change process. He understands the world-view and the long-term importance of instigating a change process rather than the short-term urgency of it. Short-term urgency must be distinguished from long term importance. Initially, most significant change processes are not urgent. But they are important.

Crisis change management is both urgent and dangerous, but the SARAH process can help people understand and identify the steps of change to be managed. The Change Leader, however, realises the implications of the external driving forces in initiating a change process and that it is an investment in the future.

The Internal Champions, or Change Champions, are the key team of people responsible for the implementation of change. They use a planned systematic change management process such as the entrepreneurial management skills described in this book to unlock the potential of themselves first, then other individuals and their team(s), and ultimately the entire organisation.

They, in effect, manage that critical transition stage from the current reality to the desired new position. They are vital to the success of the change process. Internal Champions can work effectively with outside consultants. All the other stakeholders, but especially employees at all levels, are the other key players in this challenging and exciting game.

My own consulting group works with organisations in creating business advantage and are involved in major change initiatives with small, medium and large enterprises. Our experience shows that a number of factors need to be considered:

1 INVOLVEMENT OF CHANGE LEADERS

The Change Leaders must not only be involved in the project, but must be seen to be involved in the project. In one organisation where we implemented an outstanding customer care culture, the chief executive introduced the programme and listened to the current situation analysis of delegates for the first hour of each introductory programme. He encouraged them to speak their minds and give feedback on the real issues that were blocks to their delivery of outstanding customer care.

The main problem that the front line employees identified was poor internal communication and lack of feedback. The chief executive continued listening and learning for the following two years, and was centrally involved in staff and customer focus groups. His involvement and his willingness to listen to sensitive feedback was key to the success of the project.

2 DISCIPLINED METHODOLOGY

There is a natural human inclination to resist change. In order to cope with this resistance a disciplined change methodology is very important. It's the 'doctor' approach. Examination, diagnosis and prescription are essential before any treatment or medication is contemplated. Any attempt to short-circuit the 'doctor approach' is malpractice. Do a thorough examination of all the vital functions, then give a careful and professional diagnosis to the problem using a systematic approach and only then prescribe the solution.

People resist change for a variety of reasons:
- They fear losing their jobs, status and good working conditions.
- They don't understand or see the need for change.
- They don't like the Change Leader or the Internal Champion.
- They see the change as a personal criticism or a poor reflection of their jobs.
- It's a bad time!
- They have negative feelings anyway.

People accept change more readily if:
- They will be better off in income, status, or conditions.
- They have more opportunities for growth, recognition and promotion.
- The change offers more challenge and excitement.
- The change is needed and the timing is right.
- They like the Change Leaders.
- They like the way the change is being introduced and have input and involvement.

3 NEW BLOOD, NEW CULTURE

How comfortable is comfortable? The natural human tendency to gravitate towards what's comfortable and safe has to be considered in any change process. The new desired state may not culturally suit everyone in the organisation. Some will leave because they can't make the transition on a personal level. Expect at least a 10% fall-out from a major change process. This, of course, allows new blood to enter the system. In turn, this makes a contribution to developing the new culture. But initially, this fall out causes concern and fear. Will everyone abandon ship?

Hold firm at this point. Listen! Don't panic! Keep your eye on the big picture and the overall process. Appreciate that any outward gnashing of teeth and blaming is caused by the inward fear of loss - loss of money, job, safety, status and identity.

4 HOW TO MAKE A REAL CONNECTION

Managing change successfully means making a *real* human connection. Make no assumptions about the process until the human dimension is under control.

Three principle are vital in the change management process:

1 EMPATHISE

Step out of your role as manager for a while and put yourself in your employees' shoes. Try to empathise with them. How will they feel and react to suggestions for change? Approval by employees is critical for successful implementation. I ask managers to do an Empathy Chart, which is a list of all employees who will be affected by the change. I get them to categorise expected responses under six headings as follows: 'Resent', 'Resist', 'Neutral', 'Accept', 'Welcome', and 'Don't know'. The Empathy Chart can give you an indication of how fast to proceed or what the best approach might be.

THE CHANGE EMPATHY CHART

ORGANIZATION / DEPT. _____

NAME:	RESENT	RESIST	NEUTRAL	ACCEPT	WELCOME	DON'T KNOW
_____	0 1 2 3 4 5 6 7 8 9 10					_____
_____	0 1 2 3 4 5 6 7 8 9 10					_____
_____	0 1 2 3 4 5 6 7 8 9 10					_____
_____	0 1 2 3 4 5 6 7 8 9 10					_____
_____	0 1 2 3 4 5 6 7 8 9 10					_____
_____	0 1 2 3 4 5 6 7 8 9 10					_____
_____	0 1 2 3 4 5 6 7 8 9 10					_____
_____	0 1 2 3 4 5 6 7 8 9 10					_____
_____	0 1 2 3 4 5 6 7 8 9 10					_____
_____	0 1 2 3 4 5 6 7 8 9 10					_____
_____	0 1 2 3 4 5 6 7 8 9 10					_____

2 COMMUNICATE

Communicate verbally and in writing. The written word gives legitimacy to your message. The reasons Why are often more important than the nature of the change itself. Allow space and time for communication to happen. Answer questions in full no matter how obvious the answers seem to you. Give feedback and updates.

One advantage of communicating with a group is that everyone gets the same information at the same time. No one is likely to suspect that managers are telling one thing to one person and something different to someone else. With the group approach, people can ask questions and everyone hears the answers. There is much less chance that the grapevine will distort the messages. And the group approach saves time.

Using a one-to-one approach to communicate has the advantage of giving managers a chance to convince people individually that change is desirable. The one-to-one approach also encourages individuals to express their personal opinions without the inhibitions that can arise in group settings. And managers can use the opportunity to show a personal interest in each worker.

Whether in groups or one-to-one, managers must show concern for everyone involved and gain their understanding.

3 PARTICIPATE

A complaint that employees commonly make about change is that 'nobody asked ME'. Feeling that they lack input is a serious problem for employees. Some managers and organisations have recognised this problem and have instituted 'participative management' as a solution. They realise that participation benefits the organisation and the employees.

An example of participative management is IBM's PRIDE programme, which is an acronym for People, Responsibility, Involved, Developing and Excellence. Perhaps the origins of participative management were the quality circles that were used in organisations throughout the world, although not always successfully.

Managing change through participation can be done in two ways:

The first is that before change is introduced, managers receive input from all staff, weigh the input, and then try to sell the change to the people who provided the input. It's been said that 'people will support what they help to create'. This approach also allows managers to retain control of decision making.

The second way takes more of a problem-solving approach. Under the leadership of a manager, a group arrives at a decision about change. This approach generally gains stronger commitment in the end, but it can be risky when the manager doesn't have the final say.

People are the key to change. The success of any change effort greatly depends on whether people resist it or accept it. Managers can influence people's attitudes by managing the change process using the principles of empathy, communication and participation.

FOUR APPROACHES TO CHANGE

Before embarking on a strategic planning process you should carefully consider the scope and impact of the change you require. How you assimilate change into your culture is very important.

There are two variables to consider – one is the scope of the change and the other is the impact of the change. These two variables can be presented as a double matrix. This matrix forms quadrants which categorise four extremes or approaches.

This matrix may give you a framework to think about the scope and impact you require in any change initiative that you undertake. The Important/Urgent variables could be superimposed on the Scope/Impact matrix as outlined.

Each of these defines four readily identifiable approaches:

1 Total Strategic Innovation: Macro Change with High Impact

2 Personal and Procedural Change: Micro Change with High Impact

3 Routine Change: Micro Change with Low Impact

4 Continuous Improvement Process: Macro Change with Low Impact

QUADRANT 1 TOTAL STRATEGIC INNOVATION: MACRO CHANGE WITH HIGH IMPACT

Macro change with high impact can totally change the way you do business. It requires a total rethink about your marketing, how you deploy your resources, your processes, technology and infrastructure. This kind of change is transformational, important but usually not urgent. It requires a major rethink about 'How we do things around here'.

Major resistance may occur unless the rationale for such sweeping changes is communicated through several channels and over time to everybody in the organisation. Such changes could include re–engineering, major restructuring, downsizing or strategic innovation. A move from traditional line management to a project or self-directed work team model could be an example of total strategic innovation

THE SCOPE AND IMPACT OF CHANGE

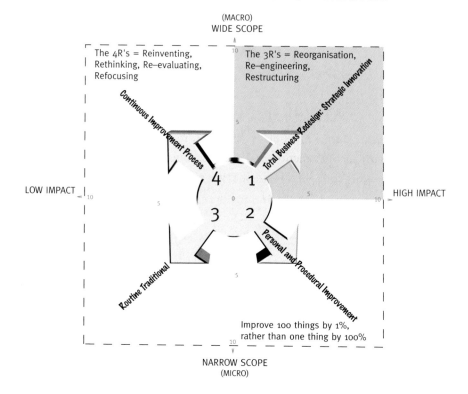

Change can take many forms and can have many dimensions from a wide scope, to a narrow scope, and from making a big impact across the total organisation to a more confined impact. Resource deployment, process management and systems engineering will depend on which emphasis to make.

Most business executives have difficulty in identifying where and how to begin business change. So map yourself on the north-south and east-west axes to determine which quadrant you are in right now. More importantly, what quadrant should you be in for the future?

QUADRANT 2 PERSONAL AND PROCEDURAL CHANGE: MICRO CHANGE WITH HIGH IMPACT

Doing 100 things 1% better can have more impact than doing one thing 100% better. A micro change can have high impact. This inevitably means better management of the moments of impression and inter-relationships between colleagues. Small procedural improvements consistently worked at over time can have a cumulative effect. Everything counts. Everything adds up.

'What kind of place would this be if everyone around here did things just like me?' If everyone first identified their own 'areas for improvement' and concentrated on improving them, wouldn't this make a difference? Everyone has tasks within their own area of control, which only they can identify. For many, personal change is perceived as unimportant and not urgent – a mindset of 'I'm OK in my Comfort Zone'.

QUADRANT 3 ROUTINE CHANGE: MICRO CHANGE WITH LOW IMPACT

A micro change with low impact is regular, routine and safe. It may regularise workflow or production procedures. Such change is well within everyone's comfort zone. If routine changes and improvements do not occur, they can actually cause anxiety and a sense of unrest. In overall strategy terms, however, it is of operational rather than strategic importance. In some industries - for example, the retail trade - there are regular seasonal requirements for change. Such examples could include coping with annual peak production periods or servicing.

QUADRANT 4 CONTINUOUS IMPROVEMENT PROCESS: MACRO CHANGE WITH LOW IMPACT

Performance improvement initiatives such as the total quality process, the installation of ISO 9000 Standards, and the development of self-directed work teams have been carried out on a macro scale in many organisations but with, in general, low impact. Some organisations benefited from them, but most have had a low net impact effect on companies.

Continuous macro changes are important improvement interventions. Above all they bring concentration and collective focus to bear on creating business advantage. Humans have a natural tendency to be diverted or become sloppy. So always be on the lookout for a better way not just for the improvement itself, but for the focus it brings.

THE PITOC™ CHANGE MODEL

This book is built on the principle of getting control of five critical aspects of your business – personal mastery (P), interpersonal relationships (I), team building (T), organisational development (O) and customer orientation (C).

I have developed the PITOC™ model in order to give you an understandable system to put change and growth and development in a personal and business perspective.

You must constantly look at two aspects of change. The first aspect is the factors that you have most control over – the PITOC™ factors. The second aspect is the converging external forces over which you have little control. Obviously, these global external forces have a massive influence in driving change.

THE FIRST ELEMENT OF PITOC™ IS P, PERSONAL MASTERY

All personal change starts with you. With you maximising your potential. With you clarifying your purpose and developing your competencies. With you balancing your values and attitudes. Personal mastery is at the very core of the PITOC™ model and at the core of your success in business and family life.

THE SECOND ELEMENT OF PITOC™ IS I, INTERPERSONAL RELATIONSHIPS

Your ability to influence, communicate and form interpersonal, one-to-one relationships, at every level of your business activities, drives everything that is happening in your business today. You can't take it for granted or leave it to chance anymore. Your ability to build trust and understanding is critical to success today. It is in fact an intellectual asset in its own right. More and more business deals are based on intangible link-ups, and intellectual properties are often held together by strong interpersonal friendships.

THE THIRD ELEMENT OF PITOC™ IS T, TEAM BUILDING

The natural extension of strong personal and interpersonal capabilities is to spread these capabilities into larger groups – into teams. You know that good teamwork works in sport. You also know that team synergy reduces stress, wastage and costs and increases value, morale, energy, sales and productivity within a team. How do you maximise the potential of your team?

THE FOURTH ELEMENT OF PITOC™ IS O, ORGANISATIONAL DEVELOPMENT

Your ultimate goal in any change management process is of course to maximise the potential of your organisation to reach its strategic goals. An organisation is made up of individuals and teams. Mix these together and you have to deal with an elaboration and complexity on a grander scale.

Management of this mix demands leadership, innovation, marketing, deploying resources, installing systems and processes, managing strategic thinking and planning and acknowledging cultural differences. Your ultimate challenge as the entrepreneurial manager is to manage individuals and teams through change and create sustainable strategic advantage from that change.

THE FIFTH ELEMENT OF PITOC™ IS C, CUSTOMER ORIENTATION

Your customers are the ultimate electorate. They are voting for you or against you all the time. Today, customers know they have choices as never before. Loyalty is hard earned. It never ceases to amaze me how companies spend small fortunes on attracting customers and then treat them as of no importance when they come to do business.

THE RIPPLE EFFECT OF PERSONAL MASTERY

Let's suppose that you are 20% effective in your personal mastery dimension. My contention is that this will have a ripple effect on the other four dimensions. Your interpersonal relationships will struggle, your team will be ineffective and ultimately the whole organisation and your customer interactions will reflect this outward ripple.

The place to start with changing the current situation or with performance improvement is, therefore, with yourself. Watch the ripple effects. Stop making excuses for gaps in performance and blaming the market, your customers, your company's culture or structure, your close interpersonal interactions. Work harder at defining, measuring and developing your own competencies than at looking for the answers in other people, situations or external circumstances,

By just starting to work on your Personal Mastery, you will experience immediate improvement all around you. Your perceptions will change. Your new beliefs, attitudes and thinking framework will energise you. You will realise that 'as without, so within' – if your external world is a mess, it's just a reflection of your internal mastery. All the secrets of personal mastery have been available for thousands of years. It's just that you may never have availed of them.

THE PITOC™ CHANGE MODEL

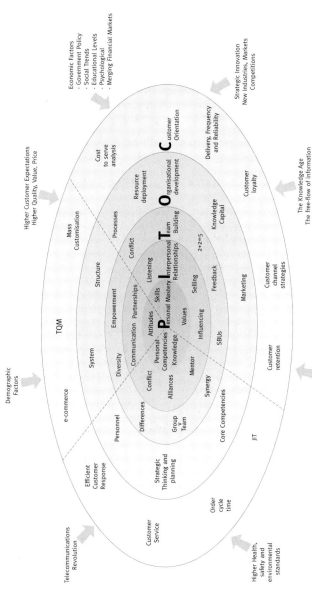

Telecommunications Revolution

Demographic Factors

Higher Customer Expectations
Higher Quality, Value, Price

Economic Factors
- Government Policy
- Social Trends
- Educational Levels
- Psychological
- Merging Financial Markets

Strategic Innovation
New Industries, Markets
Competitions

The Knowledge Age
The free-flow of information

Globalisation

Higher Health, safety and environmental standards

Customer Service

Order cycle time

JIT

Efficient Customer Response

Strategic Thinking and planning

Personnel

Differences

Group v Team

Conflict

Alliances

Synergy

Core Competencies

Customer retention

Customer channel strategies

Marketing

Customer loyalty

Customer Orientation

Delivery, Frequency and Reliability

Knowledge Capital

Organisational development

Resource deployment

Cost to serve analysis

Mass Customisation

Processes

Structure

Empowerment

System

Diversity

Communication Partnerships

TQM

Personal Competencies

Attitudes

Knowledge

Values

Mentor

Influencing

SBUs

Feedback

Selling

Team Building

2+2=5

Interpersonal Relationships

Skills

Listening

Conflict

P ersonal Mastery   **I** nterpersonal Relationships   **T** eam Building   **O** rganisational development   **C** ustomer Orientation

If you don't learn the techniques of change, you will lose the ability to survive, improve, grow and develop yourself and your business. Mastering change means learning to manage five factors – personal mastery (P), interpersonal relationships (I), team building (T), organisational development (O) and customer orientation (C) – and cope with a host of converging external forces such as globalisation, and economic and demographic factors. All change and improvement starts with you. The only factor that you have total control over is your own Personal Mastery (P). Your degree of personal mastery has an outward ripple effect on your Interpersonal Relationships (I). Excellent teamwork (T) is the natural progression of personal mastery and interpersonal communication. This ripple effect continues into the total culture of the Organisation (O). In turn, Customers (C) are the unwitting recipients of the full ripple effect of the other four factors. Converging on these five PITOC factors are the external forces that are largely outside your control. Like a ship in the storm, you must adjust to and manage these uncontrollables in a different way.

CONVERGING EXTERNAL FORCES

Converging on these five factors are several external forces, which are constantly adding turbulence to the whole change revolution. You must constantly stay alert to these forces almost as you would prepare your home for a hurricane. The five elements of PITOC™ are more controllable. Notice that they become less controllable the further you move from the centre. (The factor that you have most control over is your own Personal Mastery.) The factors you have least control over are the converging external forces, yet you must be in a constant state of preparedness to deal with them.

Major external forces adding wind to the sails of change are:
- Economic factors such as government policy, social trends, educational developments, cultural issues, political harmonisation and monetary policy in Europe.
- New industries are emerging today almost at the rate at which new companies emerged ten years ago. This creates new markets, new competitors, new products and new challenges.
- Many companies are entering established industries and redefining how business is activated within these industries. It's total strategic innovation. The borderless world and globalisation are major factors in the free-flow of knowledge and information. We haven't even scratched the surface of the impact that this will have over the next ten years. Many of the world's leading economists have predicted that the biggest market economies of the 21st century will be today's Third World countries.
- Higher safety and environmental standards that are being institutionalised worldwide will have their own implications on every business over the next 10 years.
- 'I am absolutely certain that the most fundamental issue facing us in the first two decades of the 21st century is Demographics', stated Peter Drucker at a conference that I attended in London in September 1998. For the first time since the Black Death, populations in the developed countries are declining. Drucker argued that this will have a number of effects, including an increased emphasis on education for the few, 'precious' children, and political turbulence as the ageing population fights to keep its entitlements. Companies have to adapt to an ageing workforce, with an average retirement age close to 80, whose members will want to work in a variety of increasingly flexible ways.
- Worldwide economic integration is another major trend, Drucker said,

as markets react to extreme and unprecedented currency fluctuations. Combine this increasing political fragmentation and you can see that the corporation as we know it today will fundamentally change.

• The telecommunications revolution is really only starting. We know enough to be aware that this is an irresistible force for the better. The trend towards everything being better, faster, cheaper, easier, newer, different, smaller is unstoppable and will affect your life, your career, your community, and your business. It will affect everything. You must prepare for it. Otherwise, your business will be wiped out.

At a Dublin seminar, Lloyd Cole, European Brand Manager of 3M, told the audience in graphic terms how change has taken place and how the future may look. He contrasted the recent past with the current present showing what has changed in media, in distribution, in pricing and in consumer attitudes within a few years.

MARKERS OF CHANGE

FROM ATOMS TO BITS
Atoms–Bits
Physical–Virtual=less bricks, more stores
Patents–Brands
Mass Produced–Mass Customised
Products–Solutions
Environmentally Safe–Environmentally benign.

FROM ANALOGUE TO DIGITAL
Analogue–Digital
Words–Pictures
Static Information–Variable Information
2D–3D
Colour–Hi-Fi
16 million shades–65 million shades
Broadcast–Narrowcast
In-Home, Out-House–Path to Purchase
(Truck–Street–Floor)
Stand-alone–Integrated
Corporate Identity–Brand Identity
Media–New Media

FROM LOCAL TO GLOBAL
Local Regional–Global
Quantity Discount–Loyalty Discount+More
Market Share–Share of Customer

FROM MASS TO ONE-TO-ONE
Mass–One-to-One
Customer Service–Integration
National–Global
Reseller–Value-added
Days/Weeks–Minutes.

FROM BROCHURE TO INTERNET
Brochure–Internet
Exhibition–Seminar
Photograph–CD
Newsletters–Direct
Mail–E-mail
Lists–Databases
Media–New Media

From Presentation by Lloyd Cole, 3M, (Europe)
at VICOM Seminar, Dublin, November 1998.

- Convergence of technology for example will make it difficult to define the difference between a television and a personal computer. Hybrid industries will form between computing, communications, and software; or between chemicals and electronics; or between retailing and financial services.
- Customer expectations and customer needs are increasing. Not too long ago it was argued that if you provided two of the three variables of quality, value and price, you commanded competitive advantage in your market place. No longer is this true. Today, you must have all three variables flying in formation to achieve a competitive edge.

This is a model to help you think about managing change from a strategic viewpoint. No matter what your current position is you must endeavour to think strategically at all times. The rest of this book is about creating and keeping that strategic advantage.

YOUR ACTION STEPS FOR CHANGE MANAGEMENT

This entrepreneurial management system is practical. Each chapter contains action steps for you to complete. They are designed to get you moving and to get you working on the tools and techniques outlined. If you do not implement the ideas and use the tools and the toolbox outlined, they will be of no use to you.

You must discipline yourself to do the exercises so that you can receive the full benefit of their cumulative effect.

STEP 1

Accept and acknowledge that we are going through a change revolution. Consider: How does it affect you? How prepared are you to deal with change on a personal and family, career and business level? Purposeful action is the key to managing change as an opportunity.

STEP 2

Take a sheet of paper and score yourself out of ten on your level of preparedness in each of the five (PITOC™) areas. Then write out three action steps that you should take immediately to move forward from your current position.

STEP 3

Make a plan to invest more time in gaining the knowledge necessary to prepare for change. How can you master change rather than become a victim of change? What actions could you take in the next 12 months to ensure that you are in a better position? How much money will you need to invest in your career to add value and strength to your current situation? Action favours the bold. Do it.

DOING WHAT 'THE DOC' SAID

'I worked so hard. I did the work. I met the deadlines. I had even suggested changes over years to the management. But they did nothing. I did everything that I could possibly do to get more out of the production line. The line-workers worked so hard too.

'Then one morning, the managing director called me to a meeting in his office. He told me that he had employed a team of experts to examine where the company was going and if productivity could be increased. Their conclusion was that the production line would have to be closed down. Everything was going to be changed around here.

'I was shattered. Then I told the workers. They were shocked. They immediately downed tools and they called in the Union. One of my work colleagues was an old veteran – a father figure. They used to call him 'The Doc'. In his previous job he worked on the buildings in London before he joined us on the production line. He had saved someone from death. He was sound as a bell and solid as a rock. He had worked through the bad times.

'He met us in the pub. He told us first of all that what the management did or did not do was nothing personal. Next, he told us that we should try to step into their shoes. Then he said: "What would you do if you were the managing director?" "How must the MD be feeling?" Next thing he told us was, before we took any action, we should get the facts and figures.

'So, we asked around. And sure enough, what we found out was that a new company was being set up in town. They had new state-of-the art systems. We were no competition for them. They were going to wipe us out. So we sat down and wondered would we go on strike, would we seek redundancy, would we buy out the company.

'We put a plan together based on what we knew. We decided that the best approach would be to ask the managing director and the management team to meet us with no hidden agenda, hands free on the table.

'They did. We told them that we understood how they must be feeling. Then we told them that, if they were willing, we would help them fight the opposition.

'They agreed. Times were tough for a while after that. But we got there. Some of the staff left, but most of them stayed. The management invested in a new production line. Although we didn't quite beat the new company in town, we held them at bay for many years. Then we diversified. Now we're bigger and better. And we're still at work.

'We were talking with a management expert about our experience. He told us that our approach to the change was exemplary. After the initial shock and anger we had followed the classic route of success. First step was empathy. We had achieved that with the managing director and with management. The next step was communication. We met them face to face. The next step was participation. They allowed us to get involved.

'We will be grateful forever to "The Doc", for his cool head and his wisdom in our time of crisis.

From an interview conducted by Century Management with an employee from a client company. Published with permission.©

ב

MAXIMISING
YOUR
SIX RESOURCES

A friend of mine felt pain in his back, shoulder, neck and legs. The pain was, he thought, due to flu, overwork and being run down. His symptoms were common and his doctor prescribed medication accordingly to reduce the pain. However, the pain persisted.

He tolerated it for more than four months ('I'm too busy to get it treated, I've a business to run'). His doctor eventually referred him to a specialist who diagnosed that it was neither flu nor overwork nor being run down, but gallstones. Within a day he was in hospital. A successful operation followed. Within a week, he was feeling better.

The health problem that had prevented him from performing at his best in his business, and from enjoying a good quality family life and playing golf, had been identified. Until his specialist identified the exact cause of the problem, his entire body was affected, his entire business was affected and the previous pain-relieving treatment was useless.

As soon as the problem was diagnosed and treated correctly, he was already on the way to full fitness. Within a month he was physically and psychologically better than he had been in a very long time.

ELIMINATING CHOKE POINTS
You arrive one morning at your office door to find that you haven't got a small piece of steel of about an inch and a half in length to allow you to enter. You hear the telephone ringing within. Lack of a small piece of steel prevents you from answering a caller who has a million-euro order. All you required was the key.

A choke point is a constraint or an obstacle that prevents the easy movement from one point to another. It prevents you from going from A to B directly and along the least line of resistance. It has the effect, eventually, of slowing down 'best performance' within your system. Managers and business owners struggle to manage change and maximise performance without removing their organisation's choke points. They don't have the key.

The length of time that it takes to process a sales order can have a huge impact on your sales. One of my clients traced the journey of a sales order. The company's sales order department processed the initial order within 30 minutes and within two hours the accounts department had further processed it. But the despatch department held the product for five days before packaging it for delivery to the customer. This delay was previously unknown to him. And unknown to him, customers perceived his company's service to be slow. Sales were lost.

He removed the choke point by simply re-organising the storage and throughput system within his warehouse. Customers could now receive their orders within two days. At one stroke he eliminated huge delays and other costs.

As an entrepreneurial manager, you must find the choke points that are slowing your organisation's performance. What could be your major choke point?

THE SIX LINK CHAIN OF RESOURCES

A CHAIN IS AS STRONG AS ITS WEAKEST LINK

Your ability to identify and strengthen, or, if necessary, remove the weakest link in your chain of resources will probably be your most important task of the year in creating business advantage. By eliminating one choke point, you may free up all other parts of your processes and systems.

One weak link in the chain of an organisation's resources can weaken, render ineffective or destroy the entire organisation. Most managers are unsure

40

of where to look for their weakest link. Most businesses have developed a functional blindness to their own defects.

The simplicity of this concept may account for the fact that it is so often overlooked as a business improvement solution.

What are the determinants of superior performance in your marketplace? Are industry conditions causing them? Is it internal organisational factors? Why are there profitable companies in unprofitable industries? Why are there unprofitable companies in profitable industries? What are your strengths? What are your weaknesses? What are your opportunities? What are your threats? Many answers to these questions can be found in a resource-based view of your business.

I have learned from working with thousands of business leaders and managers that most people have the solutions to their own problems within their own capability. The reason that they don't solve them is they don't resolve the significance of their choke points. More importantly, they don't know how to identify their choke points and resolve the problems caused by them. The chain-links analogy is a valuable thinking tool in the entrepreneurial management tool box.

YOUR SIX LINK CHAIN OF RESOURCES

The first place to look for your choke point is in the six link chain of resources that your organisation uses on a daily basis. It's an excellent management thinking toolbox.

Utilising your resources

The six links in your chain of resources are: Money, Product, Physical, Intangible, Time, and People. Every under-performing organisation has a choke point in one or more of these resources or links. Review this six link chain of resources within your organisation and you should soon identify your choke points.

For maximum impact, these six resources in your business must work in balance and operate in an integrated, co-ordinated, harmonious way. If one of them is out of synch, the rest will fail to function properly. It's like driving a car that has a soft tyre. All other parts of the car, the engine, the electrics, the bodywork, are in perfect working order. But the soft tyre slows down the car's overall movement. The six resources of your organisation may be similarly affected. Let any one of them be 'soft' and all the others are immediately affected.

Examine each link to identify if it is a weak link or contains a choke point. A chain is as strong as its weakest link. By replacing the weak link with a stronger link you will immediately strengthen the whole system. However, by improving, strengthening or replacing a link other than the weakest link, you do not improve the overall system. This is critically important and a practice that managers engage in all the time. They fix the 'wrong problems'. It's equivalent to fine-tuning the engine of the poorly performing car when all you need to do is put some air in that 'soft' tyre.

Let's look at each link of the chain of resources.

THE MONEY RESOURCE

Managers usually give the money resource great attention. Bookkeepers, accountants, auditors, the revenue commissioners and the Government force business organisations to give attention to money management.

Profit and non-profit organisations have been obsessed with financial measures of performance for generations.

Despite this, the money resource may suffer from major choke-points caused by a lack of working capital, over-borrowing, numerous debtors, poor cash flow management, extended credit, unrealistic costing and over-generous budgeting. Many excellent businesses are customer-focused, market-driven and excellent at getting sales but there is an apparent paradox within their business. 'We are getting the sales, we are getting the margins, and the customers love us. But why are we hurting so much?'

In many entrepreneurial small and medium enterprises in particular, the driving force is sales and marketing. They get the sales and the turnover. However, the turnover may be vanity. Profit is sanity.

What is the point of driving your car forward when there is a permanent roadblock up ahead? Awareness of the obvious roadblocks, and the potential roadblocks, is the mark of the entrepreneurial manager. It's what separates the winners from the average performers. It's using your brain, not your brawn. It's not confusing busyness with business. I am continually amazed at people, in many small and medium business in particular, working so hard on the wrong resource. They realise much later that they have been up a cul-de-sac.

More than half of all businesses in Ireland fail within the first five years of their start-up. The major reason is bad management. An ineffective manager can remain undetected for a long, long time. However, the ineffective manager eventually gets caught in the financial snare that causes liquidation and bankruptcy.

In 1995, the Institute of Chartered Accountants in Ireland carried out a survey of 208 companies which went into liquidation. The survey found that bad management was the main reason for 65% of failures and bad financial control was the main reason for 24% of failures.

All five tyres on your motor car (including the spare) must be constantly monitored. If air pressure drops below the recommended level, pump them up. Maximising performance in your business is similar to maintenance of your motor car.

An entrepreneurial manager uses financial ratios and check systems to analyse the money resource. He or she gets good financial advice to ensure that the money resource is not a potential flat tyre.

PERSONAL FINANCIAL MASTERY

Your ability to create personal and business financial advantage is central to entrepreneurial management. Money has a bad reputation because most people don't have enough of it. To justify their lack, you will hear them say, 'Money is the root of all evil' or 'Money can't buy happiness'. Both of these ideas are completely wrong. They are used only to rationalise the failure to have money. Money is not the root of all evil; disastrous money management could be! In fact, money makes sense in a language all nations understand.

Do you want to be rich or wealthy? There's a big difference. There's a lot of pseudo symbols of richness, like the school or college you attended, or the prestige attached to your occupation, or the neighbourhood you live in. Rich can be status oriented.

Being financially independent or wealthy is building a lifetime asset. The best measure is your net worth. Net worth is the current value of your assets less your liabilities. Wealth generation requires more an attitude of mind and is the result of a lifestyle of hard work, perseverance, planning and, most of all, self-discipline.

The one-sentence key to financial success is 'Spend less than you make.' Wealth is not income. High income people make big money but also have big mortgages, heavy taxes, penal repayments.

Big wage earners often get their wages to spend to maintain their high status lifestyle. They are often prisoners of a high standard lifestyle. Status-seekers in other words. Most wealth generators, on the other hand, have a self-employed attitude and use their money to invest in their business or for future personal and family enrichment. The sad part of this is that many high income earners have small levels of accumulated wealth. They live from paycheque to paycheque. My own guesstimate is that the average household in Ireland has a net worth of less than €13,000.

I was recently working with a high income client (earning more than €120,000 per annum) whose finances were in a total mess. Living beyond his means for years and with a seemingly total inability to spend less than he was making, his affairs were debt ridden, stressful and putting his whole career on a knife edge because of his inability to concentrate on key performance factors.

This highly educated professional, with two university degrees under his belt, was paralysed at the idea of personal financial mastery. His net worth was negligible and his robbing Peter to pay Paul philosophy was causing tremendous problems in his marriage and a total confusion in his own mind between the fact that he could earn such a high income and yet be in such a mess.

I worked closely with him over a 6 month period to get his attitude changed and helped him make some basic but key financial decisions.

FINANCIAL INDEPENDENCE

Your goal as entrepreneurial manager is to become financially independent – even wealthy. Only about 2% of Irish households are financially independent. Financial independence probably means a net worth of €1 M or more. That's only about 2,000 people. If you were to sit down and brainstorm some of the high profile media names and business leaders, you would probably come up with 200 millionaires at the most. That leaves another 1,800 ordinary millionaires. How have they become wealthy? What are their secrets? Who are they?

I have learned from personal experience the folly of not developing personal mastery skills in finance. If you make personal financial mastery a hobby and combine it with discipline, you actually enjoy the journey to building your financial independence. The discipline is doing the things you have to do. When you have to do them. Whether you like it or not. Nowhere is this discipline thing more appropriate than in financial management.

In the best selling book *The Millionaire Next Door,* Thomas Stanley and William Danko (1998) say most people have it all wrong about how you become wealthy. They say that 80% of America's millionaires are first generation rich. After studying millionaires for more than twenty years they discovered they have a lifestyle conducive to accumulating money under the following seven denominators:

1   **They live well below their means.**
    Many of them are in dull normal types of business such as welding contractors, auctioneers and dry cleaners. They drive ordinary cars. They are planners and meticulous budgeteers. Their national anthem is Frugal, Frugal, Frugal … Websters Dictionary defines frugal as behaviour characterised by or reflecting economy in the use of resources. Wasteful or a lavish lifestyle is its opposite.

2   **They allocate their time, energy and money efficiently in ways conducive to building wealth.**
    They invest wisely and employ professional money managers. Their goals are to educate their children, pay their taxes and retire comfortably. On average they spend nearly twice the number of hours per month in planning their financial affairs than the average person

spends all year. There is a strong connection between investment planning and wealth accumulation.

3   **They believe that financial independence is more important than displaying high social status.**

They live in middle-class neighbourhoods and wear ordinary clothes, watches and accessories and believe you aren't what you drive. Their motto is 'If your goal is to become financially secure, you're likely to attain it ... But if your motive is to make money, to spend money on a good life ... you're not gonna make it'.

They believe money should never change your values ... making money is only a report card. It's a way to tell how you're doing.

4   **Their parents did not provide economic out-patient care.**

They teach their children to fish, rather than giving them fish. They realise that children who receive an easy handout from their rich parents may well lose out in the long term. Rich kids often feel their parent's capital is their income ... in care to spend.

5   **Their adult children are economically self-sufficient.**

Most are surprised to realise that their parents are wealthy. They continually teach their children frugality and rarely talk about inheritance or the gifts their children will receive after they die. They stay out of their adult children's family matters. They tell their children that there are lots of things more valuable than money.

6   **They are proficient in targeting market opportunities.**

Why is it that you're not wealthy? Perhaps it's because you are not following a niche in the market and specialising in delivering a service to that sector. The millionaire next door does!

7   **They chose the right occupation.**

They know the best paid people and the wealthiest in the world are the self-employed. More than 80% of the affluent in America are self employed business owners, including self-employed professionals. (The other 20% of affluent households, by the way, are headed by retirees.)

What type of businesses do millionaires own? Good question. After twenty years of asking this question, Stanley and Danko conclude that the character of the business owner is more important in predicting their level of wealth than the classification of their business. This is totally consistent with everything in my book. There is no magic business or formulae – other than a media invention. You are the secret.

CREATING FINANCIAL MASTERY

I have worked with more than 1000 business owners in Ireland and with many thousands of professional managers at a very close level, and I believe it is possible to become wealthy from both positions. I have sought and received advice from every available quarter on financial mastery over the last 20 years and I have suffered, and enjoyed the fruits of my labour in different ways.

Here are my personal nuggets for your absorption. Take some or all of them and I can guarantee improvement in your financial affairs. Stop looking for the one big kill that will make you rich. The Lotto mindset is a deadly disease. Most of these financial nuggets can be translated into your personal or business affairs. My experience is that if somebody is financially sloppy at business, you can virtually take it for granted that they are sloppy at home. I can tell you story after story of sensible people who have holes in their financial affairs that would frighten you – like the man with a beautiful house and no contents insurance, or the cash rich retailer with no pension plan, or the number of people who never get around to making a will. Here are the best ideas available:

FIRST, SET A GOAL TO GET OUT OF DEBT IMMEDIATELY

If you have a hand-to-mouth attitude, a robbing Peter to pay Paul mindset, you must stop it immediately. Sit down with a blank sheet of paper and ask yourself why do I have such a shortfall? Why am I struggling? It's critical that you think on paper with your finances. Addition and subtraction tell the real truth about your current situation.

There are two sources of money mismanagement. One is spending your money too freely when you are doing well and the other, borrowing when you are overextended.

If you have accumulated debts, go to your debtors and work out a plan to pay them off over a period of time. Do some horse trading. Get out of the clutches of money lenders. Even if you're broke, you don't have to be poor. Set a plan to pay off your debts over time.

Stop buying on credit. Pay cash or do not have that product at all.

Perform plastic surgery on your credit cards. If you can't afford something, don't buy it. If you're in a financial mess, get rid of all your credit cards (bar one at most).

Start this financial mastery process immediately. Then continue what you've started. Not as easy as it looks. How many ventures have you started and not continued. Dozens? Probably.

THREE STAGES TO ORGANISE YOURSELF

How do you start to organise yourself? First, sit down and figure out 'What is net worth'. This is relatively simple. If you were to sell off all your assets, pay off all your debts and you fly to Australia with the balance in cash, in one suitcase in the morning. That's your net worth. You need to open a file and start writing this down with your partner in life and/or your business partners. Second, you need to figure out your cash flow and become totally focused on cash flow management. You need to spend less than you make. Are you spending less than your nett income? You may need to squeeze more cash out of your current operations. You may need to avoid carrying excessive costs. You may need to upgrade your operating procedures to plug cash leaks.

In the business world, you may need to recognise obsolete and excess inventory and how to turn it into cash. Could you be cash discounting too much when you could give away something of low value to you but high perceived value to your customer? Could you be kidding yourself about customers who appear profitable but are actually draining your bank account? Could your sales techniques be fine-tuned to get your money in quicker? How are you deploying your other resources? Time is money. Wastage costs.

In a nutshell, you need to get to grips with your cash flow management. Cash flow management is much more important than profit and loss statements, balance sheets and most other financial ratios and formulas.

The third step in organising yourself is to set investment goals over three periods. Short-term investment goals (two years and under €8,000); medium term goals (two to six years); and long-term goals (seven years and beyond). Choose your investments according to your goals. Determine your investment by the level of growth you want (short or long term will usually decide this), the level of safety you want (in general the safer the less the potential return), and how easily you can get your own hands on it. If you are in a financial mess, your first goal is to get out of debt. If your income is currently low, you can start off small. But start. Save 10% of whatever you are making – no matter how much you are making. If you can't cut your expenses or raise your income to meet this requirement you really are in serious trouble. But I'll bet it's more a mental problem than financial. Some researcher indicated that the average person spends less than 29 minutes per year working on their personal finances. No wonder only 3% become wealthy and 15% rich.

Here's the critical long-term question. How much money will you need in your retirement to support the kind of lifestyle you want to lead?

As the entrepreneurial manager you need to choose a financial advisor like you would choose a baby-sitter. Be patient.

Your financial planner is like an airplane pilot. When you fly you want him to take off and land safely. You want him to get you where you're going and you want to get there on time. That's very similar to the financial planner's job. But remember, if something goes wrong the pilot didn't build the plane. In other words, he can't control everything. Financial planners, like pilots, react to the weather, they don't create it. You must stay personally involved. You must learn the basics of financial travel. Never ever hand over total responsibility for your financial affairs to a financial planner.

NET PROFIT INCREASE

From a business situation the critical question is: How do I increase my net profit? And, of course, there are three critical ways to do this:

1 **Buy at a cheaper price.**

   Always be negotiating. It never ceases to amaze me how lackadaisical people become with purchasing materials for themselves, personally or for their business. Learn negotiation skills and shave (large) percentage points off your purchase price. Learn better purchasing techniques.

2 **Sell your products and services at a higher price.**

   Price is always relative. Surround your offering with good value and outstanding customer care. Use everything we talk about in this book and you can probably get an extra 20% on your margin. I have yet to see a business that went bankrupt by over-charging but I have seen hundreds go bankrupt by under-charging. Convenience, added-value, snappy service, old fashioned friendliness, responsiveness are often more important than price for most goods to most customers.

3 **Reduce your overheads.**

   Go ballistic on every aspect of overhead reduction. All costs walk on two feet. Everything can be reduced from electricity and telephone bills to staff costs. At home the average family probably spends 30% on non-essential foods and spur-of-the-moment purchases that are, in most cases, unnecessary. Frugality is a discipline. To delay gratification is being able to resist immediate temptation and focus on long-term gain. The words gain and profit are defined similarly in the dictionary.

Overheads are subtle and crippling and have a habit of sneaking up on you. How could you reduce your fixed overheads? Keep them as low as possible. Negotiate for a better deal on everything you buy. Virtually every household and business could dramatically decrease overheads by a minimum of 20% by a simple brainstorming exercise (see chapter 7). If you were told that you had three weeks to get your affairs in order or you would go bankrupt, what would you go back to doing? What would you cut out? What would you discipline yourself to do? One of the secrets of overhead reduction is close control. I'm not talking about a yearly review or a quarterly or monthly historical review! I'm talking weekly and daily overviews of spending. Our memories become very flaky when we're out shopping or making spending decisions.

Learn The Investment Game

A certain mystique has developed around the business of investing. Many people have seen it as something that other people do. Like every other area of life, it's an area that with information and knowledge you can become sufficiently expert in to make wise choices.

There are basically four areas of choices to take for the ordinary investor. In the investment world they call them asset classes and usually a spread across all four is advisable. Every choice, of course, has its own consequences. It's in your interest to know what they are.

These are:

1   **Cash Deposit Accounts.**
    Deposits are excellent for ready accessibility and very secure to meet those short term goals. The interest rate you receive on your deposits, of course, does not offset the ravishes of inflation over time. In Ireland, inflation has been as high as 20% and has been averaging out in the 1990's at just over 2%. In other words, if you kept €120 cash under your bed, over a 30 year period, it would probably be worth about €1 today. So your question is: How much money are you leaving in this asset class for far too long?

2   **Investing in the Stock Market**
    Investing in the Stock Market means you buy shares or equities and effectively get part ownership of the company. Your payback comes in the form of an annual dividend or in the growth of the share price. The more confidence people have in the success of the company, the more growth you will see in the share price. Over the long range high quality shares have been one of the best forms of investment.

However, there is risk and I think nothing frightens away the ordinary investor more than pronouncement that the market has collapsed such as on Black Friday (October 1987). However, the long term returns are far more favourable. The only question is in which equity should you invest. An analyst once told me 'Look in your bathroom and see what product you use (and everyone else uses) every day. Invest in these kinds of companies and ride the up and down waves.'

3   **Bonds for Security.**
Bonds are effectively ways that Governments (and indeed big companies) use to borrow money. They issue bonds. You can then buy and sell bonds on the stock market. They are obviously for the security conscious ... but security costs.

4   **The Property Affair.**
Ireland has one of the highest home ownership rates in the world and our love affair with land and property will undoubtedly continue. There is a constant debate as to whether equity or property investment provide the best return over a twenty/thirty year period. The property lobby and the equity lobby produce arguments and charts that in my view only serve to bamboozle the ordinary investor.

It's best if you spread your investments over all the asset areas. Ultimately, you have to decide how much risk you want to take. And then take a very deliberate and conscious decision to enjoy and smile at the wins and suffer and get on with it when you take a hit. The key thing is not to let one circumstance or bad investment, or downturn in the market lead to a reactive, knee jerk response. Take a long term view. If you are any way stressed or worried about your investments you are probable doing the wrong thing.

The bottom line on investments is to study the subject, talk to the advisers, read the financial news and become your own best advocate. Economists and full time financial whiz-kids, who have their hand on the pulse every minute of every day, get it very wrong as well. So all you can do is your best.

PERSONAL PROFIT CENTRE

Business executives over-measure business performance by profit and financial ratios virtually all of the time. However, you are also a personal profit centre. You must set financial independence as one of your major goals, not just for the money but to be free to concentrate on higher order goals and strategies. Peter Drucker says that the task of a business is to provide adequately for the cost of staying in business – by earning an adequate profit.

Profitable objectives therefore measure not the maximum profit the business can produce but the minimum it must produce. As the Entrepreneurial Manager you must think of yourself as a profit centre and establish some ratios and measures for your personal affairs. And here are some basics for financial mastery:

1   Review all your insurance policies. Get several independent assessments. Plug the gaps. How you structure your various insurances from life cover to mortgage protection is critically important.

2   Get rid of your personal banking overdraft. Your goal should be to live within your means and totally eliminate bank charges.

3   Do you have a pension? Is it adequately funded? Can you maximise your tax relief by making additional voluntary contributions? Only 25% of self employed people have pensions. In Europe there are four workers for every one pensioner. By the year 2040 the ratio will reduce to two workers for every one pensioner. This has serious implications for your financial affairs in the future.

4   Are you claiming all your tax reliefs? Millions of euros in reliefs are unclaimed each year.

5   Write a will. The amount of so-called responsible citizens who work 60-70 hours per week to feed their family and then leave them in a disastrous situation if they die because of a total oversight regarding their will is totally folly. My experience is that as high as 50% of all executives have no will.

The principles of financial success are eternal and in the first instance you should develop a very clear understanding that financial independence is more a psychological discipline than any other function. It is the medium by which earthly success is measured. Set a goal therefore to read half a dozen to ten books on the psychology and mechanics of money management.

You must also stay abreast of the mechanics of modern day money management. Money markets are volatile. Even the experts are struggling to keep up as politics, economics and even individual idiosyncrasies can rock the global economy.

In a nutshell, get to grips with your personal and business finance resource.

THE PRODUCT RESOURCE

Many managers do not realise that a product may be a combination of products. One may be the core product itself which you might manufacture. Another may be the actual product with packaging and design and a third may be the augmented product with delivery, guarantees and service. Product is a major resource of your business.

Most managers manage the physical products well. If you have a bad physical product in today's marketplace, you get 'found out' pretty quickly. People just won't buy it or give you repeat sales. Warehouse managers have inventory systems and they manage the packaging, distribution, storage and stock control in a reasonable manner. However, the accompanying service is often delivered in a substandard way with the effect of demeaning what may be an excellent product.

A quality product by itself is not good enough today. To capitalise on a good quality product, you must deliver not just good service but exceptional customer service. Quality is standard and expected by everybody. Yet the majority of companies are unclear about this. When you ask them: 'Why should I buy from you?' they invariably still reply: 'Because we have a good quality product at a great price.' Wake up! Everyone else has good quality product. Find other reasons that make it worthwhile to buy from you rather than from your competitor!

What your customer considers to be value in your product can be fundamentally different from your viewpoint. Be 100% clear on this point.

The physical side of customer needs of packaging, design, delivery and quality is met reasonably well these days. Customers in all walks of life have high expectations of how they want to be sold to. They will therefore reject products that are less than the highest quality standard.

Furthermore, sophisticated customers are ruthless in discriminating against suppliers of products and service that are good but whose presentation, back up and delivery are poor. Their consumer rights are reinforced by the legal system, which they use to maximum effect.

E-mail has a revolutionary impact on how products and services are delivered and is fundamental to all future promotion, distribution and communication strategies. E-mail will become a critical customer interfacing system. The rise of the Internet, World Wide Web and E-Mail technologies is unstoppable and requires well thought-out strategies to maximise its impact. Massive and immediate action is required towards E-commerce by many organisations.

One of your choke points may be the delivery of outstanding customer care. How do you know? What would you have to do to find out? When did you last ask your customers in a scientific, objective manner what they really think of you? Don't assume that you know your customers. Customers lie all the time.

Many organisations get caught up in fixing the wrong problem in customer care. They believe that customers want a better quality, better-designed product, and they spend fortunes giving this to their customers. Other organisations have a fixation about price, and are constantly using an external factor, such as their competition, as a basis for setting their own price. Yet it has been demonstrated over and over again that price is not the major buying motive for most customers. Price is a factor for only about 6% of commodity type purchases. How you deliver the product to the customer is often more important than what the price is.

Are you fixing the wrong problem? What is your potential choke point in your product and service delivery? Many ordinary managers, preoccupied with daily and short-term activities, fail to realise that outstanding customer care will not just happen. If it is to become outstanding, customer care must be managed by whatever medium!

The number of truly service-oriented companies in Ireland is few. Most give good service, but not outstanding service. About 20% just give bad service. These bad companies are of course blind to their choke points. They even insist on investing large sums of money on three, four or five of the links in the six link chain of business resources in the vain hope that it will make the overall organisation run better. It's similar to waxing and polishing your car in the vain hope that it will compensate for the soft tyre!

THE PHYSICAL RESOURCE

The physical resource is made up of three primary elements:

1 **Place**

2 **Equipment**

3 **Technology.**

1 Place. Your office, plant or building, the place where you conduct your daily activities, is an important resource of your business. Any good estate agent will tell you that there are three primary considerations when buying property – location, location, location. Yet it's not just location; it's also how you present your premises.

You will have seen many excellently located businesses present their properties in a shabby manner. Good marketing and good communications are best measured by the response they get. Your job as entrepreneurial manager is to create perceptions of unique added value in the minds of your customers. You set the benchmark in terms of how you manage your premises in terms of occupancy, maintenance cost, rental income, and geographical suitability. Your best competitor sets the benchmark for quality prices and service standards. Your site and location, however, present unique opportunities to differentiate yourself.

If my first impression, largely determined by my visual inspection, is that your premises are shabby, then my mental tendency is to make massive conclusions from even small observations, that your service will be shabby too. It's how perception works, fairly or unfairly. Beware. Customers easily jump to conclusions.

I have seen many potentially successful businesses with excellent products, excellent people and excellent financial management systems sabotage themselves by poor presentation of their businesses. Paint the exterior of the office, update the external signage, clean up the car park, redesign the reception area and you may totally change the customers' perceptions. Quality and speed may have been key variables in competitive advantage in the 1980s and 1990s. Presentation and design may be the 21st century winning edge variables.

2 Equipment. Equipment is the second element of the key physical resources of your business. It includes office, transport and production equipment. We live in the age of communications, but some businesses are still using the old tools of the industrial age, which have been superseded by the newer tools of the knowledge/communications age. Today's tools and equipment are designed to do everything better, faster, cheaper, easier, newer and different.

Wireless technology and electronic commerce mean instant access and immediate connection. 'Anything, everywhere' is the motto and expectation for the 21st century. But, do we have the equipment and technological resources to deliver information, service or product in a faster, better or easier way? Could the use of obsolete equipment be your choke point? If so, what can you do about it?

3 Technology. Technology is the third element. The present computer capability in most organisations is under-utilised. In many cases, companies buy computer equipment that is unnecessary. Lack of investment in training and time to explore the current facilities of computer equipment may mean that your computers are an under-utilised asset.

In most cases, it simply means reading and maximising the capability of the software. Invest time and explain to a software specialist what your specific needs from the equipment are. The calibre, capability and user-friendliness of your current computer equipment is critically important in serving the other five resources of people, money, time, product and intangibles. In today's better, faster, cheaper, easier world, obsolete computer equipment and out of date computer software should not be your choke points.

There are, of course, important items of equipment in your fleet of transport and your production line. Different businesses have different raw materials and physical resources which need to be managed.

In earlier times, land was the key resource and became the power symbol. Labour, ironically, was also seen as a physical resource in the sense that a person was seen as a 'lifter and shifter' – a bit like a machine is seen today. Natural physical resources like coal, oil, timber and steel also dominated economic life … but not anymore. The dominance of the physical resource is over.

THE INTANGIBLE RESOURCE

You can't feel them. You can't see them. You can't taste them. You can only measure their effects. They seem to be abstract constructs. They're intangible. Yet they are valuable resources that produce results, that in turn translate into products and productivity and market share and profits. Investment in your intangible resources can pay off in multiples far greater than your original investment in them.

Staff morale, *esprit de corps* and level of motivation, respect, recognition, knowledge and intellectual property, culture, company philosophy and ethos, 'unwritten agendas', corporate image and goodwill may be regarded as intangibles. You can't see staff morale, but you can measure its effects when you apply tried and tested incentives or disincentives to staff. It results or doesn't result in increased productivity.

You can't see corporate image, but you can measure the effects of employing differing corporate identity materials and approaches in, for example, the number of new customers it attracts long term or the level of consciousness of your product or service among the general public.

You can't see goodwill, but you can measure its effects in the length of time that a number of customers remain loyal. Accountants have another meaning for goodwill which is the difference between your book value and your current market value.

Knowledge has become the most important factor in economic life and foremost of all the intangibles. It may well be the key wealth creator of the 21st century. For the 21st century, effective knowledge management will be a core competency.

You must invest time and money to develop this competency. It will totally change how you do business. It will involve major changes in your processes, cultures, infrastructures and measurements. Learn the new tools, techniques, skills, framework and expertise to make this happen. Transform your capacity to create, classify, apply, exploit and value knowledge to improve performance and create business advantage.

Implement strategies based on innovation and intellectual capital. Your organisation could take a huge step forward if only you 'knew what you know', that is if you utilised your in-built but dormant knowledge. Bottle your know-how. Draw out, capture, share, and write up and apply the experiences of each employee.

Microsoft have something far more valuable than physical or financial assets. They have intellectual capital. People buy intangible assets when they invest in Microsoft. The market capitalisation of Microsoft in November 1996 was $85.5 billion with physical assets of only $900 million. By contrast, IBM's market capitalisation was about $70.7 billion but with $16.6 billion in physical assets.

Intellectual capital is defined by Thomas A Stewart in his book *Intellectual Capital* as 'intellectual material – knowledge, information, intellectual property, experience – that can be put to use to create wealth'. It is collective brainpower. It is intangible. Knowledge management is about fuelling this capital so that it becomes a catalyst for change, innovation, motivation and business advantage.

In the industrial age, land, natural resources (coal, oil etc), human and machine labour were the ingredients from which wealth was created. In this new age of information and communication, wealth is the product of knowledge. Therefore you must become a knowledge manager.

IMAGE AND IDENTITY

Your corporate image is one of the most powerful intangible resources. It can be one of the most visible and powerful statements and actions you can make about the present set-up and the future direction of your business.

Investment in corporate identity that in turn creates your corporate image yields one of your greatest returns on investment. The identity business is, however, shrouded in confusion for the ordinary manager. Its mystique has caused many managers to shy away from exploiting it.

Further, there is major confusion about the terminology and language of the industry because many of the consultants purporting to practise identity stem from different backgrounds – some from public relations, some from design, some from marketing.

Words and concepts such as image, design, brand identity and brand image, corporate identity and corporate image and reputation confuse even the people in the industry themselves. So it's not surprising that the ordinary manager is confused.

The entrepreneurial manager realises that corporate identity is a valuable resource and, when used properly, it has a major influence on all the other resources and functions within the business. Corporate identity programmes complement and help to accelerate behavioural change interventions within an organisation. They can be linked closely to early wins. It's often easier to see visible environmental change than behavioural and attitudinal change. Therefore, it is a major enabler of change and should not be sidelined in the restructuring, reorganisation or re-deployment of any of the other business resources.

Identity has the capability of not only helping the change process but visibly demonstrating that it has, in fact, taken place when it translates into image. It can influence internal and external stakeholders. It is a cost-effective resource to bring to life because most organisations are already carrying out various aspects of identity. However, many of them are doing it in an uncoordinated, mixed-up way.

You cannot NOT communicate. Everybody and every organisation has an identity. It's what you present to the world. Image, on the other hand, is the perception your 'publics' – customers, suppliers, the community, shareholders, bankers – receive from your identity. Identity is made up of brand, colour, reputation, behaviours, culture, history, style, standards, values, quality and character. Identity management is the way you manage the interactions and transactions between you and your various stakeholders. You manage them rather than let them unfold in an unsystematic way.

How you want the world to perceive you and how you present yourself is your identity. Identity communicates four things about you:

1 Who you are
2 What you do
3 How you do it
4 What you represent

There are four obvious and visible places within your business where you can study identity. I call them the 4 P's of corporate identity:

1 Products
2 Place
3 Presentables
4 People

Products: includes your services, manufacturing, distribution, selling and marketing.

Place: your premises and the environments in which you do business.

Presentables: the paperwork, signage, livery and basically how you communicate and explain to your audiences/ publics what you do.

People: your people transmit messages through their behaviours and actions about 'how we do things around here' on an ongoing basis.

Management of the identity resource is a very weak link for many small and medium enterprises in Ireland. Major corporate companies have made the investments in most cases. Just as financial management systems and, in more recent times, information technology systems are regarded as essential to growth and development, so also will corporate identity.

It is an important resource for differentiation in this competitive age. You should study it carefully for your own business. Hire corporate identity experts and give it the allocation of professionalism that it deserves. Otherwise you, your employees and shareholders will earn a tarnished image that will be extremely difficult to shine. Remember that products come and go. So do people. But your reputation is hard earned and a very valuable intangible asset.

OTHER INTANGIBLE ASSETS

There are other intangible assets and capabilities that are essential to exploiting new ideas, innovations and achievements. As an entrepreneurial manager, you need to recognise these intangible assets and capabilities and continually ask the question, 'How under-utilised are they and how could I deploy them better?'

For example, many businesses have downtime or off-peak time in their businesses. How could they use this time to create business advantage? What about using staff to make proactive phone calls to customers rather than have them 'just sit there twiddling their thumbs all morning' as one business woman explained to me. Another rented out a corner of his shop to a complementary business.

Your list of intangible assets and capabilities should include:

• The goodwill and the potential of your current customer base.

It takes between five and 15 times more time, cost and energy to get new customers than to keep the customers you have already. Customer relationships, developed your way, are an intellectual property.

• Intellectual properties in the form of patents, licences, agreements, technologies, royalties, franchises, trade secrets, copyright and brands. How much is the Kellogg name worth for instance? Or Guinness? Or Waterford Crystal?

• Your know-how, processes and bank of experience could be one of your most valuable intangible capabilities. They are usually resident in the heads of too few people. However, this fact is not fully appreciated by the management team. Your solicitor, for instance, sells pure brainpower. You buy his knowledge and experience.

• Your methods, culture, business philosophies and 'how we do things around here' are also assets. 'Our people are our greatest asset' is a well-worn cliché. The teamwork, the competencies, the total quality thinking, the responsiveness, the friendliness, the health, the skills that they have developed are assets. At the heart of this valuable resource is a network of strong relationships or implicit understandings. It's an ongoing educational process to keep this alive. Even the Accounting Standards Board, which guides accountants in these islands, puts research and development under the category of intangible resources.

• Commitment and loyalty of workforce are assets. Invest in those assets by fostering them. Don't waste them by causing undue stress. Stress costs the Irish economy an estimated €300 M per year, €200 M of this is due to time lost from work.

Your foremost question is: 'How do you continually create business advantage and are these intangibles drivers of competitive advantage for your business?'

Intangibles are assets because you cannot produce results without them. You will find that the reason you are not maximising your potential or are not 'No.1' in your marketplace has quite a lot to do with how you utilise your intangible resources.

THE TIME RESOURCE

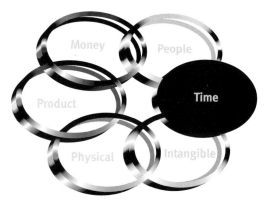

All people, businesses and organisations waste time. All of the major challenges facing businesses today in a fast-changing environment are in some way linked to time.

There are 168 hours in every week. Everyone gets exactly the same number of hours. The dilemma faced by most managers is 'How do we optimise this critical resource?'

Fiercer competition is being driven by potential improvement activities such as Just-in-Time or World Class Manufacturing. All are driven by an insatiable desire to transfer information and products faster, better, cheaper and more easily. The development of the global marketplace is about optimising all resources, but ultimately the greatest impact is made around the Time resource.

Workers seek a more flexible use of time. Part-time work, job-sharing, and contract work are fast becoming the norm. Fewer people have the luxury of the '40-hour per week job for life'.

For most of the 20th century, members of the workforce changed jobs five times in the same career. The demands of the global market economy will dictate that it is more likely that in our lifetime that they will change career five times.

Most people will have to rethink how to use their personal time, family time and career and work time. The demands of the upside-down organisation, and the revolution in the social and business world are driving the need to manage time as a scarce resource. Higher customer expectations and demands will make service more time-critical than ever.

A distributor to pharmacies recently told me that now he makes up to three deliveries per day to pharmacies in Dublin, and once per day to country pharmacies. The pharmacies expect these deliveries because their customers expect it.

'We'll deliver it tomorrow' is no longer acceptable. Everyone wants it now. The Instant age is here. And the Instant age is all about managing the critical resource of time by the second, by the minute, by the hour, by the day, by the week.

For many, time is a more valuable resource than money. Twenty years ago, there were few couriers in the cities; today there are numerous couriers delivering goods at speed, direct to homes and businesses in every city, town and village in Ireland. You can get almost anything anywhere, nationally or globally, within 24 hours. 'Anything to anyone anywhere today' is a key driving force for many organisations.

Thoroughly examining how to get 'the goods out of the woods' and by brainstorming ways to improve your channels of distribution can, by itself, have a major impact on your business. Getting a reputation for 'a quick response' to everything from a phone call to electronic communication to deliveries, can by itself differentiate your organisation from any other.

Domino Pizza, a major American pizza corporation, made its reputation on fast delivery time. They promised that if the pizza was not delivered within 30 minutes, there would be no charge. Time was the critical factor. They realised that when people ordered a pizza they were hungry. The quality of the pizza was not as important as how fast you got it to them.

All of the major improvement activities of recent decades are directly or indirectly involved in maximising the use of time. Prominent methods include Total Quality Management, Strategic Process Management, Self-Directed-Work-Teams, Re-engineering, Bench-Marking, Learning Organisations, Best Practices, Kaizen, ISO 9000, Just-in-Time, World Class Manufacturing, Environmental Standards. All have the purpose of continuous improvement and getting your product or service from A to B better, faster, differently, more cheaply and easily – but above all – faster.

In the printing business, for example, fast production and fast delivery are expected. Twenty years ago, it might have taken ten different, laborious, painstaking processes and a time frame of three months to print this book. In the year 1999, it took just three steps and less than one day to print the first edition.

GET TIME IN PERSPECTIVE

The challenge in this age of faster change is to embrace and control time by appreciating just how vital the time resource is in maximising your potential. Could the management of time be your own personal choke point? Could it be an organisational problem?

More than 80% of all managers and business owners regard the management of time as their biggest single challenge. Because there is a constant supply of this resource, it is probably one of the most abused resources in the six link chain of business resources.

Is time the choke point for members of your staff? Is it the reason that you fail to rectify other choke points in finance, product and service development, or the other physical resources? Is it the reason that communication is not so good in your organisation, and is it a contributing factor to low morale, low trust and high stress levels? Is there a connection between low levels of creativity, innovation, common sense and initiatives being taken? Is there a connection between wastage, high turnover, low sales, bad profits and all other ills in your business? You could probably trace the cause of all of the ill-effects outlined above back to a poor appreciation, awareness and understanding of the critical resource of time.

Many managers constantly moan that they haven't got enough time or there are never enough hours in the day. Therefore, time is not the problem – it's how you use it. Time is the most predictable resource for you as a manager. It has a fixed amount and a fixed rate of expenditure. However, once used, it is irretrievable.

Decide to become a time management expert right now by listening to audio tapes, by reading books and by attending courses on the use of time. I am a fanatic about time management techniques.

LEARN TO THINK AND PLAN PERSONAL STRATEGY

Please understand that the major reason why people under-perform and fail to achieve their full potential personally, as a team leader or in an overall organisational context, is because of unclear thinking and planning. In a word, it's fuzziness.

In order to clear your thinking you can easily use the six link chain of business resources as a framework or checklist when developing a personal strategic plan. Do a current situation analysis of yourself on several levels. What is your current financial situation? What about your Corporate Identity? How do you present yourself to the world? Are you professional, the proper weight, well groomed? What about your clothes? What about your poise and style?

What about you as a product or service? Are you an attractive product or service? What are your personal assets, distinctive capabilities and your personal liabilities?

How do you utilise your time? Do you confuse *busyness* with *business*? Do you confuse activity with progress? Do you have balance in your life?

Are you reactive or proactive? What worthwhile accomplishment have you achieved in the last 18 months? Have you set out in writing clear goals for the next 12 months?

Have you arranged your physical resources to give you personal advantage? Do you have a study room or library at home? Do you have an implementation system, not just any old-fashioned diary system, to plan your private work and business life? Are you computer literate?

Where do you conduct your continuous learning and education? How much time and money do you invest in your own personal, professional and business development each year?

Write all this down and whatever else comes to mind under current situation analysis. For most people it's a frightening, but truth-telling experience. Effective time management is not just about using time productively. It's also about making progress.

Becoming an outstanding time manager takes concentrated effort over an extended period of time because, ultimately, effective time management is a state of mind.

When you have completed the current situation analysis, continue with the strategic formula outlined in Chapter 5 for yourself personally. What has your personal and career history been like? Update your Curriculum Vitae to check your achievements. More importantly, what are your values, what is your mission, and what are your visions, strategic goals and tactical plans?

BECOME AN OBSESSIVE GOAL SETTER

As an entrepreneurial manager you become an obsessive goal setter because you know that setting and achieving your definite goals is the definition of success. If you understand this statement clearly, you will immediately propel your thinking onto a new level. If you get up each morning and do an honest day's work, you will achieve goals. You will make progress.

However, success and fulfilment is determined by achieving the goals that you set out to achieve rather than those things that happen to you because you work hard. There is a big difference.

Most good, honest, hard-working managers will achieve lots of personal, career and business goals. Your satisfaction, success and the entrepreneurial management feeling will come from achieving the goals that you have set. It requires strength of character and the ability to stick to the decisions and goals you have set long after the enthusiasm with which they were set has left you.

It's disciplining yourself to do the things you have to do when you have to do them, whether you like it or not. This, combined with using the proper tools and techniques of time management, is the secret of achieving above average success.

I have met so many managers who use diaries, organisers, schedulers and time management systems, post-it stickers, To Do lists and pieces of paper to organise themselves. Some use combinations of all these simultaneously. I have personally used the most complicated time management systems and the most basic. Go beyond the diary organisers to a total, integrated implementation system.

We're all busy – too busy. Whether the objective is business process reengineering, continuous improvement or to implement cultural change, you need to:

Remind yourself of Key Result Areas (KRAs) all the time and book time to make KRAs happen.

The logic is blindingly obvious – the things you lose sight of are not remembered and therefore you do nothing about them. You major on minors and you lose focus. You need to 'visually' see on an everyday basis what your key result areas are.

EIGHT KEY QUESTIONS ON TIME AND LIFE MANAGEMENT.

Here are eight great questions which you should ask yourself over and over again to maximise your time.

Q.1 AM I BEING REACTIVE OR PROACTIVE?

The 80/20 rule, which is also called the Pareto principle, tells us that 20% of the input into any process commonly generates 80% of the output. For example, 20% of your customers may account for 80% of your total business turnover. Or 20% of your product lines may account for 80% of your sales. Do you take the initiative with your 20% key customers or do you get drowned out (reactive) with the 80%.

It follows that 20% of the time you spend doing things produces 80% of your results. When and how you use this 20% is obviously vitally important. If you take some time for planning and preparation during the time management process, you can cut down considerably on the amount of time required to complete each task. The result is that you can accomplish much more with that vital 20% of time invested. This is a key point when you consider the importance of finding the time to do important tasks.

By examining a cause-and-effect situation, you can isolate key factors for remedial action. In other words, by identifying 'the vital few' (the 20%) over the 'trivial many' (the 80%) you can find the secret to your long term success and improvement. Be careful of reactive management!

A manager, who completed a comprehensive three month-long analysis of his time, told me that 18% of his incoming telephone callers took up 74% of his total telephone time. This startled him. He immediately set in motion ways and means to do business in a different and more concise way with these callers. He was reactive to every call.

Another manager explained to me that his company had comprehensive information on absenteeism but management had never sat down and analysed who were the main absentees or the potential causes of absenteeism in their business. Because he had the information on hand, he spent several hours analysing the absenteeism of the previous year. He found that 22% of his staff (absentees) accounted for 84% of all lost time. He decided to be proactive with this information!

When he analysed it further through discussion with his supervisors and staff in general, he found that the major cause was a group of young mothers whose major problem was looking after young babies. The solution was simple. He financed the building of a creche in an old office within the factory. Over the following six months, the absentee rate dropped by 55%.

Many other examples of the 80/20 rule can be seen in other aspects of industry and business. We know from training sales people across a wide range of industries that sales representatives spend only about 20% of their time in front of their customers. More than 80% of time is spent in the office, travelling or wasting time. Sales representatives who just increase time in front of the customer (selling face-to-face) by 5% or 10% may be doing enough to make a significant bottom line difference to sales. Most sales representatives have never analysed their time in this regard. Most of their managers have not done so either. Time techniques of territory management or better telephone usage alone will have significant benefits. Think it out. Be proactive.

A key executive in a client organisation just couldn't find the time to complete important tasks. Together we analysed his time management. He travelled 28,000 business miles the previous year. In his reactive mode, he felt his job was to 'jump in the car' to solve every problem. Calculating that he travelled at about 40mph, he spent about 700 hours or the equivalent of 17 work weeks in his car – that's like driving non-stop from January to May. He was astonished with this information and its implications and set about reorganising his journeys. He cut them down to 14,000 miles.

YOU'VE GOT SIX MONTHS

Bill, the sales manager in one of our client companies, was the best salesman in his field. He was not alone sales manager, but he also outsold each of the other members of his 11 member sales team in most months of the year. He had been promoted three years previously and he was delighted with the extra recognition and responsibility. Three members of his team outsold the other eight members. Every month, he held a one-day sales meeting and focused on operational issues of budgets, product updates and of course sales figures.

But the managing director said to Bill, 'Get your house in order (or else). You've got six months'. The managing director had correctly identified that all except three members of the sales team were failing to achieve their potential and that there were inconsistencies everywhere in their approaches to prospects and customers.

Sales are the lifeblood of any business. The sales manager has the pivotal role in a sales oriented company. In this company, Bill didn't really understand his job. He failed to get exceptional sales performance through his team. He had no concept at all of the difference between being proactive and being reactive.

We immersed him in a sales management programme, which included mentoring. Within four weeks, he had fired two of his representatives and within four more weeks, he had hired two to replace them. Within 16 weeks, sales had increased by 35%. One previously average performer hit a 76% increase. Within nine months sales per month had doubled.

Your application of the Pareto discipline to your time management, to mark out time to do important tasks and goals, is critical to success. Doing the wrong thing very well, is the height of folly. Think about your reactiveness!

Q.2 AM I EFFICIENT OR AM I EFFECTIVE?

One of the most important questions you should continually ask yourself is: 'Am I efficient or am I effective?' Most managers are so busy cutting wood that they don't take the time to sit down and sharpen the axe. Just hitting harder and going faster doesn't necessarily mean you're more effective. Confusing busyness with business is a major blind spot for many managers.

The efficient manager gets involved in everything. He is obsessed with making an impression: 'Look at how busy I am and how hard I work.' He suffers from the 'martyr' syndrome. The effective manager concentrates on key result areas – the 20% important, vital, few tasks. Focusing on these tasks moves you to a fundamentally better position in overall strategic terms.

Map yourself on the productivity matrix as follows: On the North (Effective)/South (Efficient) axis first – just put an x where you believe you are right now. Then the East (Proactive)/West (Reactive) axis. Then simply link the two lines for your position. Now, make some decisions around this information. Could you be deluding yourself? Ask other people to map you independently. This should reveal the real truth.

THE PRODUCTIVITY MATRIX

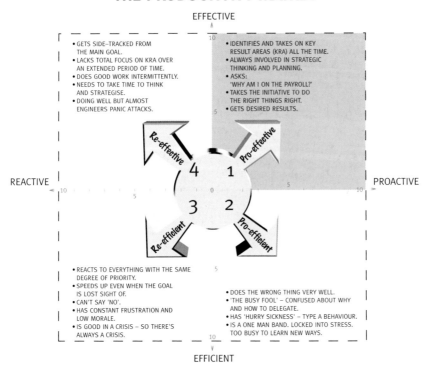

A constant challenge for all entrepreneurial managers is to maximise productivity on a personal level and on a business level. The master key to conquering this challenge is understanding and mastering the difference between effectiveness and efficiency and being re-active and being pro-active. Gaining clarity on this productivity dilemma is central to maximising your resources. Your objective should be to reside in Quadrant 1 for at least 50% of your time.

As an entrepreneurial manager, you are clear about the difference between being efficient and being effective. Being efficient means doing the job right, whereas being effective means doing the right job right. There is an enormous difference between the two. But it's a subjective judgement call in many cases. Only you can decide.

Q.3 DO I CONCENTRATE ON URGENT TASKS OR IMPORTANT TASKS?

As the effective entrepreneurial manager you identify through your strategic thinking and planning process the important success areas of your job, career and business. You are a delegator par excellence. You can see the wood from the trees. You learn to say no. You know how to lock yourself away for hours or even days of concentrated thinking and planning time. The tuned-in entrepreneurial manager does this every week and almost feels cheated if he hasn't scheduled a certain portion of time to important long-term strategic and vision-related activities every week.

THE DECISIONS MATRIX

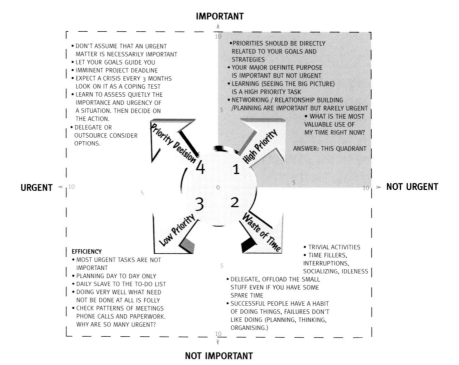

IMPORTANT

• DON'T ASSUME THAT AN URGENT MATTER IS NECESSARILY IMPORTANT
• LET YOUR GOALS GUIDE YOU
• IMMINENT PROJECT DEADLINE
• EXPECT A CRISIS EVERY 3 MONTHS LOOK ON IT AS A COPING TEST
• LEARN TO ASSESS QUIETLY THE IMPORTANCE AND URGENCY OF A SITUATION. THEN DECIDE ON THE ACTION.
• DELEGATE OR OUTSOURCE CONSIDER OPTIONS.

•PRIORITIES SHOULD BE DIRECTLY RELATED TO YOUR GOALS AND STRATEGIES
• YOUR MAJOR DEFINITE PURPOSE IS IMPORTANT BUT NOT URGENT
• LEARNING (SEEING THE BIG PICTURE) IS A HIGH PRIORITY TASK
• NETWORKING / RELATIONSHIP BUILDING /PLANNING ARE IMPORTANT BUT RARELY URGENT
• WHAT IS THE MOST VALUABLE USE OF MY TIME RIGHT NOW?

ANSWER: THIS QUADRANT

Priority Decision 4 1 *High Priority*

URGENT — 10 — 0 — 5 — 10 → NOT URGENT

3 2

Low Priority *Waste of Time*

EFFICIENCY
• MOST URGENT TASKS ARE NOT IMPORTANT
• PLANNING DAY TO DAY ONLY
• DAILY SLAVE TO THE TO-DO LIST
• DOING VERY WELL WHAT NEED NOT BE DONE AT ALL IS FOLLY
• CHECK PATTERNS OF MEETINGS PHONE CALLS AND PAPERWORK. WHY ARE SO MANY URGENT?

• TRIVIAL ACTIVITIES
• TIME FILLERS, INTERRUPTIONS, SOCIALIZING, IDLENESS
• DELEGATE, OFFLOAD THE SMALL STUFF EVEN IF YOU HAVE SOME SPARE TIME
• SUCCESSFUL PEOPLE HAVE A HABIT OF DOING THINGS, FAILURES DON'T LIKE DOING (PLANNING, THINKING, ORGANISING.)

NOT IMPORTANT

Making important decisions requires a thinking framework that helps you to justify some things you need to do (Urgent things) and guides you away from things you should not do. Your ideal decisions are high in importance and low in urgency. Focus on the decisions that are directly related to your goals and strategies.

An important task is a high benefit task. An urgent task is time-bounded – if you don't do it by a certain time the benefit of doing it will be lost or reduced. Watch out for the urgent task crowding out the important task. Schedule time for the important jobs during your personal best time. For me this is early morning – it's when I'm freshest and clearest. Writing this book was not urgent for me but it was important and I wrote most of it between 6 p.m and 8 a.m.

Ask yourself the questions: 'Am I being Efficient?' or 'Am I being Effective?' and 'Do I concentrate on urgent tasks or important tasks?' at regular times every day.

One of the best exercises that I have ever conducted was to write these two questions on the top of my diary page six months in advance. Every day when you open the page, these questions stare you in the face. There's no escaping them. It's also good to write the questions on a flash card and stick it onto the dashboard of your car or on to your desk.

Q.4 WHAT IS THE MOST VALUABLE USE OF MY TIME RIGHT NOW?

You will have great difficulty with honestly answering this question for yourself if you are unfocused. It will cause you great stress and turmoil if you are confused about the words 'effective/efficient', 'proactive/reactive' and 'important/urgent'.

You will have great difficulty answering the question fully if you haven't got the answers to Question 5 clearly sorted out and written down as outlined in your personal and business strategy. The key to personal leadership and top performance is clear purposeful action. Coincidentally, it's also the cure for stress and other illnesses. To answer this question fully, you must consider the power of purpose. What is your overall purpose? Why do you get up in the morning? What motivates you? Are you going through the motions or are you living out your dreams? What is your calling? Where do you fit? What difference are you making to other people's lives? What are your expectations?

Q.5 WHAT I AM DOING TODAY TO MOVE ME CLOSER TO THE ACHIEVEMENT OF MY GOALS?

If you don't know where you're going, there is no doubt but that you will end up somewhere. What are you doing today to move you closer to achievement of your goals? The secret, as the entrepreneurial manager, is not that you end up somewhere, even if it is a better place than before, but that you end up at the place that you set out to end up. Please don't fool yourself. If they're not written down, they're not goals, they are nice ideas. Today a step in any direction will not do. You must ensure that each step is in the right direction.

Your mind is capable of storing thousands and thousands of facts and ideas but it can only focus on those important things that you are reminded of on a continual basis. It is not possible to be proactive and focused clearly on the important and the effective without beating away the other thousands of trivial pieces of information and demands on your time.

Q.6 WHAT MAKES ME PRODUCTIVE? SUPPLEMENTARY QUESTIONS ARE: 'WHAT IS MY JOB?' 'WHY AM I ON THE PAYROLL?'

To help you answer this question, draw a 360 degree blank circle and start to divide it into sections regarding your job. How much long-term thinking time have you allocated in there? You must allocate it and slice it into your scheduling and planning system.

What are your strategic goals? Focus and clarity are key competencies for your success. You cannot honestly answer the 'What makes me productive?' question unless you are clear and totally focused on your major definite purpose.

I speak to thousands of managers each year at public and in-house meetings and seminars and I ask them what's their single biggest day-to-day and ongoing challenge. Their answers are invariably 'overloaded', 'too busy', and 'not enough time in the day'. Many of these managers are very efficient, productive people but they are not effective or not proactive and they are not entrepreneurial managers.

Q.7 WHAT CAN I, AND ONLY I, DO THAT IF DONE REALLY WELL WOULD MAKE AN EXTRAORDINARY DIFFERENCE TO MY OWN DEVELOPMENT, AND THE DEVELOPMENT OF MY CAREER AND BUSINESS?

Everyone should have primary responsibilities for key tasks. In other words, have you established what your own key result areas (KRA) are and do you know what the KRA are for everyone in your team and in your organisation?

Your ability to concentrate and focus on these key result areas will set you apart from everyone else in terms of bottom line outcomes and results.

During my talks and seminars, I ask managers to engage in a practical exercise to demonstrate my 'zoom in/zoom out' focus technique. I ask them to hold their index finger about 18" in front of their face and to focus all their attention on that finger. They can clearly see their fingerprint lines. I now ask them to become aware that everything in the background and on the horizon is blurred and unclear. I then ask them to zoom out like a wide-angle zoom lens of a camera and bring the distant horizon and background into full view.

They still keep their finger in place but are now aware that it is quite difficult to zoom in on the finger and keep a crystal clear picture of the background. Move your finger a few inches from left to right in front of your face to demonstrate the need to adjust and be flexible in moving towards the big picture.

You will have figured out the purpose of the exercise by now. It is the ability to zoom in on short and medium term requirements while at the same time having the ability to focus on the wider horizon and bring it into crystal clear vision at a moment's notice. You must be able to align the short-term projects with the medium term projects and with your big picture vision.

Q.8 THE ZERO-BASED QUESTION

The eighth and final question is a zero-based question. Zero-based questions help you to make up your mind about critical issues, and therefore save enormous amounts of wasted time, stress and people problems. Apply a zero-based question as follows: 'Knowing what I now know about this person that I have hired, or this situation that I've got into, or this product that's not selling, would I still get involved with it again?' If the answer is 'no', you need to decide to either rectify the situation or get out of it. Learn to terminate situations that are on the slippery slope to nowhere.

I have personally made numerous mistakes in hoping that the people I have hired or have been in association with would work out. When a relationship goes negative, it's very difficult, and often impossible, to bring it back to positive.

You should never wrestle with a pig because both of you get dirty, but the pig likes it! Be careful about getting into long drawn-out tangles with the people that are not in line with your strategic thinking and planning. Finish the relationship. It's best for you.

TECHNOLOGY SAVES TIME

This is the final point on maximising your time resources. It's to use all the technology available. Invest the time to upgrade your skills on computers. Use anything that will give you a personal advantage, such as mobile telephones, E-mail, Intranet, Internet.

You write at about 20-30 words per minute. A good typist can type at about 55-60 words per minute. You are capable of speaking at about 120-150 words per minute. Your mind is capable of thinking at about 1,500 words per minute.

I was amazed recently to find a senior manager handwriting a 5,000 word document and giving it to his secretary for typing. He was encouraged to invest in a dictation machine. (Perhaps he could dictate with faster results by investing in speech recognition software that would allow him to dictate direct to his laptop or PC.) Now he finds that he can get his work completed five to six times faster than in the old traditional way and is far more effective. This is a perfect example of time being more valuable than money. He frees his time to focus on his central role in management.

Using Intranets, E-mail, mobile technologies, telephone and video-conferencing all save time. Use them.

THE PEOPLE RESOURCE

The sixth link in the six link chain of an organisation, and the most difficult one in which to detect weak links and choke points, is the People resource. The other resources – money, product, physical, intangible and time – make things possible. People make things happen.

Businesses may have different products and services but, ultimately, every business is in the 'people business'. Yet here we are likely to find the biggest choke points on a personal level, between individuals, within teams, on a total organisation level and, of course, with customers. The choke points are usually psychological and cultural rather than technical and physical.

A physical choke point, such as in a production line, the design of a product or in a building or piece of equipment, can be physically removed and re-engineered, whereas emotional, psychological and cultural choke points embedded deep within people's psyche are far more difficult to identify and eliminate. All too often, unfortunately, they are not dealt with in any meaningful way.

Using the analogy of a car again, they are more like a soft tyre than a flat tyre. The 'car' continues to move forward, and even reach a high speed, yet the pull on all other resources, especially financial and time resources, is immense.

Time and money are lost at an incredible rate in some organisations. Wastage can be as high as 30% of sales in some organisations. There are people implications at all levels. It is often hard to measure, and difficult to prove, the cause of the bad effects of the people resource and it is therefore difficult to quantify its down side.

A critical learning point and insight is that to be productive, the other business resources can be managed both directly and indirectly. People manage the physical resources, time, the products and service, money and the intangible identity and reputation of the business. The leading questions for managers for the 21st century are: 'How well do we lead people?' 'How well do we lead ourselves?' 'What are the choke points for individuals, teams and organisations?'

SELF-LIMITING COMFORT ZONES AND CHOKE POINTS

One of the major choke points for the individual is a lack of personal empowerment – a lack of self-confidence and self-belief. Most people in the workforce today believe that they are limited in some way and therefore probably only perform to about 50% of their capability. The cause of their own inadequate performance has got more to do with their mental makeup than lack of opportunities, lack of skills and knowledge or any external factors.

Most people have only a vague idea of how to unlock their own potential and be thoroughly fulfiled in their personal and career development. This is the root cause of low performance, frustration, absenteeism, dissatisfaction with work and career development, and leads to stress, mental illness and family problems.

Happiness has been defined as the progressive realisation of a definite goal. The human being is a success being and is only really fully motivated when working towards personal, career, or business goal attainment.

Unfortunately, most people have only a vague idea (or no idea) how to unlock their success system. They don't know how to dismantle the block to progress along the road to their personal and professional development. This road-block or choke point impacts on all other developments.

Answers to the question of how to achieve personal, professional and business excellence and how to unlock your potential and understand the psychology of achievement are given in the many excellent programmes by management expert, Brian Tracy. I have worked very closely with Brian Tracy and his techniques and can vouch for their success. His programmes are 'How to' systems. They are a toolbox for life management, for empowerment, for success and achievement. This toolbox is further described in his excellent book *Maximum Achievement*. Each of its tools must be studied and practised just as a carpenter would practise his use of the tools of his trade.

For most service organisations, the financial investment and salaries in the people resource costs more than any other resource, sometimes as much as 80% of total expenditure. Yet most organisations invest very little money and time in improving the resource. Many managers rationalise this by saying: 'Well, we hire good people' or 'we hire people who are trained.' This is dangerous thinking. The learning and education of yesterday is already out of date and must be reviewed continuously, adapted and updated. Managers invest money in the up-keep of buildings, servicing of vehicles and the operation of finances and inventories, yet pay only token response to their own ongoing development and the development of their staff.

In Ireland, businesses invest about 1% of payroll in the development of the people resource. In France it's 3%. In Germany, about 5% of the payroll is invested in training and development.

Some managers are plugged in to the change revolution. They read newspaper and magazine articles and books, attend seminars and realise that change is the only constant. They realise that change is imminent but are unsure, don't know how, or more than likely are afraid to embrace change. Like everybody, they have a natural resistance to anything new. It's an emotional resistance. They prefer the safety of the comfort zone. To move out of your comfort zone requires the courage to take a risk, and then another risk. And so on.

EXPANDING YOUR COMFORT ZONE

'I'm OK'
'Playing Safe'
'I've always been that way so ...'
'I'll try'

COMFORT ZONE

'I'm not able to'
'I can't'
'I'm alright'

Risk Zone 1 · Risk Zone 2 · Risk Zone 3

Wallowing in the Comfort Zone will be the greatest single inhibitor to human performance improvement in the 21st century.

There is a natural human tendency to stay in your 'safe' comfort zone and justify this with excuses. To grow and develop means taking risks and pushing out the comfort zone boundaries. Risk is the breakfast of champions. It takes enormous courage.

The choke points of people are usually firmly embedded in their psyche and mind-set. Miscommunication, bad feeling, whispering discontent, 'blame the boss' negativity and 'an excuses mentality' have their roots within their minds.

If the causes of the people resource choke points are in the mind, the mind is the first place to start reducing these choke points. The second place is within the interpersonal and inter-connected team system.

A good team should contribute an 'extra personality' – an extra dimension and capability – free of charge to each team. It's not logical or mathematical. But then human potential is enormous. It's 'two plus two equals five' rather than four. All organisations, as we have said, are communications systems and everyone works in a communications system, whether it be a team, among colleagues on a production line or among the office staff.

The third major choke point within organisations is the difficulty of getting departments, teams and different offices to 'fly in formation' – to communicate effectively together while striving for the common mission, vision and strategic goals of the organisation. How do you get an entire organisation of five, 50 or 5,000 people focused and working towards a shared strategy?

It is a major choke point for most organisations. Owners, managers and employees get preoccupied with internal office struggles and factory floor politics, the grapevine, the rumour machine, past history, and the 'them and us' and 'nobody appreciates me' syndromes. They are deflected from the fact that the real enemy is out there in the marketplace and is probably scheming to steal their market share or eliminate them.

Organisation inertia, persistent staff morale blocks, bureaucracy and the barnacles of history can be overcome. A more successful path to the marketplace can be made and organisational choke points can be freed. This requires a systematic, integrated, organisation-wide approach. This book is really a system on how to remove the obstacles to success and get all departments, teams and business units plugged into a permanent mode of creating sustainable business advantage mode.

GET INTO YOUR HELICOPTER FOR THE STRATEGIC VIEW

I wear many hats in my work with businesses and organisations. I wear a marketing hat, a change agent's hat, a consultant's hat, a strategist's hat, a leadership hat. But ideally I like to position myself as a businessman. I'm in the business of helping other businesses maximise their potential; to, in effect, help them capitalise on rapid growth/expansion or free their choke points on the journey towards meeting their mission, vision and strategic goals.

I have the advantage of being able to 'look in on' hundreds of organisations from the 'helicopter' point of view. From this perspective, I tend to see the same mistakes being repeated in business after business and sector after sector, primarily because businesses are using the same techniques and methodologies that have been indoctrinated into their business owners and managers for the past 100 years or more.

Behavioural change initiatives on their own are not enough to help an organisation to run smoothly and work towards achieving its full potential. There is a need to look at all the resources as well as the structures, the systems, the processes, the functions and styles and align them with the overall strategic change management process. This analysis process has an important role in any overall strategic change management process.

AVOID FIXING 'THE WRONG PROBLEM'

The doctor/medical parallel with a business is always useful. I have seen numerous businesses invest large sums of money, time and human effort in fixing the wrong link in the chain – fixing the wrong resource. They have the 'If it ain't broke, fix it anyhow' approach. I remember asking the senior management of a business that was 'unwell' where the business was hurting. They were unsure of where exactly it hurt, but they set off to fix something, anything, anyhow. It's equivalent to the surgeon in the hospital operating theatre saying 'I don't know what is the cause of your pain, but here, let me operate somewhere anyway'.

I am familiar with the case of a business owner who knew that his business was 'unwell'. My diagnosis, however, showed that there were many contradictory symptoms in the business. Sales were good, but the finances were in a mess. The product was good but the service was bad. The staff were good but they were constantly stretched on delivery times. I noted that the number of hours that key executives were working was causing stress and even burnout.

Based on his own analysis, the business owner built a 3,000 sq. feet extension to his warehouse at a cost of €72,000. Most other people in that business sector were outsourcing and contracting out aspects of their work. This business owner decided to 'fix things' by building an extension. He diagnosed that limited space was his problem.

But his 'pain', constraining factors and problems did not go away. They increased. Now he had extra financial pressure and the frustration and confusion that nothing had really improved. He had, in effect, strengthened one of the strong links in the chain. The weakest link was still untouched – he had failed to deploy his staff properly. There was no overall benefit to the total system.

The answer to the question: 'Where does it really hurt?' can be the single most important answer that the entrepreneurial manager seeks in the year. It may take days, weeks or months to identify exactly the source of the hurt. It is time well spent. I believe that most organisations have developed a functional blindness to their own defects. They are not suffering because they cannot solve their problems but because they cannot see their problems.

In the quest to relieve financial pressure, organisations typically borrow more money or increase their bank overdraft when the real solution lies in tightening up on working capital, cash flow, debtors, sales arrangements, forecasting and budgeting.

In my view the cause of most long-standing payment problems originates in poor salesmanship and poor education of customers. Your customer relationship is an asset that must be managed for both future sales and for early payments. Irish business people almost feel (morally) obliged to have a bank overdraft to facilitate customers who are slow debtors. Set a goal to be always in the black. Manage your customer relationships so that your debts are paid on time.

Another typical response to pressure is to take on another product line or agency in the expectation that this will increase sales, performance or customers' affection. An extra product line or agency inevitably requires extra space, equipment, money, time and allocation of people. Everything affects everything else in a system. Every action has an impact that may demand three or four more actions.

A common response to 'the pain' is the installation of highly sophisticated computer equipment without allocating the time, training and people resource that is necessary to maximise the computer's potential. Many excellent computer systems have been effectively 'sabotaged' by bad attitudes and because of poorly planned installation processes. Developing a sense of buy-in and ownership among operatives and staff in general is as important as installing the 'right' equipment and technology.

The first major mistake in people resource management is hiring the wrong people. Trying to put 'square pegs' into 'round holes' is bad management. Such mistakes stem from failure to think out the requirements of the person required on the one hand and the job description and competencies on the other hand. In other words, the cause is the lack of a systematic recruitment policy that is appropriate to your business or business ethos. Hoping that everything will work out is not management. There are now many tried and tested systems and approaches to optimising the recruitment process.

The use of assessment systems and the measurement of values, skills, attitudes and intelligence is critically important in the hiring process. Put simply, there is a person for every job in the world. Square pegs (the person) should fit into square holes (the job). The manager doesn't realise he's putting a 'square peg' into a 'round hole', and the new employee doesn't realise it either. The employee suffers, the manager suffers and the organisation suffers. This is a major choke point for many organisations.

I asked a zero-based question to a group of 50 sales managers. 'Knowing what you now know about the members of your sales teams, how many of them would you re-hire if you had the chance to do it again?' Each manager had at least three people that he/she would not recruit again. The average negative response for the group of 50 managers, who had cumulative sales teams of 420, was 23%.

Many of them had hoped, and prayed, that they could eventually or inevitably fit 'square pegs' into 'round holes.' It rarely works. It costs enormous amounts of time, money, stress, customer damage and sometimes sabotage of the company.

Many sales managers have a major blind spot in the hiring of staff. It's usually their puffed up egos! Their belief that a low-performing person will transform to high performance is a poor belief. They listen to excuses and promises for the future. They delude themselves into believing that the decision they made in recruiting the person in the first place was right. This is 'ostrich' or 'head in the sand' management. It is a major mental choke point and requires somebody with courage to realise that a mistake was made and that both parties are suffering as a result. The ability to say: 'I made a mistake, I was wrong' goes to the heart of personal development.

All high performing, deal-with-the-real-issues managers have high self-esteem. Fear of making a mistake and inadequacy and inferiority complexes are firmly put in the bottom drawer. Entrepreneurial managers accept mistakes and failures and setbacks as part and parcel of development and growth. They refuse to accept them as personal inadequacies. They refuse to feel guilty. They deal with stress by taking purposeful action to sort out challenges.

FLY IN FORMATION

As an entrepreneurial manager you learn to juggle the six business resources of money, product, physical, intangible, time, and people so that they fly in formation. You learn to identify the choke points within the resources. You focus your attention, energies and other resources on eliminating the choke points. You realise that this may take three or four attempts on different resources and that you may need to get outside help. Your job as an entrepreneurial manager is to maximise the output from these resources. The bottom line today is always the outcome, the result.

Creating business advantage is, of course, a relative term but it ultimately relates to advantages in which your customers place some scale of importance or worth.

The six resource model gives you a framework for prioritising and classifying your resources. Your people resource and your 'intangibles' are less likely to be copied by your competition than your more visible and accessible tangible resources. They may therefore be the key to sustainable growth and building advantage.

The story of the six blind men who each grasped a different part of the elephant illustrates the danger of appraising each of the six resources solely from your own perspective. The first blind man felt the tusk and assumed it was a spear. The second felt its side and thought it was a wall. The third felt a leg and said it was a tree. The fourth felt its trunk and thought it was a snake. The fifth made contact with an ear and thought it was a fan. The sixth thought the tail was a rope. Each blind man reached his own conclusions solely from his own perspective. How would the collective perceptions of the six blind men have changed, I wonder, if the elephant had moved?

Resources do not confer market supremacy by themselves. They are only good when strategically applied and brought to the market. You must act as the catalyst to convert them into something of value. You must first identify them. Then develop and protect them. Finally, you must effectively deploy them in the marketplace to create sustainable business advantage.

Change is a problem if you decide that's how it will be for you. Change is not just a challenge either – it's an opportunity to grow and develop and create business advantage in all aspects of your life. The rest of this book further develops the tools to do just that.

APPLY THE PROCESS

1 Using the Six Resources model do an analysis of your business.
- How are you deploying each of these resources?
- Is there an obvious weak link?
- What can you do about it immediately?
- Are some resources more important than others in your industry to create business advantage?

2 Talk to the experts for a deeper analysis. Just talking doesn't cost anything in most cases. Think about the range of experts. They include financial/taxation experts, corporate identity experts, marketing experts, logistics experts, safety and human resources experts, knowledge/information technology experts, and legal experts. You can't be an expert on all the areas yourself and you will only spend money anyhow with these specialists if you get a good return on your investment. So talk to the people who know.

3 To organise yourself, organise your environment. Clean up. Dump all that stuff around you. Categorise information. File and label information. Build storage space.

4 Write everything down. Start with your personal strategy plan.

• Your Net worth?
• Your Goals?
• Your Activities?
• Your Purpose?

PITOC™ RESOURCES

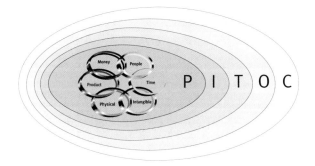

A resource-based view of the world can be applied to personal mastery, interpersonal relationships, teamwork, organisational success and customer interactions. A gap between your current reality and your expected performance can almost always be identified in the strain on the chain of resources.

3

THE

COMPETENCY

CHALLENGE

You have the secret within you! Your most controllable and powerful life force is your personality. You must unleash its potential to achieve personal mastery. But how? What do you have to do to be the best you can possibly be? What are the characteristics required for entry level or adequate performance? What are the differentiators of superior performance?

Your personality is the engine-room of your success. It's your personal distinctive character. It's the 'turbo charger' in your career and business success. Awareness, understanding and implementation of your enormous personality potential can propel you forward on the entrepreneurial management journey.

Your team's personality can also be defined, measured and developed. A team is any group of people who need one another to get something done. It's the key operating unit within your organisation.

Your organisation's personality is its culture and philosophy, and value system. It's what gives it energy and passion. What are your unique capabilities that differentiate you from your competitors? What is your ethos?

As an entrepreneurial manager you must walk, talk, eat, sleep and drink the creation of personal and business advantage. You must look constantly for better, faster, cheaper, easier, newer, different ways of achieving your goals. You must work in a systematic manner. Do not confuse busyness with business. Do not confuse activity with progress.

To succeed, you must work persistently in developing personal (P), interpersonal (I), team (T), organisation (O) and customer (C) success habits. It's a journey. It's a challenge. It's a learning process and it never ends.

To develop personal and business success habits you must first have a thorough understanding of your own personality, the personalities of other individuals, the techniques of team development and your organisation's culture. In a nutshell, you must learn to define, measure and develop personal, interpersonal, team and organisational competencies.

YOUR COMPETENCY FRAMEWORK FOR EXCELLENCE

So what are competencies? Competencies provide an integrated framework for the behaviours, skills, knowledge, abilities, attitudes and values that create and sustain business advantage and this chapter demonstrates how these competencies can be identified, learned, encouraged and improved.

The Competency Model is a system for maximising the collective capability and learning power of yourself, your team and your organisation. It provides a 'map' to understand competencies.

Maximising organisational performance is a function of having clearly defined competencies.

THE COMPETENCY MODEL

The Competency Model is made up of three main segments. One is nature – your inborn observable behaviour or temperament. The second is nurture – your motivators, beliefs, attitudes and values. The third segment is your learned practices which you have acquired formally or informally. Your ability to understand the integration of all these elements goes a long way towards maximising the competencies of an individual, a team or an organisation.

The Competency Model provides a framework to define, measure and develop personal, interpersonal, team and organisational competencies.

85

The Competency Model provides an internal, common framework for organisations to clearly understand what skills, knowledge and behavioural benchmarks are required to meet their strategic objectives. By defining their competencies, employees, managers and leaders can grasp what is required to reach new levels of excellence and performance.

Once the competencies are defined, competency based tools and applications are designed and implemented. The Competency Model is a flexible system and toolbox which harnesses and integrates individual, team and organisational competencies.

The Competency Model has three dimensions (like three aspects of your personality). I will deal in depth with each one of these dimensions (natures) in turn.

1   Your *first nature* or disposition is Temperament. It affects your manner of acting, feeling and thinking. It's how you go about doing things. It's your observable behaviour.

It is unlikely that you will reach your full potential unless you are performing in a way or in an atmosphere that comes 'naturally' to you. But do you understand your tendencies, emotions and preferences? Unfortunately most individuals do not understand their own nature and often struggle with being competent *against* their nature. Why fight nature? Temperament answers the question HOW you and your team will tend to communicate or approach a situation or a problem.

Most schools of psychology agree that your temperament is fixed before the age of five years. Because it is most likely that you will only reach your full potential and be totally fulfilled by doing what comes naturally, temperament is given a special treatment in this chapter.

2   Your *second nature*, or what has been nurtured, is made up of your personal interests, expectations, attitudes, values and beliefs. These are the reasons WHY you do things. They are your hidden motivators.

There are quantitative and qualitative techniques to help individuals, teams and organisations to appreciate and utilise its values, integrity, self-image and motives. This is more of a 'nurture' process and answers the question of why you are motivated to do the things you do.

3   Your *third nature* is made up mostly of learned practices and acquired attributes. These include your skill, knowledge and education which are critical to influencing your personality development.

Your level of intelligence is a controversial issue because many people link it to how well they fared in intelligence tests or in examinations. You shall see that real intelligence has little to do with traditional stereotyping of how smart someone was at school or college (ie academic achievement).

Your past and present experiences obviously have a major influence on your life and professional career development to date. Cultural and environmental factors also influence your personality. Your present situation is a sum total of everything that has happened to you over your life period.

Individuals, teams and organisations have an enormous collective experience base. If we only 'knew what we know' and implemented it, we would accelerate our learning and task-based competencies at an almost exponential rate. This third dimension answers the question WHAT we need to do and learn to propel us forward.

There are also unknown factors, for example, heredity that, no doubt, have an influence on our personalities.

I worked in Switzerland with managers from ten European countries. We concluded that there is no doubt that the decisions by each individual were influenced by their country's culture. Germans tend to be more structured and professional. The Portuguese tend to be less serious. Cultural and environmental factors do influence behaviour. In society, for example, we know that 80% of prisoners come from the same socio-economic level and from the same geographic areas.

Let's start now with a deeper study of each slice of your competency make-up. Let's study the Competency Model in some depth.

1 TEMPERAMENT: MEASURING NATURAL OBSERVABLE BEHAVIOUR

Have you ever been totally misjudged by another person? Have you ever misread another person or known someone who just irritates you? How many times have you had a conflict with another person and struggled with the *real* cause of that conflict? How many times have you had an almost instant connection? Someone you just clicked with? Let's see can we find some of the answers to these questions in this section.

THE TEMPERAMENT COLOURS

Once upon a time, a man was sitting on a rock watching people. He began to notice incredible similarities in the people who passed by. Although each one looked physically different, there were great similarities in how they acted. Some seemed relaxed and friendly, while others were all business and more direct. Some talked more than they listened. Others just observed.

An idea popped into his mind: 'If I become like the person I am talking to, maybe I can get to know more people and really make a difference in their lives.' Methodically, he jotted down all the similarities and found four ways in which people behaved and colour coded them for convenience.

1 Some people were forceful, direct, results oriented (Red).
2 Some people were optimistic, fun, talkative, expressive (Yellow).
3 Some people were steady, patient, relaxed, caring (Green).
4 Some people were precise, accurate, detail oriented (Blue).

He found that many people had characteristics of two or even three of the behaviours, but that one behaviour seemed to be the strongest. To test his new theory, he was outgoing and friendly to the talkative, expressive people. He put on a serious face and discussed the deep details of life with those of precise, accurate behaviour. To those who were direct, he picked up his pace and got right to the point. Last of all, to those of steady, patient behaviour he was laid back, relaxed, and listened. Incredible! Fantastic! He noticed his communication became more and more effective and people began to seek him out!

He soon realised that a person who understood people was in great demand. He became a well-respected citizen of the community, making many contributions to better the lives of the people around him. One thing people always said about him, was that they felt so good when talking to him.

Later in life, as he pondered his accomplishments, he smiled and said: 'All this I have done just because I took the time to open my eyes and watched how people expressed their natural competency.'

© Reproduced with permission from The Universal Language by Bill Bonnstetter.

Albert Einstein, (1879-1955), scientist and author of the *Theory of Relativity* wrote: 'Everything should be reduced to its simplest form, but not simpler.' Einstein's statement is particularly relevant to the study of temperament and its application to knowing yourself better, to upgrading interpersonal communications processes and to building high performance teams and organisations.

People are different. That's why it's so important for the entrepreneurial manager to develop a structure or a system for understanding both the similarities and the differences between human beings. Otherwise, it can be a lifelong scramble to figure them out. You haven't got a lifetime to learn this. You must get a system that you can understand and, more importantly, apply. In this section I will give you such a system.

Scientific research has proven that people of all races and religions have similar characteristics in 'how they act.' The study of temperament is the study of a universal language of observable human behaviour. Just watching people proves its validity. Every day, we live in a wonderful laboratory where we can observe people and learn how to communicate better.

OUR DIFFERENCES AND STRENGTHS

Great thinkers throughout the ages have attempted to describe the different ways in which people act. These include: Hippocrates (437- 460BC) the father of modern medicine; Carl Gustav Jung (1875-1961) the father of modern psychology who identified and described different 'types' of people in 1921; and Catherine Isabel Briggs, developer of the Myers Briggs system. The challenge has been to devise a method of turning the psychological theory into practical use.

In 1928, William Molten Marston developed a theory that is in common use today and is the basis of our temperament model. According to Marston, who was the inventor of the lie-detector, individuals tended to behave actively or passively, depending on whether they viewed their environment antagonistically or favourably.

He modelled this behaviour along two axes of a four-quadrant model. Each quadrant describes a behaviour pattern: dominance (D), inducement (I), steadiness (S) and compliance (C). This model became known as The Universal Language DISC. I have added four colours – the temperament colours red, yellow, green and blue – to help in the visual and practical use of the model. In this book, they are shown in different tones.

THE UNIVERSAL TEMPERAMENT LANGUAGE

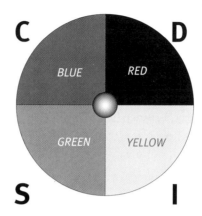

Temperament is your inborn observable natural behaviour. It's how you or your team will tend to communicate or approach a situation or a problem.
The four colours – Red, Yellow, Green and Blue – match the four behaviour patterns.
First described by William Molten Marston in 1928, every person is mapped somewhere on the Temperament Wheel and a knowledge of your colour and that of your team greatly improves your ability to operate in a team and maximise performance.

In the 1970's, Bill Bonnstetter set a blistering pace by his development of DISC language. Combined with continuing, intense research and validation, in 1984, he introduced a computerised and personalised report on DISC.

Up to the 1980's, psychological approaches seemed to be applied to people stricken by severe illness and not to those with excellent performance. Bonnstetter and other creative thinkers have combined psychological study and research to provide methods of identification of behaviour patterns. The result is that it is now much easier to focus on the strengths, differences and infinite possibilities of your own behaviour and of those you interact with.

READING BEHAVIOUR AND EMOTIONS

The theory has been put into practice. Your objective as the entrepreneurial manager is to create personal, career and business advantage by unlocking human potential. Use of the Temperament colours in identifying the strengths and tendencies in personal performance, interpersonal connections and organisational development gives entrepreneurial managers tremendous human relations advantage.

In order to accept, appreciate and honour the differences in people, it is not enough to say that each person is 'unique.' It is, in fact, the logical result of a few basic observable differences in mental functioning. One of these basic differences concerns the way people prefer to use their minds. It's about how people perceive things and make judgements and assert themselves.

An understanding of the Temperament colours helps you read the universal language of behaviours and emotions. It is the language of how you 'act out' your behaviour.

Research has consistently shown that behavioural characteristics can be grouped in four main quadrants. People with similar styles tend to exhibit specific types of behaviour common to each quadrant. This is not acting. Your behaviour is a necessary and integral part of who you are. In other words, much of your personality and best competency practices comes from nature (your inborn temperament) and much from nurture and learning (the rest of the Competency Model).

An important point to note is that you can adapt or 'stretch' to deal with people in adjoining areas without too much difficulty. A 'Yellow' style, for example, can take on the mantle of the Green or the Red without too much difficulty. The real challenge is connecting with your opposite, for here may be your blind spot. Ironically, it's also your greatest opportunity for improvement. So our Yellows will find their greatest challenge in dealing with the Blues.

THE STRENGTHS (+) AND THE WEAKNESSES (–)
OF THE TEMPERAMENT STYLES

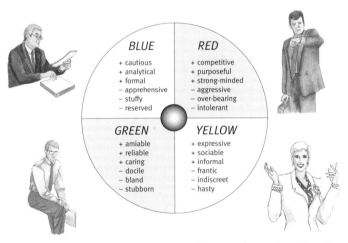

Most people have one dominant colour. This style has natural strengths and weaknesses. A strength overused sometimes becomes a weakness and a weakness is often an undiscovered strength. Many people have two or three colours and are therefore 'naturally' more flexible. Underline the words that best describe who you are. This is probably a best guess as to which is your dominant colour.

BENEFITS OF THE TEMPERAMENT COLOUR LANGUAGE

Your personal and professional competencies – who you are, what you do and how you do things – have their origins in your temperament profile more than any other single factor. Understanding the power and benefits of this temperament language is, therefore, critically important to defining, measuring and developing your overall competency make-up. The benefits are helpful in:

1 GAINING COMMITMENT AND CO-OPERATION

People tend to trust and work better with those who seem to be like themselves. The most effective way to gain the commitment and co-operation of others is to 'get into their world' and 'blend' with their behavioural style. For Reds this may mean stretching their behavioural style to connect with the Greens – it means becoming more relaxed, steady and patient (for that interaction at least).

Observe a person's words, tone of voice and body language – 'how' they act and interact with others. Notice clues in their work or living area. By applying the Temperament language, you will immediately be able to adapt to their style.

2 BUILDING EFFECTIVE TEAMS

People tend to be too hard on each other – they continually put value judgements on behaviour. Therefore, team development tends to be slowed or halted due to people problems.

An awareness of behavioural differences has an immediate impact on communication, conflict resolution, and motivation for a team. For example, a group of Blue Engineers were wondering why they were regularly stuck in progressing major projects. They had no idea that the reason was personality (Paralysis by Analysis) rather than engineering factors. When one of their team left they hired a Red (Let's do it quicker) and transformed their throughput within months. It was only with the benefit of hindsight that they really appreciated the impact of the temperament factor.

Investment always precedes return. Investment in training your team on the Temperament language gets an immediate return in team development. Most teams never make it to high performance without training in a behavioural model. Most team problems are behavioural, not functional.

3 Resolving and Preventing Conflict

Understanding behavioural similarities and differences can be the first step towards resolving and preventing conflict. By meeting the person's behavioural needs, you will be able to diffuse many problems before they even happen. People prefer to be managed in a certain way. Some like structure and some do not. Some like to work with people and some prefer to work alone.

A 'Shot in the dark' or 'Treat everyone the same' approach will put you at a distinct disadvantage on the entrepreneurial management journey. The computerised Temperament report will teach you more about a person in ten minutes than you can learn in a year without it.

4 Gaining Endorsement

Have you ever met a person who just annoys you? Have you been able to isolate the reasons why they irritate you? When you see that person coming, do you dread the interaction? If so, it is because their behaviour has caused them to lose endorsement with you. Every interaction you have with a person either increases or decreases your endorsement.

The Temperament language allows you to behaviourally 'stack' the deck in your favour. By knowing a person's behavioural style, you can immediately adapt to that style and gain credibility. You can appreciate and honour the difference they bring to the interaction. Your colleagues, family, friends and customers are all plotted somewhere on the Temperament wheel.

SIX ELEMENTS THAT IMPACT ON YOUR ENDORSEMENT

The following six elements greatly impact on your endorsement, or how much 'sanction' or 'approval' others will give you. Your overall performance is directly proportional to your level of influence. Your ability to influence others is a key entrepreneurial management competency.

1 Personal and positional credibility

Your position affects your endorsement. If you are managing director or chief executive of an organisation, you will gain a certain amount of 'positional' endorsement simply because of your position. Positional endorsement gives you a certain amount of credibility. This endorsement can then be increased or decreased based on 'how' you act and 'what' you believe. In other words, your personal credibility and influence has to be earned but adds enormously to your positional endorsement.

2 APPEARANCE

Your appearance greatly affects your endorsement. People notice the way you dress, your grooming, your sense of style, your eye contact, your handshake and your walk. Anything a person 'sees' can positively or negatively affect your credibility.

I meet many sales people who send an unprofessional message just by the way they dress and groom themselves. Unmatched shirts and ties, dirty shoes and a messy briefcase are a few examples of things that can negatively affect your endorsement.

I do not wish to dictate what you should wear, but to inform you that whether you like it or not, appearance does affect your endorsement. The elements of professional appearance can be learned.

3 PROFESSIONAL ATTITUDE

Your attitudes and beliefs impact on your level of credibility either positively or negatively. If you are a person who has a reputation for doing what you say you will do when you say you will do it, and with a sense of urgency, you will have a major advantage over a 'wishy-washy' type person.

A 'straight shooter' will develop a greater level of endorsement because of their reliability and trust worthiness, especially with Reds and Yellows.

Professionalism is important, and a person who is professional will gain more endorsement than a person who does not have a strong set of positive, consistent beliefs. Everyone who interacts with you keeps at least a mental endorsement score card on you.

4 TASK OR FUNCTION COMPETENCY

Your technical ability influences your endorsement. Your level of learning, expertise and problem solving capabilities in your field is how many people will measure your credibility level, especially Greens and Blues. You will be 'listened to' if you establish these credentials.

The entrepreneurial manager learns the hard and soft technical skills. Organisations all over the world look for those who can motivate people and transform an ordinary team into a great one. Professional coaches who can lead a team to victory are in great demand. The great coaches have the ability to form strong people relations. Your ability to develop outstanding people skills is vital to your credibility. It's a learnable competency.

5 ORAL PRESENTATION SKILLS

Have you ever sat through a talk or seminar that put you to sleep? Was it because of the constant, boring, droning of the presenter? Have you ever sat through a meeting where the time just flew by? Was it because of the excitement, knowledge and skill of the presenter? The first presenter described will lose your endorsement. The second will gain it, and you are more likely to recommend and 'sell' the second. If you stand up to speak and are unable to effectively present your ideas you will have trouble gaining endorsement. Oral presentation skills can be learned.

6 GIVING AND RECEIVING FEEDBACK

Feedback is the receiving and acting upon various forms of information from others. Your ability to give effective feedback (one-on-one) greatly impacts on your credibility. If you have ever communicated effectively to an employee (or child) with positive information on their performance, or lack of performance, you will know the power of feedback. Many employees receive little feedback on their performance, and therefore cannot make appropriate adjustments. The manager then loses the employee's endorsement and the relationship eventually ends. Most people want to do a good job. Your task is to give effective feedback and thus allow the employee to make appropriate changes.

PRODUCTIVE INTERACTION

You can learn the Temperament language to assist you in the area of communications, people relations and team building. It is very powerful in one-to-one communications, negotiation, recruitment, sales and management development. Everyone who interacts with a customer should know the colours language instinctively.

You should learn the language to create personal and business advantage in your area of expertise. Not to communicate behaviourally is to 'shoot in the dark,' hoping to hit the target. By understanding such a language, you will be enabled to direct your communications and team effort to be more on target.

You adapt your behaviour daily to those around you, so behavioural adaptation is nothing new. The Temperament colour language merely provides a valid model that can be adapted immediately to whoever you interact with.

The Temperament language is to communications what a turbo-charger is to a fine-tuned engine. You can do well without the turbo-charger, but if you want to be on the fast track, you must put the turbo-charger on. This language is the turbo-charger for your personality and communication competency development. To interact productively with people, create business advantage and journey toward being an entrepreneurial manager, you need to acquire a knowledge of such a language.

THREE STEPS TO GREATER ENDORSEMENT

The following three steps will help you to achieve greater endorsement from those around you:

1 KNOW YOURSELF

First, know yourself. Awareness of your own behavioural tendencies provides the basic foundation for increased communication. You have certain inherent behavioural tendencies that make you unique. To be aware of these tendencies provides you with the knowledge required to modify your behaviour. For example, some people are very direct and to the point when speaking. They're even blunt. If you are aware of this, you can consciously learn to listen more and wait before responding. Others hold back. Some avoid disharmony and conflict at all costs. Both behaviours may need adjusting at appropriate times. Knowledge is power – if you apply it. Once you have developed a heightened awareness of your behaviour, you can begin to consciously control your behaviour.

2 APPRECIATE AND HONOUR DIFFERENCES IN OTHERS

Know yourself first, then learn to recognise behavioural differences in others. This heightened awareness allows you to create more win/win situations. These interactions allow you to concentrate your energies on your long term vision and maximise short term focus rather than negative absorption in win/lose encounters.

We tend to get irritated with the behaviours of our opposites – Reds with Greens, Blues with Yellows – unless we learn to respect and honour those differences. This is one of the great personality challenges. Your ability to work successfully with your opposite is a significant indicator of how well you have embraced this concept.

3 APPEAL TO OTHER'S BASIC NEEDS

Before you can appeal to a person's basic needs, you must know their needs. By knowing their basic needs, you can intentionally do something that will appeal to these basic needs, giving you greater endorsement. For example, if you know that a person likes details (behavioural trait), then you can make sure that you bring all the details to their meetings. Another example is that if you know that a person likes to be direct or in control, you can prepare for a meeting and get to the point quickly and in order.

Temperament profile analysis allows you to understand the HOW of human actions and provides a framework and insight for developing your critical task and character competencies.

2 YOUR HIDDEN MOTIVATORS

THE COMPETENCY MODEL

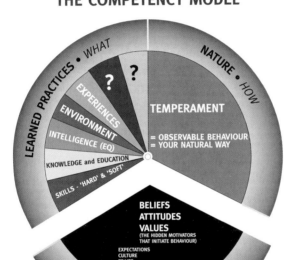

The second part of The Competency Model is your hidden motivators – your beliefs, attitudes and values system. Your personal, team and organisational motivators are central to entrepreneurial management success.

A value system is desirable and important to you as an individual. It provides you with a framework, a philosophy and a purpose. It provides a basis for action. Once clarified, a personal value system will provide purpose and focus for your life and your work.

By contrast, individuals, teams and organisations that have no direction are typically those without a coherent set of deep down shared beliefs and values.

They tend to look only at the short-term, observable, measurable results in quantity terms.

Value-driven individuals and organisations express their core beliefs in quality terms such as 'customer satisfaction', 'high standards of professionalism', 'healthy relationships', 'personal growth', 'high self-esteem' and 'great life satisfaction'. They achieve clarity, they have vision and they set long-term strategic goals to realise their vision.

When Tom Peters, co-author of *In Search of Excellence*, was asked for 'one, all-purpose bit of advice' to help an organisation achieve excellence, his response was: 'Figure out your value system. Decide what your company *stands for*. What does your enterprise do that gives everyone the most pride? Put yourself twenty years in the future. What would you look back on with the greatest satisfaction? What is your motivation?'

VALUES GIVE FOCUS

A great blockage for most individuals, teams and organisations is lack of a structured, well thought-out focus and goal-direction. The underlying cause of this is lack of a value system. Well thought-out, clear values add focus and energy to all our actions and goal achievements. They are the fuels in the fire of achievement.

Champions in sport practise focus. Practitioners of martial arts become experts on focus. The secret of the Karate blow is that all the energy and force is centred on a very small area such as the edge of your hand. That's why black-belt Karate experts can smash through stacks of boards or bricks without pain. All psychological and physical energy is totally focused on the breakpoint.

If someone threw a basin of water at you, you would get very wet. But if the same water were shot at you through a high-powered water hose gun, you might also get injured. The only difference is concentrated power and focus. You will find that all the successful applications of the elements of this book emerge from a clear understanding of your values.

Many ordinary managers struggle for much of their time with conflicting values. The entrepreneurial manager writes his values down on paper or in a diary and reviews them on a regular basis. These written-down values provide parameters for deciding on a position. They help you to leapfrog procrastination, fear of failure and negativity blocks. They help with your communications, motivations, strategies and learning.

A miscellaneous, unordered list of values that may help you to begin this process is given below. It's important that you choose your values without influence from anyone else. They need to be consistent with one another. You need to consider alternatives/options and grade them in order of importance. Do you feel good about these values? Are you willing and proud to talk publicly to other individuals, your team, your organisation and to your customers about your value positions and views?

Be prepared to give these exercises a significant amount of time and thought. In the first instance, just underline or highlight about 20 that you feel best represent your values. You may want to add some of your own.

I value …

honesty	involvement in politics
integrity	my religious beliefs
professional success	good manners
open-mindedness	individual freedom
success and achievement	winning
my family's happiness and success	law and order
keeping my thinking on social issues	orderly home life
standing firm on matters of principle	being decisive
having a wide range of friends	having a balanced life style
financial independence	musical excellence
peace of mind	self-sufficiency
marital harmony	credibility in my profession
being creative	doing something worthwhile
health and energy	serving the less well-off
keeping careful records	loving relationships
being a leader	understanding other people
intellectual growth	being a good listener
personal excellence	trust in God
being funny	tolerance of others
being a good team player	artistic talent
ability to make things happen	dressing well
my problem-solving ability	my influencing ability
being purposeful	discipline
my sense of fairness	being a risk-taker
preparing my children for adulthood	being patriotic

Now rank your top ten values in order of importance. Pick the one that you feel is No.1, then No.2 and so on. When you have to make a choice on a matter, this is the test as to whether you really believe No.1 is more important than No.2. This exercise is designed to get you thinking about your values.

Question: How much time do you spend thinking, talking about and generally acting in a way that is consistent with your top values?

VALUES CLARIFICATION

Many people find values clarification to be a particularly difficult exercise. They overlook it or totally avoid it. As an entrepreneurial manager you welcome this self-examination. You also welcome the team examination process. In fact, you are fully aware that self-revelation and self-examination is the first critical step to any improvement process, especially the personal and team growth process.

Some key questions to help you identify your core values are given below. Before you answer them, please keep in mind that:

1 Values are critical to personal, interpersonal, team, organisational and customer success (PITOC™ again!). It is very difficult to create a lasting personal and business advantage without them. Without values, people tend to become 'wandering generalities rather than meaningful specifics'. Ultimately, all reactive and unproductive management can be traced back to unclear values.

2 It isn't easy to sort out values. A value clarification exercise takes considerable time, and may raise issues that will cause conflict on a deep personal level.

The process of thinking, and in particular writing out your own values, is a personal growth experience. You will see the importance of values clarification in creating business advantage in the strategic planning process later in this book.

Here are key questions to consider in terms of values:

Q1 If you are unclear or confused about your values, what are the reasons?

A_____

B_____

C_____

Q2 If there are contradictions or conflicts between the values you have picked and what you preach, write down examples of where you succeed in this and where you fail.

A_____

B_____

C_____

Q3 Give three examples of how this values exercise helps you.

A_____

B_____

C_____

Q4 Give three examples of how this values exercise hinders you.

A_____

B_____

C_____

Q5 Who were the main influences in forming your core personal values? How did these people, situations or events help form your values?

A_____

B_____

C_____

VALUES ARE THE FOUNDATION OF GOAL SETTING AND ACHIEVEMENT IN TEAMS

I believe that all successful events and achievements can be traced back to strong core attitudes, beliefs and values. The bedrock of all good effects are good values. Clarity of values leads to good planning and goal setting. In turn, good goal setting is the basis of good time management. Clearly ordered values give 'purpose.'

Good time management practices create communication and strategic advantages in your personal and business life. You can't hit a target that you can't see. If you don't know where you're going, you'll probably end up somewhere else.

The major reason that teams do not achieve their potential is lack of trust and poor communications skills. Lack of trust is directly related to the value system within the team.

For team and organisational development, clearly defined core values:

1 provide opportunities for people to function as human beings rather than as resources in the productive process;

2 provide far more opportunities for each team or organisation member to develop to their full potential;

3 seek to increase the effectiveness of your team or organisation in terms of its goals;

4 tend to create an environment in which it is possible to find exciting and challenging work;

5 provide opportunities for teams to influence the way in which they relate and contribute to their work, the organisation and their environment;

6 treat each human being as a person with a complex set of needs, all of which are important in their work and personal and private life.

However, there is often a conflict between people and work. It is particularly acute when organisations right-size or re-engineer to meet competitive pressures and financial survival. Yet many organisations continue to espouse in their annual reports that 'our people are our greatest asset.'

This experience has reflected the swing to much more 'practical' values concerned with being clear about terms and conditions of employment, priorities, standards and budgets for equipment, finance and time. These values place emphasis upon effective and efficient delivery of customer care as opposed to the more general values of human potential and employee satisfaction.

The great value struggle for many individuals within the organisation seems to be the inconsistency between what the people at the top say and between what they do. On the other hand, most people leading organisations are well intentioned but constantly struggle with implementation. 'How do I implement these ideal scenarios?' 'How do I get poor performers to tune in?' 'How do I tell my sales manager that he is past his sell-by date?' 'How do I create the super team?'

As an entrepreneurial manager you should embrace the values concept on a very personal level and in all one-to-one communications. This awakens the 'Why?' question. All too often, the 'What (should we do)?' and 'How (should we do it)?' questions are sought out and answered, but never the 'Why?'

This values-concept becomes really powerful in building trust, togetherness and then *esprit de corps* in team building. And, of course, it's the essence of building a positive, open culture within any organisation.

Most managers skip over this stage of development. They, of course, grapple with the consequences down the road. The entrepreneurial manager takes it on board as another basic tool to gain a competitive edge. It's at the very heart of personality, competency and strategy development. (See Chapter 5)

ATTITUDE

Your attitude is central to creating personality advantage. Your attitude is the way you see things and approach challenges. It's personal to you alone. *YOU* make YOU think and feel and act the way YOU do. You decide whether you see an event or a person as a problem (negative), as a situation (neutral), as a challenge (positive) or as an opportunity (proactive), to live out entrepreneurial management.

The great challenge for most people is that they are unclear about their own attitude. They misread it. On a scale of one to ten, they are convinced that they have 'good attitudes' when, in reality, if we were to scientifically measure their mental state of mind, we would find that they have blind spots to their own development and their perception of the world.

Most people have no measures against which to assess their attitude. They have no toolbox, or are not even aware that there is such a toolbox to change or develop their thinking competencies. This is the intelligence trap and being caught in it in the Age of Information and Communications is equivalent to a life-time sentence of mediocrity and struggle.

As an entrepreneurial manager, you make it your business to become an expert in attitudinal management, starting with your own attitude development (intrapersonal), and continuing to one-to-one interactions (interpersonal). Attitude management is a personal management competency. The natural extension of intrapersonal interaction and interpersonal interaction is development in a team context. We all work in teams. Your ultimate challenge is to get your teams working well within your organisation.

One person, you the entrepreneurial manager, can influence the direction of a whole organisation. One entrepreneurial manager can create business advantage and move business mountains. Someone once said: 'Show me an organisation that's doing something exceptional and I'll guarantee you there's a monomaniac loose in there somewhere'.

A business owner asked me to help him develop a sales culture within his organisation and to develop the skills of his management team. He was prepared to pay me a significant amount of money to set a process in motion to do this. But he didn't want to get involved in the process itself. I said this was not my approach but he persisted. Eventually he asked why it was so important for him to be involved? I answered, 'Because your personality is plastered all over this place. Everyone and everything around here is totally influenced by you'. I knew this as I had just completed a customer and staff attitude audit of his company.

THE IDEAL EMPLOYEE COMPETENCIES

I have conducted the Ideal Employee exercise with thousands of managers and staff all over Ireland. The results are invariably the same across a range of industrial sectors, different types of businesses and different cultures. I simply ask the audience to brainstorm with me the attributes and qualities of the ideal employee.

If they were to hire this ideal employee to help them optimise their own performance, say as an assistant, what would the essential qualities of such a person be? I encouraged the audience to use descriptive words, at random, to identify their 'ideal' employee. The descriptions are similar in virtually every case.

THE IDEAL COMPETENT EMPLOYEE

Century Management have asked thousands of managers, and non-management personnel to give qualities / attributes of the ideal employee. These are the words used to describe the ideal employee:

ACTS INTELLIGENTLY	ENTHUSIASTIC	INITIATIVE USER	PUNCTUAL
ADMITS MISTAKES	ETHICAL	INNER PEACE	QUESTIONING
AMBITIOUS	EXCITED	INNOVATIVE	QUICK WITTED
ASSERTIVE	FLEXIBLE	INTUITIVE	RELAXED
BALANCED	FLUENT	JOB KNOWLEDGE	RESOURCEFUL
CAREER ORIENTATED	FOCUSED	JOB SKILLED	RESPONSIBLE
COMMITTED	FOLLOWS UP	LATERAL THINKER	SECURE
COMMONSENSE	FORGIVING	LEADER	SENSE OF URGENCY
CONFRONTER	FRIENDLY	LEARNER	SETS DEADLINES
CONSCIENTIOUS	FUN LOVING	LIKABLE	SMART
CONSIDERATE	FUTURE ORIENTATED	LIKES OTHERS	SOLUTION ORIENTED
COURAGEOUS	GENEROUS	LITERATE	SPONTANEOUS
CREATIVE	GOAL ACHIEVER	LOVES WORKING	SUPPORTIVE
CUSTOMER FOCUSED	GOAL SETTER	LOYAL	SYSTEMATIC
DECISIVE	GOOD MEMORY	MOTIVATED	TEAM PLAYER
DELEGATES	GOOD VOCABULARY	OPEN MINDED	THINKER
DETERMINED	GUTSY	OPEN TO CHANGE	THOUGHTFUL
DEVOTED	HARD WORKING	ORGANIZED	TIME MANAGER
DILIGENT	HEALTHY	OUTGOING	TOLERANT
DISCRETE	HELPFUL	PASSIONATE	VERBALIZES
EAGER	HIGH SELF ESTEEM	PERCEPTIVE	WELL SPOKEN
EFFICIENT	HONEST	PERSISTENT	WILLING TO LEARN
ENERGETIC	IMAGINATIVE	PLANNER	WRITES CONCISELY
ENJOYS CHALLENGE	IMPROVER	POSITIVE	WRITES EFFECTIVELY
ENJOYS JOB	INDUSTRIOUS	PRACTICAL	WRITES LEGIBLY

People are often hired for their knowledge and skills. Almost invariably they are promoted, succeed or de-hired because of their attitude, and their personal competencies.
It is easier to give people with the right attitude the right knowledge and skills, than it is to give people the right attitude even though they have the right knowledge and skills.

Go through the checklist above for your own situation and put an A beside an Attitude description, an S beside a Skill and a K beside Knowledge. Count the words under each heading and write the total beside the three circles of Knowledge Attitude and Skills. This indicates the ideal employee mix for you. Are you hiring, training and promoting to this ratio?

Ninety per cent of the words are attitudinal and value-based in nature. Skills and knowledge based competencies don't pop to the forefront of a manager's mind when asked to outline the requirements of a key employee.

The moral of the story is that managers tend to hire for knowledge and skills and educate and train for knowledge and skills. But, how do they recruit and train for attitude? Most managers and business leaders don't know how to do this.

They try new trends such as total quality, empowerment, team building, and self-directed work teams. Inevitably, they become frustrated in their efforts. The majority of Total Quality initiatives have not succeeded in achieving their intended goals, mainly because they failed to deal with the people issue appropriately.

Your key to attitude success is to take winning edge actions that other managers do not take. The actions that you take may already be clear! Most senior managers and business owners that I work with agree that poor communications, low morale, trust and attitude problems could be improved upon and that such improvement could reduce unnecessary costs, absenteeism and wastage, and increase sales, productivity and profits. If managers know this, why don't they solve it? Answer: They don't know how or they don't have a proven toolkit. It's as simple as that and my contention is that these underlying motivators are competencies that can be defined, nurtured and developed.

Another key to attitude success is that you send a rocket through any potential choke points in resources or throughput systems. In other words you remove anything that prevents you from getting from A to B faster.

MOTIVATION

As the entrepreneurial manager you are interested in more than motivating your members of staff. You are aware that the concept of motivation is gravely misunderstood and has been abused for more than a hundred years. Most managers don't even understand the term motivation. They believe that motivation is something you do to somebody else: 'My job is to motivate the team.'

They have inherited a 'carrot and stick' vision of motivation. The 'carrot' approach is where you attract the person by encouragement or incentive or a natural reward to move towards you at a certain pace over time. The 'stick' approach is where you threaten, openly or in a more veiled way, the motivatee to move in a certain direction by fear. Neither method can be classified as motivation. Each is merely movement. It moves people towards you or away from you by an outside stimulus.

Motivation, on the other hand, comes from inside the person. It's an emotion. That person is stimulated to undertake a certain action for his/her own personal reasons and benefit. You can only create the environment for this to happen more easily.

As an entrepreneurial manager you are aware of this and you develop a system for not just *motivating* individuals, but for motivating teams and the whole organisation. You realise that to get EXTRAORDINARY performance from another individual, team or an organisation, you must first get maximum performance from yourself. Otherwise, any initial success you may have will be vacuous and will be unlikely to be repeated.

The key to unlocking the potential of another individual, and changing the culture of an organisation for the better, starts within you, the entrepreneurial manager. You learn personal excellence and leadership competencies and then teach these same competencies to individuals and teams within the organisation. Sometimes the task of changing a culture and unlocking the real potential within an organisation starts with one person. Then it develops to two people, five people, ten people, 50 people and 500 people.

USE A MENTAL TOOLBOX WITH INTERNAL CHAMPIONS

The key to successful transformation of an organisation during a time of accelerated change is the systematic application of the tools in a mental 'toolbox.' It is impossible to fix the whole organisation in one fell swoop. You need help and support from people who are on the same mental wavelength as yourself. Developing these internal champions takes time, investment and total commitment to the application of this 'toolbox'. We are all cogs in wheels – one small cog helps another and so on.

CHANGING THE ORGANISATION ATTITUDE

In my view, the best place to start 'to improve things around here' is to use the human performance improvement model outlined below. It's another view of PITOC™.

Step 1: Help each individual to acquire an appropriate understanding of the Personality factors of temperament, knowledge, skills, attitude, values and intelligence etc to define, measure and develop their personal and task competencies.

HUMAN PERFORMANCE IMPROVEMENT MODEL

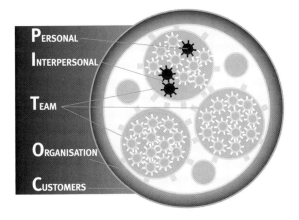

All human performance improvement starts with personal mastery. Everyone has at least half a dozen critical interpersonal relationships. Everyone works in a team. Teams interacting with other teams are the essence of organisational development. Get all this right and the customer will automatically receive outstanding customer care.

Step 2: Learn interpersonal competencies to maximise relationships internally with colleagues and with customers and other stakeholders.

Step 3: Help groups of individuals become teams. The natural extension of personal and interpersonal development and growth is team development and growth. You need to experience, learn and apply team development competencies. What are the competency levels required for different job families?

Step 4: Help organisations to provide the right conditions, environment, climate, culture and learning opportunities for teams to reach their potentials. It has a ripple effect. Ultimately leadership is about getting extraordinary performance from everyone in the organisation to help achieve its strategic goals.

However most organisations have not defined, measured or developed core competencies for the overall enterprise for now or for the future!

Step 5: The customer is the ultimate arbitrator. Customers vote with their feet every day. So keep everything customer focused. But is everyone clear what constitutes 'best customer practice?'

HIRING AND FIRING

I believe that most organisations hire staff at all levels because of their skills, knowledge and experience. They check the curriculum vitae for background experience, education, knowledge of the industry, and evidence of skill application. They use this as the means of communication to check the personality, attitudinal component through the face-to-face interview process. In many cases, this leads to disaster later on. I believe that at least 80% of people are hired (primarily) because of their skills and knowledge portfolio.

Their prospective employers give their attitudes and values little attention. Yet, 90% of all managers say that attitude is the critical success factor for most jobs in most industries.

Another perspective shows my contention to be correct. Managers confirm that 80% of the reason they fire people is not because they lack knowledge or skills, but because of their poor attitude. In most cases it's their inability to get on with other people, especially their bosses and immediate colleagues.

THE COMPETENCY WALL

Stiff attitudes and ineffective communications are the greatest choke points within most organisations. The greatest effort in maximising the performance of the whole organisation should be to attack this choke point. Most organisations, however, are unaware of this. They fix the wrong problem. Of course, fixing a link that is not the weakest link in the chain does not strengthen the overall chain. Many of those who recognise it as their choke point don't know HOW to free that choke point.

They may have been neutralised by past negative experiences. I believe the place to start is with developing total quality thinking.

The competency wall shows that the place to start with rethinking, renewal, and restructuring is with the foundations. Any physical structure that would be expected to survive tough usage over a long period of time, would, from an engineering point of view, be built on solid foundations. The deeper the foundation the higher you can build. Similarly, if you are to attempt to change the thinking, the culture and the attitudes and values within your organisation, you must start with the foundations. The foundations are mostly psychological and attitudinal in nature.

We have grown and developed through generations of bad management and faulty management structures. I believe the best place to start creating business advantage is with personal communication and attitudinal development.

THE COMPETENCY WALL

| Formal Education | Entrepreneurial Management | Developing an Outstanding Customer Care Culture | Finance | Teamwork | Negotiation | Logistics |

(Hard Competencies)

The Competency Wall is as strong as its foundations are solid and deep. Combining task and professional-based competencies with more people-based personal competencies strengthens the whole organisation. To build a wall without solid foundations is folly – cracks appear sooner or later.

THE PERSONAL EXCELLENCE COMPETENCY PROCESS

The most powerful foundation process or toolbox that I have ever used to eliminate fear and develop the personal and professional competencies of individuals, teams and organisations is a process which was created by my friend Brian Tracy, the Canadian management leader and is described in his best selling book *Maximum Achievement*, which is about personal and organisational transformation. It's about personal excellence and creating business advantage.

You need a toolbox from which to reprogramme how you do things. You need to manage the transition from the present status quo to the future vision. It needs individuals, teams and organisations to unlock potential and, like a snowball rolling downhill, it grows in pace and momentum by giving individuals the tools to understand goal focus, personal change, organisational change, employee involvement, creativity, core values, continuous improvement, innovation, quality, work and performance, and excellence.

The process used by our team of consultants at Century Management allows individuals and teams to have a forum in which to deal with the real issues and core problems that have been preventing them from moving forward at the pace at which they are capable. It allows them to look constructively at obstacles of performance blocks, barriers to effective communication and other competitive impediments. These obstacles have the cumulative effect of being a major choke point for the entire organisation.

Above all, this kind of process helps to reactivate all current competencies that are under-utilised or not used at all. 'If only we knew what we know now'. Most people have vast stores of knowledge, skill and potential lying dormant within their nature, nurture and learned practices.

The reality check for most organisations will show that the real enemy is rarely outside the organisation, but is working surreptitiously within the framework and makeup of the organisation. 'The enemy is invariably US.'

You, the entrepreneurial manager, must work persistently towards getting everyone to co-operate with you and make his or her maximum individual contribution.

When an organisation is not working in harmony, we say that the sum of its resources makes two plus two equal three.

When the organisation is performing in a successful, though mediocre way, (failing to reach its potential), we say that two plus two equals four. Your focus, your goal, should however be to gain a winning edge so that you will get two plus two to equal five or six. Or more.

When everyone is working in co-operation for the achievement of the mission, the vision and strategic goals of the organisation, it is as though many extra people are working and supporting the individuals on the teams.

3 LEARNED PRACTICES

THE COMPETENCY MODEL

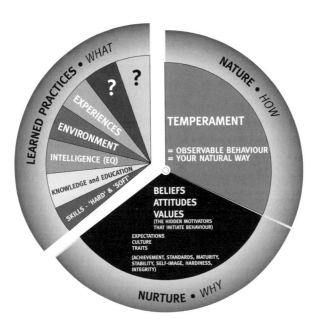

The third segment in the competency model comprises skill, knowledge, education, environment factors, intelligence and experiences – the learned practices – that you have acquired along the way. They are the 'what' task competencies, although the lines are blurred on some of them. In addition to attitudes and values, two other domains of learning are knowledge and skill. These domains have a big influence in creating personal, interpersonal, team, organisational and customer advantage. The interconnection between all of the domains of personality and learning is important to understand the competency challenge.

KNOWLEDGE AND THE INFORMATION REVOLUTION

There is more information in one of today's Sunday newspapers than the average person in the Middle Ages (500AD-1500AD) learned in a lifetime. By 1776 the amount of information learned had doubled twice. However, it doubled again during the Industrial Revolution (up to World War II).

It took 50 years for it to double again. Today, the amount of information doubles every two or three years and this is set to increase.

It's important to recognise and understand the implications of the rapid pace of change and its historical development. Otherwise, our thinking may be way out of date with 21st century reality.

Until the 1700's the greater part of human history had been an agricultural age in which mankind basically had a subsistence living from the land and bartered and traded at local level for basic needs. Land was the major source of wealth.

In 1776, Scotsman Adam Smith (1723-1790) wrote *An Inquiry into the Nature and Causes of The Wealth of Nations*. This book, one of the most important books on economics ever written, had as its central theme that markets act like an invisible hand in guiding production and consumption, and that even though people are basically selfish, their interaction in the market will be for the general good of society.

His book opened with the description of the division of labour in a pin factory. One person working alone could produce 20 pins per day. However, by breaking the task of making pins into several operations, 10 workers could produce 4,800 pins. This was 240 times more than one person.

Smith's views helped speed up the Industrial Revolution and the trend towards manufacturing as a means of production. Rural people left their rural villages for the large manufacturing centres which developed into towns and cities as we know them today. The means of production and labour became the main source of wealth.

The Industrial Revolution, said to have lasted from 1776 until World War II, had a massive influence on the development of management structures and practice. The bureaucratic hierarchical approach to management stemmed from this period and the manager/employee supervisor/worker system emerged.

This bureaucratic system has greatly affected social and political development all over the world and, in particular, business development for several hundred years. Several generations of families came to believe that this was the 'proper' way to live, earn a living and do business.

The production emphasis was all embracing, brawn power rather than brainpower. Workers were 'exploited' to lift and shift and not to think and be creative. The trade-off was job security and the 'job-for-life' culture was born.

Generations of this kind of economics became part of our culture and many people are not aware of the new age thinking.

World War II had a tremendous disorientating effect on the whole world. Every continent and virtually every country in the world was directly or indirectly affected. But because the means of production was sent into upheaval for more than six years in the industrialised world, it had the effect of helping businesses and nations to rethink, refocus and reorient how they did things. Over the next three to four decades, the Age of Service was born where the customer gradually became the master. There was a gradual shift of emphasis from the factory to selling and distributing; from production to marketing; from limited choice to multiple choice. Slowly and imperceptibly at first, but certainly during the 60's and 70's, this trend gathered pace.

The gradual shift can be best seen in the numbers of people employed in different industrial sectors in Ireland. In the 50's, 30% of all workers in Ireland were employed in the agricultural sector, 50% were employed in manufacturing plants and factories and 20% were employed in the human services and professional sectors. Today, 75% of everyone employed in Ireland works in the services sector. Less than 12% of the labour force are employed in the agricultural sector, and only 10% are employed in manufacturing.

A massive change in how we earn our living has taken place in the short period of between three and four decades. This change pattern has been similar in all industrial countries around the world. What does it mean? It means that the manufacturing sector has learned new, better and faster ways of doing what took an enormous input of manpower, money and energy in the early decades of the century. Now the production line and the machinery can pump out more with less, – less input, less resources, less people, less energy, yet with a higher output, a faster output, a better output.

Today, organisations around the world are 'right-sizing' and 'down-sizing', 're-engineering' and 'restructuring' from the system that was born during this period. It's painful, but it must be done. Not everybody understands how.

Why is this understanding of knowledge important to you in creating personality and business advantage? It's important because many managers haven't resolved the full implications of change for their own development and business performance.

Our social, political, economic and business institutions hang over us like a great shadow. Everyone now knows about change, but at what level?

Knowledge of our history and development helps. Have you considered the pace and sequence of the knowledge change and its implications for your future? If you have, you will know that we will need new knowledge and new competencies for success in the 21st century.

LESSONS FROM THE INFORMATION AGE

In the 1980's a new age was born. It was the Age of Information, driven by a telecommunications revolution, and signalled by the advent of more sophisticated computer technology. As computer hardware became better and faster and cheaper and smaller, its capability to churn out data increased at a phenomenal rate. No sooner was the newest hardware and software launched than newer, better hardware and software emerged. Obsolescence and innovation seemed to ride side by side. New competencies were defined and developed almost as quickly.

In the early 1990's, we had the means to retrieve, store and assimilate more data than at any other time in history. But the challenge to turn data into useful information was already under way. Roger Moore, the founder of INTEL, suggested that the capacity of the microchip to store information would double every eighteen months. He was right.

The computer hardware revolution quickly blended into a revolution in software, and the software revolution paved the way for the advent of a new age.

THE COMMUNICATIONS AGE

The stone, bronze and iron age lasted several million years. The agricultural age lasted more than a thousand years. The industrial age lasted several hundred years. The service age has lasted three to four decades, while the information age lasted one, perhaps two, decades. And now we are entering a new age where we can maximise the mountains of information available to us. This age is called the Age of Communications. Many will argue that these ages where one industry or emphasis dominates are now running concurrently. Perhaps they are right!

The Age of Communications will be characterised by KNOW-HOW. Do we recognise the power of the increasingly valuable resource of intellectual capital? Electronic commerce and electronic communications allows information to get to its destination better, faster and cheaper.

The challenge of the 21st century is not that acquiring the information. It is rather having the know-how to capitalise on the abundance of information and the ability to turn it into knowledge and wisdom so that we can create business advantage. Will we be overwhelmed by it or will we realise that intellectual property will be more valuable than raw materials, products and services?

As an entrepreneurial manager you are plugged into the new means of communication. You are aware of and you understand the new power play. You know that knowledge management is a new science and that this is the one advantage that will gain for you the competitive edge in the business survival and business development race.

It will require personal, professional, managerial, organisational and specialist task competencies as never before. Knowledge management is one of the new competency challenges.

SKILLS APPLICATION

The third learning domain is to obtain, build and update regularly the skills necessary to maximise the knowledge resource. Having an understanding of the techno trends of the 21st century will not be enough to give you the competitive edge for business advantage. The real challenge is: 'How can you use your technology and intellectual capital to go beyond your competitors?'

Technology levels the playing surface, even for economies and industries that have had economic, social, political or geographical constraints in the past. China and the Pacific Rim countries, India and Africa can come up to speed as quickly as First World countries in the technology revolution. So where will your advantage be gained? What are the key result areas in which to beat the competition? What are the vital things you must do to stay in front?

I believe that the decisive winning edge can be gained in the personal, managerial and entrepreneurial capability that only human beings can bring to new revolutions – intellectual capability and its application.

All the old ways of doing things should not be disregarded. On the contrary, we should rethink many of the old professional management skills and re-charge them with a fresh, new, energetic approach called entrepreneurial management. Old skills and new skills can be synergistic. Soft skills and hard skills can mix to add value to both. But define and measure these practices as Competencies. Then develop them.

115

NEW FORMS OF WORK

At the core of new, softer, winning-edge personal skills will be new learning opportunities. Self-reliance was the core of bartering and the trade and exchange economies of a thousand years ago. The electronic revolution gives us a new capability to be free again from the drudgery of the factory assembly line, office or the 'job for life'.

Employability and assembling a portfolio of skills is the new way to sell yourself. New forms of work are emerging and will continue to emerge. Contract jobs, variable pay, part-time working, job sharing and working from home are trends that are having a tremendous impact on our economies and our societies. Increasingly, we will learn to appreciate, understand and embrace the concept of self-reliance.

Today's workforce must replace the self-limiting concepts and dependency born of the industrial age with an entrepreneurial spirit of self-employment – for 21st century executives that may be a new competency to contend with. The socialist concept of 'someone else is responsible, and everyone is equal' is being replaced gradually throughout the world. Communism just did not work. Generations of conditioning, whether of the capitalist or the communist variety will not be easy to shake off. It's easier to stay inside the comfort zone of a mother organisation.

Fear of failure and reluctance to change paralyses most individuals, teams and organisations and prevents them from reaching their potential.

It's easier to engage in blame, mistrust and criticism than to embrace the new way of doing things. Everyone is capable of change, but few dare. You, the entrepreneurial manager, must dare. New thinking and application skills are required.

Self-reliance, self-employment, self-empowerment, self-confidence, self-propulsion and self-teaching will be the key competencies of the entrepreneurial manager for the 21st century. The concepts of variable pay and employability are here to stay, whether you trade your skills as an entrepreneur or as a life long employee. This requires learning hard skills like computing know-how and the skills to access the know-how. It will separate the winners from the losers. The learning organisation will outstrip the organisation that uses the traditional approach.

RELATIONSHIP MANAGEMENT SKILLS

You are on a train journey from Dublin to Cork in the year 2010. You get into a conversation with a fellow passenger about your respective businesses. She asks you: 'What is your single most important differentiating factor?' You answer, 'Relationship Management. It's our personal communications ability to maintain and develop a close relationship with our key stake-holders.'

Your questioner asks you to explain in more detail and you continue:

'We have the state-of-the-art electronic communications systems. We constantly update our technological requirements. We constantly update and upgrade our products and processes. Our financial controls are excellent yet our ability to form extra special human relations, connections with our key stakeholders, is undoubtedly the reason that we are the leaders in our field.'

'We take an entrepreneurial management approach to relationship management. We actively work to develop human communications with our customers, our staff, our suppliers, our investors and our community neighbours just as hard as we work on electronic and marketing communications.'

'We have created business advantages for our stake-holders to be part of our organisation without the formal, legal, traditional-type contracts.'

'In a nutshell, we have become masters of inter-personal communications. This is our differentiating factor. It's our key skill.'

We shall explore these inter-personal communication skills in Chapter 4.

PITOC™ OWNERSHIP

As an entrepreneurial manager you are critically aware that self-reliance is unlikely to happen until each individual feels a sense of ownership and responsibility for the overall process. This is one of your biggest challenges and it is why you must become totally absorbed in your own personal and professional competency development.

You know that you cannot take another person further than you have gone yourself. You cannot, in effect, give somebody an experience that you haven't had yourself. You must lead by example. Therefore, you must always work on your own development. Your people will then respect your knowledge and your experience and, only then, take more seriously the task and the tools that you give them. Create an environment in which productive work will be done.

INTELLIGENCE

Intelligence is the application of common sense. Unfortunately, common sense is not so common. Intelligence is a misunderstood subject and we will look at it in more detail in Chapter 8 on Learning.

EXPERIENCES

Your life experiences, obviously, help to shape your learned practices, personality and competency set. There are five major areas of influence that make up your life experiences:

1 EARLY FAMILY LIFE

Your early upbringing, experiences and conditioning will continue to have major impact on you throughout your adult life in either a positive or negative sense. Often this occurs at an unconscious level. The influence of parents is profound and lifelong. For many who carry negative parental influences it is never dealt with. It is even avoided consciously or sub-consciously. We are all 'victims' of criticism, guilt, and other negative emotions often unwittingly dished out by our parents. Frighteningly, this conditioning puts a kind of invisible wall around our belief in ourselves to accomplish things. It's like a mystery brake on competency development.

2 SCHOOL

Your teachers may have played a big part in the development of your personality. The ethos of your schools, how safe it was and the memories all add to your current beliefs, attitudes and values.

A forty-year-old business executive said to me recently that he 'hated everything about his old school' and what it represented. He had a particularly bad series of experiences with one teacher.

When I asked him to explain why he was still 'fighting' this man, it transpired that this man had the very same attributes as two colleagues whom he never got along with.

Everything has a cause. What you are today is a sum total of all your experiences. Feelings of anger, guilt and cynicism are developed from somewhere. You must let them go. Forgiveness is a tough act.

The bottom line is this – you will never be totally competent unless you 'let go' of the past.

3 WORK

For the same reasons that parents and teachers are authority figures in your early life, many people transfer their boss into this role, whether he or she wants to be seen in that role or not. Whether you like it or not, work dominates most adult life. Your work experience and your interaction with your work colleagues help to form your personality, and the key to the competency challenge is personality.

During my interventions in companies, I regularly find patterns of behaviour or hang-ups. I asked an interviewee the question: 'Of all your six bosses to date, which did you get along with least and why?' Her answer was the boss who had the same character traits that she disliked in her father and her school principal. He was too 'demanding and domineering.' Coincidence? Doubtful. We carry our experiences with us.

Be careful who you might be fighting psychologically! It's simply an enormous waste of mental energy that you should be using on more creative endeavours.

4 PRESENT FAMILY LIFE

Your experiences at home with your 'significant others' – spouses, children, and parents – do help form your personality. I don't believe it's possible to be great in the office and lousy at home.

Many of the business owners with whom I have worked have at the root cause of most of their business problems personal and interpersonal home life. I estimate that about 35% of this group have serious marriage problems or are already separated. The experience of a personal relationship breakdown causes serious stress and influences personality development.

5 HOBBIES

What you do in your spare time is a great reflection of what experiences really turn you on. What you like to do when you can freely choose for yourself might give you some clues to understanding your real mission in life.

More than half of those employed are in the wrong job – no wonder people hate work. I like work because it's my area of excellence. For me, early sporting successes and failures have always helped me have better experiences of business setbacks and teamwork. I always 'play the business game' at full speed until the final whistle or end of project. But when it's over, just as in a football match, you shake hands with the opposition, forget the misses during the game and just get on with it. What hobbies are you naturally good at? What hobbies do you find yourself drawn to? What do you find yourself talking about or reading? Everyone has a unique ability. What's yours? Your hobbies may give you a clue.

THE SECRET IS WITHIN YOU

Your personality is a given. It's the sum total of everything you are or have become. If you are an entrepreneurial manager of the 21st century, I believe you are morally obliged to be all that you can possibly be. You must learn all about your personal and task competencies if you are to unlock your potential. The Competency Model gives you a framework to meet this challenge.

More than 80% of people don't know their own capability. They think it's circumstances, or luck, or their background or a host of other factors (excuses) that has them where they are now. YOU know the secret. The secret is within YOU.

INVEST IN YOUR COMPETENCIES

Here are four steps towards developing your personality:

1 Complete a personal, career and business competency audit of your personality. To move forward and improve you must first know what areas you need to develop. Your personality development is within your control. Develop clear insights into the personality and task competencies you need to develop to unlock your potential.

2 What plan can you set in motion to define, measure and develop your competencies over the next five years? Write out 20 ideas to get you started and then pick three to get you going over the next six months. Do something. Do anything. Start.

3 Get a personal Mentor (someone you can talk to about your development.) Ask. Even pay them. Nobody is lining up to save you. Get help.

4 As with all good investments you put the effort, time or money in first, and wait for the payback or reward later. Invest in your personality up front, not later. Trust the process.

PITOC™ COMPETENCY

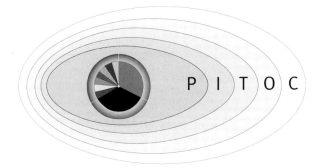

Competencies help define, measure and develop superior performance at all PITOC™ levels. 'If you cannot name it, you don't fully know it is critical to creating personal, professional, team, organisation and customer advantage. Competency development meets this challenge.

4
ACHIEVING PROFITABLE COMMUNICATIONS

'Communication takes place more in the mind and heart of the listener, than in the mouth of the speaker'
—ANON.

A warm smile, a caring approach, an immediate and consistent response, attentive listening, clear feedback channels to management, to staff, suppliers and customers may make the difference between costly communication losses and communications that enhance development and profits.

Small communications interactions can have profound cumulative effects. Bad communications cost time, money, energy, reputation, product sales, valuable staff, valuable suppliers and, more often, valuable customers.

Customers may be *consciously unaware* of why they buy more from your business or why they are loyal. It may be location or price or product or that bit 'extra' that you give. But their subconscious mind registers everything. It 'knows' that genuine exceptional communications is the icing on the cake and, providing the other 'givens' are in order, is central to creating profitable business advantage.

CASE HISTORY 1 : THE RIPPLE EFFECT

John Browne, an agent, phones to place an order for 36 boxes of materials. The order taker writes on the order sheet in his own handwriting. The six looks like a 'zero' with a fringe on top. The distribution department operative reads the six as a zero. John Browne's client receives 30 boxes, six less than what John ordered for him. The boxes had been destined for the launch by a Minister of a new product in Germany within three days.

Cost: Time lost, stress to many people, additional effort and cost in getting an extra six boxes sent by courier and by air to Germany on time for the launch. Profit on product halved. Potential loss of client. Loss of reputation as the story went the rounds of the distribution company, the agent, the exhibition staff in Germany and the Minister's office.

CASE HISTORY 2: MAKING AND LOSING SALES

In a comfortable back office of the company sit the managing director and her marketing and sales people. They are dependent on ten clients for 80% of their business. They are discussing how to increase their number of major clients. They decide to increase their marketing budget by 10% to achieve their new objectives. Meanwhile, a major client who accounts for 12% of their business is not more than 20 metres away. He is being addressed abrasively by a young staff member whom he approached to complain about a defective product that he bought.

Cost: He walks away from the company never to return. With his departure, all because of failure to handle his complaint with understanding and sensitivity, goes 12% of the company's business. The by-now-former client will talk about his experience to his friends and colleagues resulting in a further cost of potential clients to the company. Efforts in the back office are already being neutralised.

CASE HISTORY 3: OVER PROMISED, UNDER-DELIVERED

One morning, a customer phones an office in Dublin and explains his need for an urgent purchase. A company secretary answers and tells him that the service manager will return his call before midday. The company secretary passes on the message but fails to convey the urgency of returning the call that morning (her note read 'phone Bill Murphy ASAP'). The service manager decides that, since he knows the customer on a personal basis, the customer will wait until next day.

Cost: Customer does not wish to wait beyond midday. He takes his business to the competitor. What are the lessons?

CASE HISTORY 4: SPLIT SECOND

Potential customer phones office in Galway. Abrupt telephonist answers in a tone of voice that indicates indifference and even discourtesy.

Cost: Potential customer decides in one split second that she will not do business with the company. She takes her €10,000 order elsewhere.

CASE HISTORY 5: PERCEPTION DECEPTION

Man attired in dungarees arrives at plush Dublin office front desk. Receptionist is hostile because he appears to be unshaven and his hair is dishevelled. Her perception is that he is up to no good. Her attitude and tone of voice are less than welcoming.

Cost: The decent, law-abiding and successful millionaire takes his business away from the company.

Business organisations are losing valuable customers, suppliers and good staff because of their blindness to the fact that successful companies live by achieving profitable communications.

When I ask individuals and teams in organisations what are their core problems in the workplace, their first response is usually, 'barriers and breakdowns in communications.' The causes of these barriers and breakdowns are usually twofold. One is lack of effective interpersonal communication. The second is blocks in the process and channels of communication.

In our service performance and communications audits of total organisations, managers give their own communication initiatives a high rating. Non-management personnel across a range of industries give management communications a low rating.

I personally think managers believe that poor communications reflect badly on their management capability. CEOs and managing directors tend to look at profit measures. Their view is that if profits are good, everything else must be good. But how much better could their profits be? This is an endemic problem in organisations that otherwise seem to be successful in terms of marketing, image, products and profitability.

THE BUSINESS OF COMMUNICATING

The area with greatest potential for improvement in companies and organisations is internal communications. Every aspect of your business has the common denominator of people. Communications affects every aspect of business. Everyone in business is in the business of communicating.

Good communication is essential for the effective operation and development of your business. It ranges from decision-making to policy-making, from education and training to marketing and human resource management. By using good communications methods, the people or the business organisation will work effectively towards creating and keeping customers.

Good communications is about transmitting and receiving messages at the personal, interpersonal, team, organisation and customer levels. Before a message is sent or received, it is necessary to have Information, Knowledge and Understanding. Each level has an overlapping and cumulative effect on the other.

Your intrapersonal communication, that is your ability to understand and communicate with yourself, has a major impact on your interpersonal one-to-one, face-to-face communication. This, in turn, affects the ability of your groups of people to communicate effectively as a team, and in turn, has an effect on the overall atmosphere and culture of your organisation.

Your customers are the ultimate arbiters. More than any other factor, they vote for you or against you based on the effectiveness of your communication.

THE COMMUNICATION PROCESS

Everyone communicates. You cannot NOT do it. You do it naturally from the time of birth. However, few people communicate as effectively and efficiently as they could in the business environment.

Good communications is concerned with the creation, transmission, interpretation and use of information and messages. It starts with your wish to express something. You then decide how to articulate and transmit the message. The primary responsibility for the success of the communication lies with the sender.

THE COMMUNICATION PROCESS

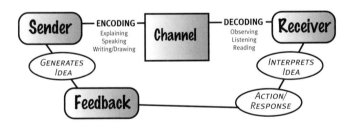

With effective communications, you can achieve virtually anything in an organisation. Most organisations, unfortunately, struggle with their internal and external communications.

Communications is about people sending messages to people. The objective is to transform data into information and subsequently into understandable knowledge.

The objective of entrepreneurial management is to achieve purposeful action from the operation of an effective communications process. Communications is ultimately a human process. Even the best technology is orchestrated by a human.

Technology is merely an enabler. Everybody communicates. Everybody is a sender. Everybody is a receiver. Learning to take and deliver feedback completes the communications loop, but the primary responsibility for communication is with the sender.

The receiver of your message will form an impression of what they have heard and interpret it against their own background of values, attitudes, beliefs, skill, knowledge, temperament, intelligence and experiences. In turn, the receiver will transmit what he or she has received to colleagues and to the wider community.

As an entrepreneurial manager, you realise that successful communication methods provide a mechanism to get exceptional results. You can spend 80% of a working day communicating with others. However, the achievement of strategic goals and plans is virtually impossible if the right people do not receive the right message, in the right way, and at the right time.

The form of communication that takes place in an organisation has a major influence on productivity, morale, energy levels, teamwork, and levels of co-operation on an informal and formal basis. These intellectual capitals are a real asset in your business. The lack of them causes time delays, wastage and costs more than any other factor. The causes of most industrial relations disputes can be traced to bad communication.

As the entrepreneurial manager, who is an excellent communicator, you become an expert in all five PITOC™ areas. You constantly work on your own development. You learn to focus mental activity in a goal-directed way. You engage in constant self-talk. 'What is my purpose?' is a great intrapersonal communications question. You develop an awareness and an understanding of why effective, face-to-face, team and organisational communication takes place. You know why customers buy repeatedly. Good communication is not a hit-or-miss exercise. You are both conscious of and competent in the methods and systems of communication, and you can therefore apply them repeatedly with effect.

The amateur communicator is sometimes successful but doesn't really understand why. He is unlikely to repeat his successes often enough. Knowledge and skill in communications methods is essential for effectiveness in entrepreneurial management. The professional communicator sets and keeps standards above a certain level and refuses to allow them to slip below minimum standards. Effective communication is a minimum requirement for virtually every other competency.

No Perfect Communicator

As an entrepreneurial manager you will understand and accept that there are no perfect communicators all the time. Everyone makes mistakes. You will also realise that good communications can be learned.

You will understand that it affects all aspects of your job, including marketing, crisis management, advertising, public relations, selling products and services, negotiations, counselling staff members, influencing stake-holder bosses and clients, making presentations, conducting job interviews, and facilitating problem-solving sessions.

As an entrepreneurial manager, you decide to become an excellent communicator. You set about doing so by gathering the information necessary and setting clear goals to achieve your communication objectives.

A core competency of every entrepreneurial manager is to know the difference between being 'a nice person' – being easy to get along with on a personal level, and getting groups of people to work effectively in organisations.

In this chapter, I will explain the elements of personal face-to-face communication and show how these elements are also elements of team, organisational and customer communications. Interpersonal communication works effectively only when the intrapersonal components are effective. For team development, you must add extra dimensions to your communications process. This is simply because more people are involved and because the potential for breakdowns to take place increases exponentially.

You will also see that for total, integrated, organisation-wide communication there are even more dimensions and components. Your customer comes second in the communication process. If all the other elements of internal communication are put in order in the first phase of the communication process, the second phase – external communication and customer service – usually happens on target and in an almost seamless, natural manner.

BARRIERS TO COMMUNICATION

Before any communication initiative takes place there will be *natural* barriers or potential obstacles to its satisfactory achievement. Your awareness of these barriers is the first step in overcoming them. A communication barrier can disrupt or distort a message to your receiver. Your receiver may therefore become less than willing to fully engage in the communication, or become irritated or defensive, or take the wrong meaning from the message.

Natural barriers to communication are:

Language Variation: Due to their education or background, some people may be unclear in their use of words. People may interpret words in different ways. How they convey words by letter, by memo, by e-mail, by brochure, press release, on multimedia, on television and video, radio or audio-tape can be the difference between success and failure in the communications process. Computer buffs, doctors, journalists, accountants and lawyers use jargon that can mean different things to different people. If you have a limited vocabulary or lack of knowledge on a particular subject, you may have difficulty conveying your ideas to another person. Making assumptions about another person's knowledge level (or they about yours) is a major barrier to understanding.

Age: Age differences may mean different values and interests. The 'generation gap' can be a barrier in itself. Today, teenagers have a distinctly different background, a different culture, different attitudes, aspirations and values from those of even their very 'young, trendy' parents. Demographic trends must be taken into account when targeting audiences and niche markets.

Background: Social and cultural differences lead to different perspectives, interpretations and understandings. For example, a rural and urban 'clash' exists in all parts of the world. The way we view the world – our perceptions – is largely determined by our past experiences. So people of difference ages, status, sex, nationalities and personalities will perceive situations differently. We often jump to conclusions and see what we expected to see rather than what is the actual reality.

Stereotyping: Stereotyping can greatly affect what and how to interpret what another person says. If someone is perceived to have authority, influence, power or expertise, we tend to believe them more readily. Criminals may speak the truth, but most people will be inclined to doubt them. Someone said to me recently, 'All accountants are the same'. Because we learn from our experiences, we run the risk of labelling different people and putting them into categories or boxes.

Personality Clashes: When two people do not 'click', the ability of one to listen to the other can distort the message or dilute the interpretation and reception of information. 'Behaviour breeds behaviour' is an old proverb. Strong views or emotions can work for you or against you in communications. They can make you totally irrational/blind to any other view or, on the positive side, can show your commitment and enthusiasm for the subject.

Race/Religion: Race, cultural and religious differences are potential roadblocks to effective communication in many cultures.

A French visitor who greeted one of my clients with a customary French embrace and kiss on the cheek, did so to a background of members of a workforce who, in ignorance of custom and culture, issued wolf-whistles.

Only the utmost good grace and exercise of delicate discretion by my client to recover goodwill prevented the loss of a lucrative deal and a good client.

Sex: Discrimination by sex prevails in many organisations. Women in particular face this barrier. Their chances of success in business are often lessened merely because of their gender. A female architect explained to me the challenges she had working on building sites where male colleagues were reluctant to accept her views.

Listening: Some individuals are great talkers and very expressive, but are poor at listening and understanding the meaning of the sender's message. Failure to listen is one of the most common barriers to good communications. You must also be aware that not everyone will be as enthused about your message as you may be. Your challenge is to present your message so that it appeals to the interests and needs of your listener.

As I walked in to talk to the staff of an engineering firm I was told that 'Nobody would talk to me and nobody would listen' because of bad feelings in the business. Within five minutes everyone was openly expressing their views and down-loading all their woes. They did not want to be preached at or lectured to – they wanted to be listened to.

Bad Health or Low Energy Levels: A group of workers told me recently in a survey on service performance and communication in their organisation that their boss was always 'waspish' and 'grumpy' after 4.00pm. This got worse on Thursdays and Fridays. When I brought this point up with the boss later, he recognised that his batteries of energy had run out at that time (due to the 7.00am start, long hours, being overweight, etc) Shakespeare said 'Fatigue doth make cowards (and grouches) of us all.'

CLASSIC COMMUNICATION EXCUSES

People give standard excuses to cover breakdowns in communications, disagreements, inefficiencies, poor service, mistakes, errors, bad feelings, conflict and other things that go wrong. These are the 'classic' excuses given in the form of staff answers/responses in hundreds of companies that I have worked with:

'Well, it was just a breakdown in communication.' This usually means that there has been a major mess-up and we don't really know the cause or how to prevent it again.

'Nobody told me.' This is an hotel classic when you have explained your requirements on the telephone (even sent written details) to a meeting room manager, but nobody else has been briefed.

'Nobody asked me.' 'I'm supposed to be in charge/control of this, yet xyz happened ...' The implication is: 'I'm not telepathic.'

'If only I knew.' A first cousin of *'Nobody told me.'*

'First I've heard of it.' 'It's not my fault. Don't blame me. I will protect myself if you do.'

'That's not my job.' Used everywhere that people don't understand change and flexibility, responsibility and co-operation.

'It has nothing to do with me'. More of the same. 'I'm not responsible.'

'We don't speak the same language.' Usually happens when double monologues have taken place. There is no understanding of the need to listen with empathy for meaning.

'Well, I might as well have been talking to a brick wall.' Same as above.

'I forgot'. This response is, at least, honest.

'She didn't hear a word I said'. Despite the fact that you explained at length and probably with some eloquence and lots of content.

As an entrepreneurial manager, you confront these classic statements as part of your day-to-day operational problems. Communication means improving relationships and leapfrogging over the natural barriers and excuses.

Realising that these natural barriers or roadblocks to effective communication must be understood and overcome, you learn the mechanics that take place in an effective communication. You set out to master the skills of both sender and receiver.

EFFECTIVE LOQVE COMMUNICATION

The effective, entrepreneurial management communicator understands all the ingredients of effective interpersonal communication. Just like a baker would understand all the different ingredients that go into baking a cake, or a mechanic would understand all the component parts that contribute to making an engine hum smoothly, so too do you need to understand the ingredients of an effective communication.

A simple way to remember the ingredients of communication is in the acronym of LOQVE – Listen, Observe, Question, Verify, Explain. I have found from bitter and from successful experiences that when a communication goes badly or goes extremely well, you can find the 'secret' in these five components. The 'secret' may be in one component or in a number of them together.

LISTEN   OBSERVE   QUESTION   VERIFY   EXPLAIN

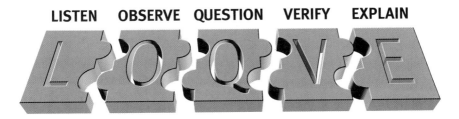

The five elements of a successful communication in a face-to-face interaction are Listen, Observe, Question, Verify and Explain.

This awareness and understanding separates the winners from the losers in communication terms.

Everyone has the capability to have an excellent exchange but most managers do not know the make-up of the exchange and cannot repeat it so the 'hit-and-miss, I get it right, I get it wrong' process continues indefinitely.

So, let's now look at the LOQVE method and the components/elements of effective communication:

LISTENING (L)

Listening is the first key element of effective face-to-face communications. Listening is different from hearing. You hear with your ears, but you listen with your mind and your heart. Listening is an intellectual, attending, emotional, mental process. Active listening takes an effort. Hearing, on the other hand, is a passive process – it is auditory, sensory and physiological.

Most adults fail to listen comprehensively. They are unaware of their inadequacies in this matter. You as an entrepreneurial manager realise this and you dedicate yourself to the study and application of the skill of listening. The implications will be enormous for personal, interpersonal, team, organisational and customer development (PITOC™).

One major difference between top performers and the bottom performers, is that the top 20% of performers all have influencing roles in society and business. They listen intently and they absorb everything that happens.

If reflection is the ability to 'listen back,' then anticipation is the ability to 'listen forward.' Listening is therefore beyond hearing. It's a combination of hearing, perceiving and understanding. It's empathy in action. Empathy is listening with your mind, your heart and your soul.

As a good listener, you try to understand thoroughly what the other person is saying. In the end, you may disagree intensely, but before you disagree, you want to know exactly what you are disagreeing with.

Effective listening takes enormous effort and practice. It involves:

1 Being more aware and concerned about the other person than you are about yourself. Listening is a discipline of self-denial. It's delaying your input to allow a real opportunity to understand. Unless the other person understands your message there is no communication. It's only talk.

2 Encouraging the speaker to tell their story, without hindrance, without conditions. Encourage the speaker with appropriate responses such as, 'I see', 'Uh-huh,' or nod your head and look attentive. Discipline yourself not to think about your response while the other person is speaking.

3 Focusing on the feelings behind the words and reflecting back to the person, the content and the emotions of their message. 'Will you ever listen to what I'm saying' or just 'Listen' probably sums up the anguish that communicators have.

The balancing scales model shows that there are two dimensions to a complete conversation. The first is hard facts, figures and information. The second more difficult side is the soft side of the emotions, ego, feelings, the meaning behind the words and body language. Your objective is to balance the scales.

Powerful listening is an elusive skill – it's an acquired attribute that can take years to grasp. It requires serious concentration and technique. In interpersonal relationships and team building, it builds self-esteem and trust – two critical bonuses in all communication.

Giving feedback to a member of staff is often handled awkwardly by a manager because they go 'off-balance' on either the facts or the emotions. Sometimes they have no examples or back-up information to support an opinion. And sometimes they have all the evidence, but forget to protect self-esteem. The first step in giving feedback is to be clear in your own head about the gap between the behaviour you observe and the expected behaviour. The second step is to consider how you will give that feedback – both sides of the scales are important.

BALANCING COMMUNICATION

Words	Feelings
Facts	Emotions
Figures	Understandings
Information	Egos
Content	Empathy
Message	Meaning

Effective Communications requires equal weighting of hard data (words, facts, figures, information, content and messages) with softer human emotions (feelings, emotions, understandings, egos, empathy and meaning).
Good communications requires a constant balance between these two sets of elements. If you overload one set, the other set will not balance. Getting the balance right is a constant challenge.

Many people aren't sure after studying the subject of listening whether they are good listeners or not. Check for your listening capabilities in the listening exercise below.

LISTENING EXERCISES

You are entitled to disagree with my point of view but only if you can first state it properly.

On a scale of 1 to 7, rate yourself as a listener:

• Do I allow the speaker to express his/her thoughts completely without interrupting?

• Do I listen 'between the lines' for underlying feelings as well as for facts?/hidden meanings?

• Do I actively try to remember important facts, names, etc?

• Do I write down the most important details of a message?

• Do I look at the speaker as well as listen to what they have to say?

• To ensure correct understanding, do I read essential details back to the speaker before the conversation ends?

• Do I refrain from turning off from the speaker or interrupting because the message is dull and boring or because I do not personally like the style of the speaker?

• Do I avoid becoming hostile or excited when a speaker's views or values differ from my own?

• Do I ignore distractions and pay attention to the communication barriers outlined earlier?

• Do I express a genuine interest in the other individual's conversation?

You may or may not be a natural listener, but you can learn to be a professional listener. Make a decision to be an outstanding listener. Get feedback from those who work closely with you. Ask them do you hear only what you want to hear? Do you jump to the conclusion before the speaker has finished talking? Do you interrupt to make your life-saving point? (This just irritates the speaker)? Do you make all sorts of assumptions from your own experience? Do you finish other people's sentences for them?

OBSERVING (O)

The second key element of effective face-to-face communication is the ability to observe everything that's happening in the communication process. The eyes are the window of the soul and they are our most powerful sense. There are twenty-two times more nerves going from the eye to the brain than there are from the ear to the brain. Yet most communicators use their eyes 'recklessly.' What's not said should be the focal area of effective communication rather than what is said.

To understand non-verbal communication, you need to watch, read and analyse the signals given out by people. Observing is 'listening' with your eyes. It's the skill of reading 'between the lines.' In his famous book *What They Don't Teach You At Harvard Business School*, Mark McCormack advises that you *'Listen aggressively and observe aggressively'*.

Here is a test of your observations. Count the number of 'f's in the four lines printed below and write the number on top of this page.

FEATURE FILMS ARE THE
RESULT OF YEARS OF SCIENTIFIC
STUDY COMBINED WITH THE
EXPERIENCE OF YEARS.

The purpose of this test is to show you that permanent items sometimes catch your attention and less important items pass it by. You tend to be selective in what you want to see. You may tend to block out things that you do not want to see and delude yourself into believing that you are being truthful to yourself.

The point of this test of course, is to show that inattention to detail often leads to breakdowns in communication. How can you persuade people to pay more attention to detail? Using a diary, checklists and, most importantly of all, thinking on paper by writing things down will all help you to become more observant.

A surgeon told his medical students that a surgeon needs two gifts: freedom from nausea and the power of observation. To demonstrate his point, he dipped his finger into some nauseating fluid and licked it, requesting each of his students to do exactly as he had done. Each student put their finger in the fluid and licked it. Appraisal time came and the surgeon announced: 'I congratulate you on having passed the first test, but not, unfortunately, the second; for not one of you noticed that the finger I licked was not the same finger that I dipped into the fluid!'

Following our test, most people see only three 'f's, some see four, but very few see all six 'f's first time. (If you still haven't seen all six 'f's, go back and look more closely).

As an entrepreneurial manager you know that your mental make-up and personality (as outlined in Chapter 3) influences your perception, and perception influences observation. Observing is not the same as seeing. You see everything that passes by your eyes but you do not record everything. Later in this chapter you will see how critical non-verbal communication is to the total communication process.

As an entrepreneurial manager, you will be aware of people's ability to jump to conclusions and see the wrong thing. You use the PITOC™ model to search for the implications and influences of such behaviour on daily activities. You, in effect, become an observation specialist, realising that by opening your mind to new learning situations you will gain the ability to observe more clearly.

As an entrepreneurial manager, you should study the effects of perception. It will help you to understand how best to present your message and yourself to your audience. Critical factors of perception are: 'How they "see" you,' 'How they may process and evaluate your style, information and ideas', and 'How they derive meaning from them.'

Here are a number of optical illusions! What are your impressions? What are the implications?

PERCEPTION AND DECEPTION

Edgar Rubin's 'reversible'.
Can you see both patterns at once?

The five vertical lines are parallel.

See my wife or see my mother–in–law!

Perception is in the eyes of the beholder. In Rubin's reversible (top) you can see a chalice or you can see the silhouettes of two human faces. In the centre illustration, all five vertical lines are straight. This may be contrary to what you see. Focus on the dark area of the picture by cartoonist W E Hill, (1915), and you'll see my wife. Focus on the lower centre area of the picture and you'll see my mother-in-law.

You receive only limited information through the five senses.

Rubin's 'reversible pattern' and Hill's 'Wife and Mother-in-law' provide useful illustrations of this point.

Rubin maintained that you cannot see both the twin boys (the black pattern on white) and the goblet (the white pattern on black) at the same time; you virtually switch off one image, then switch on the other image. Two distinct fixations or stops are made with the eye.

The same holds for W E Hill's illustration. You have to switch from the young woman to the old woman and back again. If you can only see one woman at this point, show this picture to a number of people and the possibility is that at least one of them will see the opposite to you.

Everyone has a different capacity to take in stimuli or information. Our ability to use our senses effectively and with acuity is determined by the amount of exercise we give to each of our senses. Most sighted people do not use their hands and ears as efficiently as they would if they were partially sighted or blind. Because of this perception disparity, the challenge for the communicator is enormous. How do you make a real communication connection?

Awareness and understanding are the first key steps in this process. As an entrepreneurial manager, you are aware that ambiguity in the transmission of a message is a major reason why breakdowns in communication occur. Successful message-sending is dependent in the first instance on accuracy, brevity, clarity, context, simplicity, relevance, directness and timeliness of the message. Lack of time and pressurised work environments contribute to failure in message-sending and in communication.

By listening attentively and observing aggressively and by seeking clarification where there are unclear messages, you will go a long way towards having an effective communications exchange. Listening and observing skills improve two-way communications. Two-way communications increase involvement and commitment which are essential to building trust and loyalty. Trust and loyalty are the bedrock of relationships. Good relationships create an atmosphere or culture to improve communications even further. It's that ripple effect again.

QUESTIONING (Q)

The third key ingredient of effective communication as shown in the LOQVE model is Questioning (Q). This is your ability to ask the right questions at the right time and in the right way. The skill of *appropriate* questioning is one of the most powerful management skills. By learning to ask pertinent questions for maximum benefit and by combining them with attentive listening and focused observing will, without doubt, gain the winning edge in communication for you.

Skilled questioning is important in all verbal communications. It involves both verbal and non-verbal behaviour. There are no right or wrong questions and there are no right or wrong ways of asking. There are only appropriate questions and appropriate ways of asking and an appropriate time to ask.

There are several categories of appropriate questions with which you need to become expert.

OPEN QUESTIONS

Open questions 'open up' the person who is responding to give a fuller answer. Good open questions tend to start with Who?, What?, Where?, When?, Why? and How? They tend to get the other person talking and explaining, and you listening and observing. The more listening you do, the more powerful will be the communication. Appropriate questioning and listening go hand in hand.

Some good opening phrases in the questioning process may be: 'Tell me about …,' 'What happened …?', 'How can I help you?', 'How do you mean?'

For many years, experts suggested that the 'Why?' question was too strong or even abrasive. However today, because of change and competition, you are recommended not only to ask 'Why?', but ask the question 'Why?' at least five times. 'Why do you say that? … Why did you do that? … Why? Why? Why?' Open questions are great to open a conversation and to generate discussion. In an interview situation, for instance, a person's answers/responses to them can reveal a great deal about that person's personality – how well they express themselves without guidance or prompting. They can also give a clear indication of their ability to think. Such questions are like having a camera with a wide-angle lens that gives you a panoramic view of the landscape.

CLOSED QUESTIONS

Closed questions tend to invite short answers. They tend to 'close down' the conversation. They are used for getting specific, single facts through 'Yes' or 'No' type responses.

Closed questions tend to start with phrases such as; 'Are you …?', 'Could you …?', 'Would you …?' If you are looking to develop 'possibilities' in a conversation, they have a stop/start interrogation type effect. They are usually a disaster. They are a major reason why many sales people do not sell more products and develop better relationships.

I have audio and video recorded hundreds of sales people who would swear on a stack of bibles that they don't use closed questions with customers. When we play back the recording, we find that 80% of the questions are closed. To know and not to do is not yet to know. I believe there is a natural tendency to ask closed questions and go for the facts in business commitments. Be aware of this in your interactions. Without feedback and practice, I believe that you will unwittingly and repeatedly over-use these techniques.

By listening to yourself on audio and by observing experts on video, on television, in seminars and in one-to-one interactions, you can help yourself to develop the skill of effective questioning.

Many communicators fall into the trap of asking too many closed questions. By asking open questions and by getting into the listening mode, you will get total control over the direction and influence of the conversation. If you want to develop 'possibilities' and a really good communications exchange, the more talking that your counterpart does, the better the outcome.

All good counsellors and mediators know this instinctively from their training. This doesn't mean that you say absolutely nothing. Real listening means that you alternatively absorb and express ideas in the conversation.

The classic closed question 'Can I help you?' allows the possibility for a 'Yes' or 'No' answer.

Compare this with a better customer service question such as: 'How may I help you?' It's far more difficult to say 'No' to this question.

More classics are: 'Are you being served?', 'Is it urgent?', 'Are you OK?'

Don't fall into the trap of believing that all closed questions are wrong or bad. When they are used appropriately, they are an excellent tool in the communications questioning system. Closed questions are excellent when you want a brief answer or when you want to get very specific information.

In an interview you may want to get objective factual or biographical data or to compare responses with other candidates ie their experience, or levels of skill. In photographic terms, closed questions like having a zoom lens on your camera, allowing you to zoom in on a particular spot.

REFLECTIVE/PROBING QUESTIONS

Reflective or probing questions are asked as a result of what the other person has said. These questions allow you to develop or expand a conversation. Developing the possibilities within an interaction is the essence of good communicating. It helps get examples, illustrations and explanations moving.

I heard a service engineer in a garage using a reflective question. A customer mentioned in passing that his wife was dissatisfied with an aspect of her last service. Later in the conversation, the service engineer responded: 'You said you had a feeling that your wife was annoyed about the quality of the service when she was here last month. May I ask in exactly what way she was dissatisfied?'

Here's a probing question: 'You seem to prefer the old model to the new. Could you tell me why?' The soft use of 'Why' is a great prober. It moves the conversation from the general to the specific: 'Could you give me an example of why this happened in your last job?', 'When you say you are rarely absent, how many days have you missed in the last year and why?'

The need to ask a probing or reflective question is often instigated by body language. If you are totally wrapped up in the communication, observing aggressively and listening attentively, a wry smile or a grimace can tell you more than the words spoken.

I regularly ask my clients: 'Why did you give that little smile when you said ...xyz' or 'Why did you raise your eyebrows to heaven when ...' or 'You seem to have a challenge with that explanation of ...'

Probing questions are excellent for unearthing deeper meanings or for going more in-depth to find out more details. They help flush out the real issues for discussion. If the real issues are left underground, then it's only a superficial communication. 'How do you mean?' is a great probing question, as is, 'Can you give me an example?' and 'What happened then?' Answers may also be yielded from the command: 'Tell me more about that'.

LEADING QUESTIONS

Leading questions tend to bring the other person along your chosen direction. Such questions may seem to be manipulative. 'You are well able to handle 100 this time, aren't you?' is an example.

I overheard a manager say, sarcastically, to the person responsible for purchasing a machine that had malfunctioned shortly after delivery: 'I take it that you examined it thoroughly before buying it. Didn't you?'

These are classic leading questions and are often conversation stoppers. Watch out for them being used on you and be careful how you use them in your interactions.

Some people just ask loaded questions which reveal too much emotional information. 'What do you think of the latest political scandal?' was a question I was asked by a prospective client when I entered her office some time ago. I side-stepped the issue by saying: 'It's very interesting. How do you view it?' It transpired she was a fanatical supporter of the party in question. She still doesn't know my views on the scandal nor my political affiliations. However, we have conducted a considerable amount of business together.

APPROPRIATE QUESTIONS DEMAND ANSWERS

As an entrepreneurial manager, you realise that in today's business world, success does not necessarily come to those who think they have all the right answers. It is often more important to ask the right questions at the right time and in the right way. Mastering the questioning technique will turn an ordinary conversation skill into a formidable business tool.

The reasons are simple – appropriate questions demand answers. They stimulate thought in others. They get information. They encourage people to talk. They show that you care. It is better to know some of the key questions than to know all the specific answers. Think out six key questions for your business. Write them down. Perfect them. Ask them all the time.

As I said earlier, I wear many business hats, such as business advisor, change management agent, mentor, consultant, management trainer, strategist, salesman, team leader, counsellor, manager. I have a stock of ten powerful questions that I use over and over again. They give me an avalanche of information from my clients. When I am called into a business, one of my early requests is: 'Tell me as much as possible about your business'

The response to this question alone with helpful probes can take from 90 minutes to nine hours. Just asking a question, however, is not enough. The ability to actively listen and observe aggressively is equally important.

An open question that I ask is: 'What is the biggest, single, unsolved, ongoing problem in your business right now?' This usually gets to the heart of the matter.

Probing, listening and observing are critical skills because, in most of my cases, the clients themselves haven't identified the source of their own problem. But with skilled questioning techniques, they appreciate the opportunity to seek the answers within themselves and their business. Two of my favourite questions to develop a better understanding of my client's situation are: 'How do you mean?' (Open) and 'Could you give me an example of this?' (Probing).

One of the most powerful questions in solving problems is called zero-based questioning. A client explained to me that she had an ongoing problem for several years with a member of her sales force and was in several minds as to how to solve the problem.

I asked permission (an appropriate Closed question): 'Can I ask you a question?' to ask a zero-based question. The answer almost immediately brought the client to a solution and an action that she knew she should have taken 18 months earlier.

The zero-based question I asked her was: 'Knowing what you now know about this sales rep would you still hire him?' (Closed). Her instinctive answer was 'No!'

My next question was another Closed question: 'Do you believe he can be helped or trained to improve his performance?' Her answer was again 'No!'

My next question was: 'What do you think, as a responsible, professional manager, you have to do for the greater good of yourself, this person and the organisation to solve this problem?' (Open question).

She explained to me afterwards that she had been rationalising, justifying and making excuses for her original decision in hiring someone whose personality didn't fit the job and who caused enormous stress to the manager and other sales staff, as well as cost to the organisation. Her ego had prevented her from ending the person's employment.

She thanked me profusely for taking a serious weight (stress) off her shoulders and for helping her with her decision. As importantly, she thanked me for asking her the 'right' questions. She later used the zero-based questioning technique to eliminate a problem product line from her business.

DOOR CLOSER AND DOOR OPENER

Some closed and probing questions can be classified either as 'door openers' or 'door closers'. A 'door opening' reply might be something like 'Sounds like you have a problem with that …' It encourages feelings to be shared, but only if the other person wants to. 'Could you enlarge on that?'

A friend gave me an example recently of how he came home from work and said: 'I didn't get very much done at work today.' His wife responded by saying: 'Why was that?' ('Door opening' response). On the other hand, a 'Door closing' response might be another example that I overhead in a business where one manager said to another: '*Why* on earth was Joe asked to do that job?' His colleague replied: 'I was wondering the same thing myself.'

QUESTIONS HAVE POWER

Good managers know how to use questions to win co-operation and dedication. They know how to ask themselves personal critical questions. They then learn to ask individuals good questions. Likewise, they pose strategic questions for their teams and for their organisation. Asking questions of your customer is key to establishing needs and building strong relationships.

As a businessman and management consultant, I have participated in hundreds of staff meetings, strategy sessions, board meetings, coaching sessions, international workshops, sales calls, job hiring and termination of employment, and performance appraisals. From my experience, all excellent communicators and managers demonstrate a mastery of the questioning technique. Questions have power.

VERIFYING (V)

Having Listened, Observed and Questioned, you must now Verify that both the sender and the receiver of the message or information clearly understand each other. It means knowing what the person has said. More importantly, it means understanding what the person means.

During this stage of the LOQVE process we use a method which is called paraphrasing. In other words, you rephrase in your own words, what the sender has said, conveying – to them – what *you* think *they* mean. Do not just repeat their words to them – they are bound to agree with that.

If effective communication is about having a clear understanding and an exact meaning of what was said, as well as tuning in at the feeling and empathetic level, the verifying process goes a long way towards preventing unclear instructions, disagreements, bad feelings, errors, mistakes and inefficiencies in the workplace. More importantly, the verifying step helps prevent wrong assumptions and misunderstandings being formed – the root cause of miscommunication.

You should be conscious about using two verification statements on a continuous basis. The first statement is, 'What I hear you say ...' The second statement is, 'What I understand you to mean ...' Clients spend a lot of time explaining to me the trials and tribulations of coping with change, competition, customers, staff and products in their business. Having listened, observed and questioned in the appropriate way and for the right amount of time, I summarised a recent interaction as follows:

'OK, what I hear you say is that you are under extreme stress/pressure. You are looking for a better way to manage how you do things and maximise the operations within your business. Is that correct?' or another approach to this may have been 'Now, what I also understand you to mean is ...'

I will attempt to grasp the essence and real meaning and level of intensity by listening, observing and questioning the process that has taken place. If I have been properly plugged into the emotion and content of the conversation, I will get the answers I seek 99 out of 100 times. My clients will know subconsciously that I know what's going on for them. A profound old adage is: 'Don't tell me how much you care. Show me how much you care.'

The four elements, LOQV, are all about how you gather information. Information is critical to how you respond knowledgeably to the other person. Information and knowledge lead to wisdom and give you control. Amateur communicators do not 'attend' in full to listening, observing, questioning and verifying. They tend to react to the other person. Lots of talk may take place but there is very little communication. Being aware of this and constantly working at becoming more competent and skilled separates the entrepreneurial manager from the rest of the pack.

EXPLAINING (E)

The final ingredient in the LOQVE formula is Explaining (E). People tend to explain and talk very much from how they see the world in the temperament colour language. Reds and Yellows tend to talk at about 140 to 170 words per minute and some even faster. Greens and Blues tend to be more measured, thoughtful and reflective and may speak at about 110 to 140 words per minute. Remember that people like to be communicated to the way *they are,* not the way *you are.*

The ingredients of communication that you have been reading about so far have been very much about gathering information, understanding the situation and maximising the possibility of making a 100% connection on an emotional, mental and content level. These will help you to deploy your time and efforts effectively. At some stage, however, you must do some talking and explaining yourself.

To be effective with the skill of explaining, you must speak clearly, directly and logically. Your recipient is more likely to understand and accept your ideas because they are directed to their needs and their motives – because you have LOQVE'd them. Mentally prepare your explanation before starting. Be brief and to the point. Make sure that the other person understands the message as clearly as you understand it.

THE 7 'C's OF EFFECTIVE COMMUNICATION ARE:

CLARITY	Less is More. Leave out the waffle.
CONTEXT	Timing and Situation are critical to success.
CONTENT	Prepare. Think on paper.
CONTINUITY	Over-time.
CONSISTENCY	Builds confidence. No surprises or mixed signals.
CHANNELS	The channel is clear, consistent and in context.
CREDIBILITY	Credibility builds trust and connects people.

Most people read at about 200 words per minute. With speed reading, this can rise to 600 words per minute. We can listen at a speed of about 400 words per minute. There is a big gap between our ability to take in information (400 wpm) and even the fastest person's ability to speak (200 wpm). This gap accounts for distractions, interruptions or breaks in eye contact during the listening and observing process. Be aware of this. Discipline yourself to stay tuned-in intellectually with your ears, and visually with your eyes.

Another technique is to kinaesthetically tune in. This means to use your senses, especially your physical senses. It means keeping your body aligned to the person. We'll dwell on this later regarding body language.

You can, of course, conduct a conversation within your own mind (self-talk) at a phenomenal speed of 1,500 words per minute. This is intrapersonal communication. One person explained it to me as like sending a barrage of ideas flooding through his mind at a phenomenal speed. Just think about the avalanche of ideas that flow through your mind as you drive your car on the average day. You simply cannot stop thinking, can you? As I explained earlier, you can learn to control and channel this powerful energy source towards the achievement of your goals.

You can spend as much as 80% of your day in oral communication. As much as 60% of your time can be spent with subordinates, 30% with supervisors and as little as 10% with peers. For this reason alone, you should set a goal to become excellent at presentation and speaking skills.

I have taken hundreds of managers through my Professional Presentation Skills programme. All of them report back that it not only helps them to become better speakers in a more formal setting, but helps them with their one-to-one communications in small group meetings, during interviews, during sales conversations and in resolving conflicts.

There is nowhere that you, the entrepreneurial manager, can seem to be more exposed and even inadequate than in making a formal presentation or conducting a meeting. People, who in extreme circumstances are usually brave, may be terrified public speakers. They lose perfect opportunities to shine and become exceptional managers.

HOW THE MESSAGE GIVES CREDIBILITY

CREDIBILITY IN COMMUNICATIONS

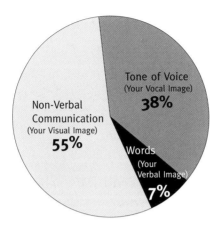

A key ingredient of effective presentations is credibility. This is determined by the consistency of three factors – the words you use (what you say), your tone of voice (how you say it) and your non-verbal communications (what you do).

To maximise your effectiveness as a communicator, it is most important that you understand three elements involved in communication. Thousands of observations and studies have been completed on how people communicate. Probably the one that has stood the test of time and the one that is still regarded as the classic was conducted by Dr. Albert Mehrabian in the 1970's. His studies showed that the three critical elements of words, tone of voice and non-verbal behaviour were essential to effective communication but it's really the proportions of 7% to words, 38% to tone of voice and 55% to non-verbals that startle most people at first.

The combination and understanding of the ingredients of communication (LOQVE) and the consistency of the words, tone and body language all come together to give you a key variable to successful communication. That key is credibility. The measure of the effectiveness of any communication is the response or the result that it gets. By building trust and credibility, you connect with your listener more easily. Good talkers may be regarded as ineffective communicators because people simply don't believe them. It's not what you say that is really important. It's how you say it and your actions (non-verbal behaviour) that often speak louder than words.

THE POWER OF WORDS

VERBAL IMAGE

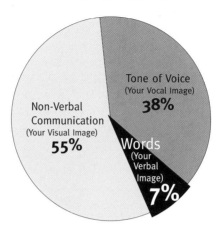

The words you use may account for only 7% of the total impact your message sends to others, particularly in first encounters. Nevertheless, use of picture words, clear pronunciation, correct grammar, the proper vocabulary and emphasis have an important bearing on your communication.

The Lord's Prayer is only 54 words long. The Ten Commandments is only 297. Some of the most powerfully written combinations of words that have stood the test of time are simple, clear and short. One of the most powerful combinations of words ever written is the American Declaration of Independence (300). Contrast all this with the EU Directive on the Export of Duck Eggs (26,911).

The Plain English Campaign is an organisation that tests the text and format of documents to ensure that they get the message across in terms that the customer will understand. They award the Crystal mark for clarity in language and design, and the Honesty mark which is the seal of approval for the content. In other words what the customer sees and reads in the words is what they get – no ambiguity or having to read the small print for the catch. Insurance companies and the legal profession, take note! Even the South Africa Government has Plain-Englished their legislation. When will the legal eagles drop their century Old World embargo on modern, straightforward, sensible English? To read a contract without mumbo-jumbo would be a joy!

Creating verbal advantage is the ability to use words precisely and powerfully. Research studies over many decades have proven that a strong command of the English language is directly linked to career advancement, to the amount of money you make, and even to social success.

To move ahead in your career, your vocabulary level must at least equal the average level of the members of your profession. To excel, your vocabulary must surpass that of your colleagues. 'Words, like nature, half reveal and half conceal the Soul within', wrote Alfred Lord Tennyson.

Every day, people judge you by the words you use. Rightly or wrongly, they make assumptions about your intelligence, education and your competencies levels. The words you use send signals about who you are and your mindset in an almost disproportionate way. 'A word spoken (or written) is past recall' is the old proverb.

Not having a strong grasp on English words can be a serious handicap. As an entrepreneurial manager, set out to command as large, as diverse, and as exact a vocabulary as possible. 'Endeavour to use the right word and not its second cousin', as Mark Twain said.

TELEMARKETING AND WRITTEN COMMUNICATION

On the telephone, your diction, pitch and inflexion and modulation become even more relevant. The words become more relevant than in face-to-face encounters. Everyone is in the telecommunication business. It should be a core competency in your business. It should be a distinguishing feature by itself. Yet all too often, organisations have a sloppy telephone manner. Remember every perception counts.

Your telephone receptionist is a key communicator. Have you given him or her the training, feedback and help that he/she needs? On the telephone, the words may account for 55% of the total impact. Tone of voice probably accounts for 38% of the impact and non-verbal behaviour may be as low as 7%.

Telemarketing is one of the fastest growing industries in the world. You could probably do more and better business on the telephone by just thinking about it. But why not make it a winning edge technique?

In written communication, the word 'probably' accounts for 80% of the impact on your message and the visual design, style, layout, pace and rhythm accounts for the other 20%. Non-verbal communication does not enter the equation.

Most people are poor, mediocre or less than effective at written communication. Despite so much emphasis on it in our education system, mistakes in basic spelling, syntax, and grammar are rife. Stuffy, formal language still pervades letters and reports (the legal profession has institutionalised this, of course) and unclear expression of ideas is everywhere. E-mail communication etiquette demands that we get good with words. Go back to basics if this is your limiting factor. Keep a pocket sized dictionary close by for quick checking. Learn basic layout, design and grammar skills. Do not let yourself down in this very exposed and visual area.

TONE OF VOICE

VOCAL IMAGE

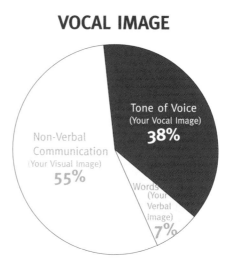

Tone of Voice
(Your Vocal Image)
38%

Non-Verbal
Communication
(Your Visual Image)
55%

Words
(Your
Verbal
Image)
7%

How you say something is often much more important than what you say. Variations in vocal pitch, volume, tempo and inflection convey meaning and emotional tone. Interpretation of vocal cues is a significant amount of the communications process.

To demonstrate the impact that the change of tone can have on the same six words, I ask delegates to say the same set of words in different tones of voice. On a flip chart, I write the words: 'I can't believe this is happening.' Then I ask people to say it sequentially in an angry tone of voice, in a happy state, with some disgust, in total confusion and with a lot of enthusiasm. The lesson is clear immediately for everyone concerned. The six words are the same, but the meaning and the emotions change with the change of tone.

Everyone has, at some point, been 'short' or curt, abrasive or unpleasant to another person. I walked into an electronics shop and as I approached the counter, the assistant curtly and abruptly said: 'Yes, can I help you?' His words were correct but his manner and tone were all wrong. The meaning of the communication for me at that time was that I was an interruption and an inconvenience to that assistant. Perception is the reality. Words alone are limited in face-to-face communications.

People sometimes squirm when Americans say: 'Have a nice day'. They interpret this as not having a lot of meaning behind it and that it is an empty phrase. How many empty phrases do you use that you are not conscious of?

I observed an introduction where the words were correct – 'It's nice to meet you,' – but the tone of voice was incorrect and the body language was in conflict with the delivery of the words. The receiver had received an inconsistent message. Remember that tone of voice accounts for 38% of the communication process.

NON-VERBAL COMMUNICATION

VISUAL IMAGE

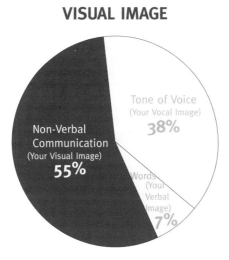

Non-verbal communication makes up 55% of the total communications process. It is essential for you as an effective communicator to understand all the component parts of this particular aspect of communications. Just as a motor mechanic understands all the component parts of a motor car and how different parts of the engine fit together, so too does the entrepreneurial manager become an expert in the parts of non-verbal communication.

Non-verbal communication is about your total image and it is inseparable from the total communications process. Lying with words is easy but it's very difficult to lie with your body. Let's look at some of the actions involved in body language.

HANDSHAKE

You will experience many kinds of handshake, some genuine, some indifferent. One extreme type of handshake may be the 'bone-crusher' where another person squeezes your hand so hard that you feel like it's in a vice. Many people interpret the 'bone-crusher' handshake as a reflection of the personality – too strong, domineering and overpowering.

The opposite type of handshake is the 'dead fish.' If someone gives you a 'dead fish' handshake, you receive messages indicating weakness or blandness or, as somebody remarked to me recently, 'You get the feeling that there is nothing inside.'

An ideal handshake should be solid and above all appropriate to the person receiving it. Obviously, a handshake with someone who is petite requires a different measure than if you were shaking hands with a professional wrestler. For me, a good handshake should be accompanied with full eye contact and a smile. The eye contact makes the handshake. My observations indicate that as many as 50% of people will not make direct eye contact during a handshake. All excellent communicators practise this until it becomes an automatic habit.

The worst communications charade you are likely to witness is where someone grumbles the words, 'Pleased to meet you', makes no direct eye contact, doesn't smile and gives the 'dead fish' handshake. This is a clue to what to expect in the communication process itself and you must adjust and adapt to the circumstances at that time. When a communication breaks down, you can bet there were clues to its happening quite early on – but were you aware of them? If, on the other hand, someone gives you the appropriate signals at the outset, gear yourself up for an intelligent interaction.

BODY POSTURE

How you deport yourself tells the other person a lot about your attitude and personal disposition. Your body, including posture, gestures and facial expressions, constantly sends messages to other people and makes powerful statements about who you are, how you are feeling and what you are thinking.

Body language can reinforce your verbal messages or it can discount them. It is often the basis on which people decide whether or not you are worth listening to. The key is to look for clusters of non-verbal actions, rather than jumping to conclusions from seeing one isolated action. People often interpret arms folding as a sign of defensiveness or resistance to the speaker. However, in isolation, this could be a restful position. So, you should look for other clues. For example, if I fold my arms, move back my seat, align my body away from you and make no eye contact, you might come to a different conclusion.

The key insight in non-verbal behaviour is to understand that you are a sender of non-verbal messages and that you need to become an interpreter of these messages for the person with whom you are communicating. When there is a conflict between what you say and your body language, we are more inclined to believe the body language. Remember that it's 55% of the impact.

A clear understanding of the natural temperament (behavioural) style of a person is important because different behavioural types will tend to use different behavioural actions. (See Chapter 3)

For example, expressive types (Yellows) will be more demonstrative with their hands and bodies to complement what they are saying. On the other hand, analytical types (Blues) will be more reserved in all their movements. But, unlike temperament, body language is more a question of nurture than nature.

So, within yourself, be conscious of body posture, and how you sit or stand. In a one-to-one meeting, keep an open, receptive posture. Lean slightly towards the person, yet remain relaxed. Face the person, but avoid a body position or stance that conveys direct confrontation.

THE USE OF SPACE

Be conscious of how close you stand or sit to another person so that you are both comfortable. By staying three or four feet apart you can achieve good one-to-one conversation. Unless you are lovers, within six inches is too close and too invading of personal space. City-dwellers are more comfortable with closer contact than people from rural areas who are accustomed to open space. Be aware of this as you may 'crowd' a person who is from a rural area and give the wrong impression by moving closer.

For a group presentation, it is important to manage the distance between yourself and your audience. 'Hiding' behind a podium or speaking from a 'height' (stage) can also send out wrong signals. Sometimes, speakers tend to have a great void between the speaking podium and the audience. This is as great a mistake as facing another person across the barrier of a huge desk. Not only does space affect the way we communicate but we also use space to communicate authority, status and sense of territory – the boss's seat is sacrosanct, 'This patch is mine' or 'Don't come any closer, stranger.'

FACIAL EXPRESSIONS

Be aware of your facial expressions. Much visual concentration is centred on this part of the body. Watch out for over use of your facial movements such as smiling, grimacing and frowning, over-use of eye contact by staring, rubbing your nose or pulling your ear.

Your face is the mirror of your mind. It's the outside part of your body that most manifests your inner thoughts and personality. It reveals your soul. It's your visual autobiography. To appropriately gaze into another person's face is like absorbing the depth and entirety of their life.

Most of us can move only two parts of our face – our forehead (brow) and mouth (jaw). The majority of your facial movements are concentrated on those areas. Consider eyebrow movements and how they communicate disbelief, anger, or happiness. Mouth movements may signal pleasure and displeasure.

HAND MOVEMENTS

In one-to-one conversations, how you use your hands can be very important. If you are very demonstrative (extrovert), you may tend to over-use your hands to reinforce verbal points. Practise and be conscious of how you use your hands and arms.

For instance, how many meanings can you take from the hand gestures: raising your hand and arm; placing your hand on your chest; your two hands clasped or joined; folding your arms; pointing with your index finger.

It is important to have clean hands and clean manicured nails. Even the quality of the pen in your hand that you use in meetings can be an important factor in supporting your communications efforts. Everything contributes either positively or negatively to your image.

THE USE OF TOUCH

The use of touch can be a very powerful non-verbal behaviour and is obviously closely related to the idea of personal space. An appropriate handshake is an accepted physical contact with another person. But putting your arm around another person may create confusion or be interpreted as either positive or negative. Giving somebody a hug may be interpreted likewise. Touching somebody's arm, holding their arm or giving somebody a pat on the back are liable to work for you or against you depending on the time and the situation and what you are trying to achieve.

The sense of touch is one of the most immediate and direct of the five senses. It communicates belonging, tenderness and warmth. We use the phrase 'that was very touching' to explain our deepest moving experiences. It physically connects us to another person in an intimate way. Used wrongly or in the wrong circumstances, it can convey a meaning of intrusion or even abuse or assault.

The use of touch and body awareness has much to do with the balance of power between the two people in question. A boss is more likely to give a member of his team a pat on the back and say 'Good man, Jack.' In the doctor/patient relationship, the doctor is more likely to touch the patient than the other way around.

I saw the power of touch in action while my wife and I were having a meal in a restaurant in Dublin. We became aware of a couple at another table, who were out of earshot. As we observed, the lady became increasingly agitated with the waitress about some aspect of the service or meal.

Although we couldn't hear what was being said, the pointing and gestures and general animation told us. The waitress left the table and emerged from the kitchen a few minutes later with the chef. Through a combination of explanation and tone of voice, the chef set about defusing the discontent. His key non-verbal action was to put his hand on the lady's arm – you could literally see the anger dissipate.

It was a master stroke from a master communicator. The light touch on the arm, combined with appropriate body posture and correct tone of voice, helped defuse a potentially explosive argument.

THE LANGUAGE OF TIME

How you use time is a very powerful non-verbal statement. Cultural differences within different organisations and between countries may dictate attitudes to the management of time. Individuals have different time scales and the value of time can be experienced in many ways. The phrase, 'Have you got a minute?' can mean totally different things to different people on different occasions. It could mean one minute or 20 minutes: or it could mean 'Let's have a chat.'

People who are continually late for meetings and other deadlines are making a statement. They may be stating: 'I'm a very important person and I've got more important things to be doing'. They may be stating: 'Please notice me. If I arrived on time and blended in with everyone else, I wouldn't be noticed. But by arriving late, I cause everyone to turn their head and give me recognition' A person who continually does this may be either inconsiderate or have low self-esteem, or be unaware of their bad habits.

THE PAUSE AND SILENCE

One of the most powerful uses of time in conversations, and particularly in public speaking, is the use of a pause. Proper use of pause or silence adds enormous credibility to a communicator but it requires mastery of the highest degree. In selling, old sales trainers used to teach: 'When you ask that closing question, shut up: he who speaks first, loses.' The power of the pause for emphasis is a skill that the great communicator works on all the time.

Have you ever been given the 'silent treatment?' It's definitely non-verbal communication. Being 'Sent to Coventry' is one of the cruellest social punishments – it's a non-verbal message. So whilst the saying 'Silence is golden' can be good, it sometimes builds the barrier to communications. On the other hand, silence used properly – listening – is really powerful in feedback situations and in resolving conflict. Silence in listening can connect us with what is unsaid and unsayable. Successful use of silence requires master skill.

ENVIRONMENT

Messages about who you are, the environment that people see you in, your office, its equipment, its location, spaciousness, presentation, colour scheme and so on come from how you think and how you do things. Impressions created from the first time you walk into someone's office or onto a production line last for a long time. Someone who has a clean, neat, organised desk sends a message that is different from someone who has a dirty, untidy, dusty desk. A world map, a quality statement, family photographs and achievement certificates presented cheerfully on your office walls create far better impressions than featureless walls that state nothing about you.

DRESS SENSE

Your physical appearance is probably your most powerful non-verbal statement. When you consider that 95% of your body is covered most of the time, you will realise the importance of grooming, appearance and dress.

The message about your business in terms of quality, responsibilities, values and service should not conflict with how you present yourself in terms of your clothes, grooming, and cleanliness.

I frequently meet managers who spend enormous sums of money creating perceptions of added-value through their advertising, brochures, packaging and public relations. On visiting their premises the greeting I receive can be inconsistent with my original perception or image of it.

The beautiful presentation of a reception area and the outside of the building may be in conflict with the human face of a frowning, cheerless manager or receptionist. I often say to senior managers that I have met well-dressed mechanics in overalls and badly-dressed business executives in suits. You and I make value-judgements based on first impressions. We think others do not see the small details within ourselves.

From the vantage point of an office window, the manager of one of my client companies and I watched a van move into the company parking lot. The driver of the van alighted and walked towards the main entrance of the building. I was astonished when my client remarked: 'He looks a bit shifty, doesn't he?' I pursued this line of thought and asked how she had come to that conclusion and so quickly. 'Well', she responded, 'look at the dirt of the van and look how he walks and slouches along. He doesn't seem to be very happy.'

This observation took place from a second floor window at 100 feet, within a time-frame of 30 seconds. Draw your own conclusions.

THE TIME WE SPEND COMMUNICATING

Most managers spend most of their working day communicating with people. Listening can take up to 45% of that time. Talking and explaining can account for about 30% of that time, reading 16%, and writing 9%.

You can see from this that 75% of our communicating time is spent listening and speaking. Schools and colleges provide little, if any, formal training in communicating (especially listening skills). The greater concentration of school activities is on traditional reading and writing skills. However, we spend only about 25% of our communicating time working on these areas. As the information revolution unfolds, it is probable that we will spend less time reading and writing, and more time in watching and listening.

SIGNALS OF INEFFECTIVE COMMUNICATION

Communication is more effective when the communication interaction is managed. Learn how to recognise the signals in the communication process. Watch out for subtle hints. Apply the LOQVE technique. Watch for non-verbal actions, the tone of voice and the words that convey the signals you are looking for.

A subtle hint could simply be the manner in which somebody answers a 'Good morning' greeting. The tone and non-verbal actions will give you the necessary clue you are looking for. Watch out for further non-verbal actions. A sad or downcast expression could be depression, or, it could be just a 'hangover.' An outward expression of uncharacteristic behaviour, a sudden change in performance or indecisiveness in completing a task may be indicators of communications ineffectiveness.

These are the finer points of excellent face-to-face communication and they separate the winners from the losers. Everything accumulates and adds benefit or loss to your overall performance.

On their own, isolated actions or series of actions such as these may not cause your communication to falter. However, the proper combination of all of these adds up to good communications. Have you ever had someone say: 'I can't put my finger on it, but something was not quite right,' or, 'We just didn't click.' Our subconscious minds have 'observed' and registered all the non-verbal behaviour even if our conscious minds do not understand the language of non-verbal communication. As an excellent communicator, you are always observing non-verbal behaviour.

HOW TO MANAGE THE COMMUNICATIONS PROCESS IN CONFLICTING, PROBLEMATIC OR STRESSFUL SITUATIONS

Have you ever found yourself in 'bad form', angry with yourself or others and not knowing why? You know that it affects your ability to communicate, solve problems and manage your time. It's stressful. But you don't know why.

As an entrepreneurial manager, you learn to apply the PITOC™ model. You learn to understand stress within yourself and in others who are acting in an irrational manner. This principle applies also to one-to-one interactions, team performance and throughout the whole organisation.

I have developed the iceberg model to give a visual representation and simple explanation of the problems of conflict resolution and communication.

Only about 10% of an iceberg is visible above the surface of the water. Likewise, the effects of bad internal communication may be visible on the surface in the form of outward, negative behaviour. However, change of the surface behaviours may solve the problem only temporarily.

ADVANCED COMMUNICATION FOR PROBLEMATIC SITUATIONS

GO BELOW THE SURFACE PROBLEMS FOR THE DEEPER CAUSES.

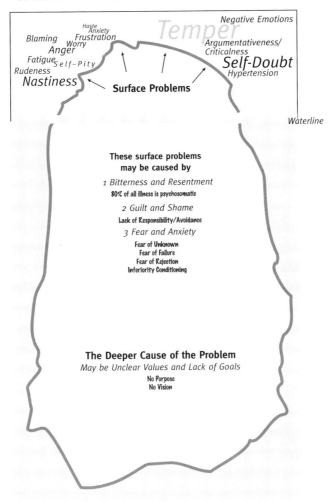

When dealing with conflict, personal problems, stress and negative people, try to look at the problem in two dimensions; one, the surface problems and two, the deeper problems. Go below the surface problems, the outward manifestation of emotions, which on the iceberg are a 10% share of the entire problem, to see the deeper causes which are 90% of the problem. By changing the surface behaviour only, you may solve part of the problem.

Many communications 'door slammers' such as rudeness, cynicism, scepticism, outbursts of anger/temper, irritability, over-criticism, hypersensitivity, blame, self-pity, worry and anxiety are symptoms of deeper causes. The professional communicator, therefore, learns to go below the surface for the emotions and deeper reasons that cause surface problems.

The deeper, underlying reasons are usually fourfold:

1 The first reason may be some form of bitterness and resentment towards someone or some event in the past. Many medical professionals today agree that as high as 80% of all illness is psychosomatic in nature – the negative condition of the mind (psycho) makes the body (somatic) sick.

2 The second potential reason may be guilt and shame. It comes from a feeling that the person has done something they know they shouldn't have done and they are now transferring the blame, anger and frustration outwardly onto other people. Aristotle once wrote: 'Anyone can be angry – that is easy. But to be angry with the right person, to the right degree, at the right time, for the right purpose and in the right way – that is not easy.'

3 The third major reason may be fear and anxiety. Fear of failure and fear of rejection are two of the greatest paralysers of human potential. Many people don't really understand the self-limiting beliefs that have conditioned their attitudes and actions. They tend to express fear and anxiety in the form of cynicism, scepticism, rudeness and anger to people that they interact with.

If you are being moody or irrational or negative in any way towards other people and hence causing breakdowns in communication, you can look for the answers deep inside yourself in the above three critical areas.

Conversely, you can search for the answers within other people by using the LOQVE method. Emotional intelligence is far more powerful than academic intelligence for the entrepreneurial manager. But emotional control is a learned behaviour and it requires awareness, understanding, practice and mastery like every other discipline.

4 The root cause of most surface communication problems, however, is a lack of focus and direction, unclear values and goals. Purposeful action is one of the best ways to eliminate worry, anxiety, fear and helplessness. If you are blaming and complaining, check yourself. You're probably not taking appropriate action, and/or your resources are probably deployed badly, your personality is being blocked and frustrated in achieving its potential.

The Iceberg model and the Strategic Thinking and Planning model (as shown in Chapter 5) can be applied equally to personal communication and leadership strategy. I use the Iceberg model all the time myself.

When I become aware that I am developing feelings of anger, moodiness, irritability or rudeness (the surface problems) I always set out to find the deeper reasons for these outward emotions. What am I annoyed over? What am I avoiding? What am I guilty about? What issue am I afraid to confront? Who am I am afraid to deal with? What is the unknown factor that I may need to take issue with? Ultimately, I go right back to my goals and values and ask myself if 'what I am doing right now is helping me to achieve my goals. Am I off-track? What is the best use of my time right now?'

Most of your below-the-surface problems will be personal, interpersonal or team issues. But nature has a great way to send you signals. It's called stress. You may need to do a self-analysis and get back on course. Most people don't know how to self-regulate and spend enormous amounts of time being 'wandering generalities' rather than 'meaningful specifics' as Zig Zigler, author of *See You at the Top,* puts it.

WALKING THROUGH THE VALLEY OF TROUBLES

'Everyone wants to give good advice, but how wonderful it is to be able to say the right thing at the right time.'

You, the entrepreneurial manager, must be capable of wearing many different hats at different times. One of these hats is that of counsellor. Another is that of negotiator. Another is conflict resolver and another is facilitator.

The Valley of Troubles model demonstrates very clearly how you must EARN THE RIGHT to give advice of any kind no matter which of these hats you are wearing.

There is a natural tendency for all communicators to rush in with their 'brand of the truth', to help people and to give freely of their advice. However, there is a wise old saying: 'The propensity to give advice is equally matched by the propensity to ignore it.' The Valley of Troubles model suggests that we need to learn to pace our travel down into the valley and up the mountainside to ensure that we make a real connection in our communication.

The meaning of any communication is the response or the outcome that it gets. Giving the very same communication, even using the right words, tone and non-verbal behaviour before you go down the Valley of Troubles and after you climb out of the Valley of Troubles can be like the difference between night and day. The key to getting safely out of the Valley of Troubles is the LOQVE formula. You must get to know people's feelings, circumstances and perspectives. Only then are you entitled or qualified to help, to speak or to give advice.

THE VALLEY OF TROUBLES

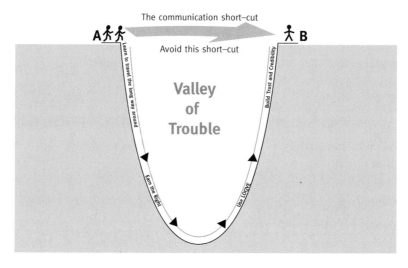

Your communication ability is put to the test at critical points of human contact such as resolving a conflict, a critical sale or negotiation, an interpersonal clash or a sensitive counselling or mentoring encounter. It is better to walk with the person through the Valley of Troubles in these more sensitive encounters. Don't jump from A to B.

As you travel down their Valley of Troubles, use LOQVE to get to know their feelings, circumstances, situations and thoughts. Only when you have walked with them through the Valley of Troubles are you qualified to help or advise them. Everyone wants to give good advice, but it is better to say the right thing at the right time.

Most people tend to take the communications short-cut by tendering instant, well-intentioned advice and help. Taking this short-cut may prevent a deeper form of communication from taking place.

As a manager, you are a counsellor. Realise that you cannot take another person further than you have gone yourself. You must earn the right. Learn how to connect at this advanced communication level.

Timing is crucial to success. Even if the answer is obvious, you must be prepared to walk down the Valley of Troubles and take ownership of the situation with the person to whom you are speaking. One of the biggest single mistakes in communication is moving too quickly or jumping in with 'Let me tell you …'

When somebody is in trouble and vulnerable, you, with your counsellor's hat on, should not confuse concern and helpfulness with trying to control the other person. Trying to 'fix' the other person often amounts to abuse of power. The causes of such a power struggle are that you want to change the other person, you want to be proved right, you want to win approval or you want to expose a person's faults. It's an ego trip. Beware of this tendency within yourself and resist it. Practice leads to mastery. Remember that personal mastery is at the very heart of entrepreneurial management.

Your goal, with your counsellor's hat on, should be to let that person come to their own conclusions and to help them walk up the Valley of Troubles on their own. The realisation that you cannot take another person further than you've gone yourself is critically important in such a delicate walk. Therefore, the intrapersonal journey for yourself must have gone on beforehand and be ongoing within yourself to really have effective communication interaction.

When you have earned the right to communicate as outlined, you can then give advice, guidance or direction. However, I believe from my experience that nine out of ten people know within themselves what the solutions are to their own problems and merely require a helping hand.

ORGANISATIONAL COMMUNICATION

If the biggest single choke-point within organisations is miscommunications leading to low morale, lack of trust, fear, conflict and poor teamwork, the biggest challenge for the entrepreneurial manager is to eliminate this choke point.

You must approach the elimination process as a challenge and an opportunity. You must synchronise all the resources and capabilities and maximise all the 'people power' so that everyone is working furiously towards the achievement of a shared vision. Only then will you achieve your organisation goals. The key question that must be answered fully is: 'How do you get everyone in the organisation to unlock their potential for the greater good and happiness of the total organisation?'

People are more likely to learn, change, grow, develop and contribute when they believe that the new 'way of doing things around here' is both desirable and possible. Your major task is to create the environment for this to happen.

There are four major challenges for organisational communication:

1 To create and communicate an overall strategy for the organisation.

The challenge for most organisations is to create and share a compelling strategy to which everyone becomes committed to. This will be outlined in more detail in Chapter 5 on Strategic Thinking and Planning. As the entrepreneurial manager, you must help to create that strategy.

Your objective is to create an open system through which managers and staff constantly question themselves, listen to others internally and externally, and observe changing circumstances. You can use the LOQVE system to do this. Entrepreneurial managers constantly study the external environment and the internal environment so that the organisation can be competitive and futuristic.

Living the values, developing a sense of mission and energising the organisation with the compelling vision is the challenge for the professional communicator and the entrepreneurial manager. The compelling vision specifies the strategic driving force of the organisation. It is central to the strategic and operational (tactical) goals.

As the entrepreneurial manager, you must have the influencing strategies and skills that will encourage everyone to play a part in transforming the vision into reality. Persuasion forms attitudes, changes behaviour, instils standards and builds a positive climate. You need all your communications skills to present the big picture to everyone in the organisation.

Communications skill techniques are empty unless they are reinforced by personal example. You must lead by example. Organisations need heroes and stalwarts in the same way that sports teams need top performers. You will be judged on the results. Stories of successes and early wins become part of the discussion around the organisation. In effect, they become part of the communications process.

2 TO GET GOAL FOCUSED

The second major purpose of organisational communication is to get everyone focused on future developments and goals. How do you get a totally integrated organisation-wide focus on future direction? How do you get everyone's energy and effort moving forward in the same direction? The need for integration and co-ordination varies with the size of the organisation and the types of work undertaken. Small organisations can be controlled by a single boss. Large organisations require elaborate systems for integration while professional, divisionalised and creative organisations have different needs. You must study and be aware of the different systems and mechanisms necessary to make integrated, co-ordinated progress in your team or organisation.

The communication mechanisms for communicating with agents, sub-contractors and self-employed stake-holders are different from the traditional hierarchical methods of communicating with employed staff. Matrix type organisations combining project and functional type structures need a different communicating style than the traditional pyramidical hierarchy. Organisations which lack well-developed and appropriate communications systems and channels may be inefficient, wasteful, incompetent, and bureaucratic in dealing with outside partners.

The geographical spread of an organisation can cause communications barriers. An individual's ability to communicate clearly can be hindered by the internal layout of his workplace. A poorly ventilated or over-heated environment will cause drowsiness, sickness and other physical ailments. Performance can be hindered by being in different offices, in different buildings and even on different sites. The result can be misunderstandings, frustration and disintegration on both formal and informal communication levels.

A major complaint that most organisations give me about their place of work is that it has a 'them and us' culture.

When I ask management what their choke point is in terms of maximising the human resource, they invariably reply, 'it's them,' meaning the workforce. When I ask the same open question of the workforce, they invariably reply 'it's them,' meaning the management. One of the major de-motivators within organisations, and a major cause of communications breakdown, is 'not knowing what's going on' and 'not being in on things' in their own organisation.

Management may assume that everyone knows everything about the company's developments and initiatives. They are often puzzled when they realise that not everyone does know, or is a victim of misinformation and disinformation. Rumour is invented to fill the void caused by lack of communication and lack of information. Be aware of this.

You realise that you must communicate information downwards and let people in on things. You realise that you must encourage upward communication by asking people for their views and opinions, and you must facilitate the use of lateral communications in which people may share, discuss, analyse and decide on information without the presence of management. You must observe their reactions, and listen carefully to non-verbal responses. In turn, you must verify facts and ensure that misunderstandings are eliminated. This brings personal communications expertise to practical benefit for organisational development.

3 TO CREATE AND MAINTAIN A HEALTHY, HAPPY, SELF-CONFIDENT ORGANISATION.

How do you get every single person within your organisation to focus on the vision and the implementation of strategic goals within your organisation rather than engaging in energy-absorbing negative communication activities? Office politics are a major contributor to absorption of time, energy and stress within organisations. The great tragedy is that they are given a licence to continue by managers who do not practise LOQVE and are simply afraid to risk rocking the boat.

The fundamental reason why communication breaks down, sometimes irreparably, within organisations is a gradual breakdown of trust. Low levels of trust between management and staff are the root cause of all ineffective communications in organisations. Low trust leads to low morale and low self-confidence, and ultimately, low productivity, wastage, accidents, absenteeism, unhappiness and lots of frustration for everyone concerned.

An organisation that has ineffective communications systems stemming from low trust and low morale is a low self-esteem organisation. You know that there is no wave of a magic wand that will change mistrust to trust overnight. Mistrust invariably invades an organisation like a cancer and once it takes hold it's difficult to remove. You can sort out the physical resource problems of an organisation in a short period of time. You can do likewise with the financial resources and likewise with the time resources. Careful identity-management can change your external image. However, to change the mindset and the culture of an organisation takes time, expertise and patience, and a systematic integrated organisation-wide approach.

The first step towards the objective of a healthy, happy organisation is the building of trust. It's virtually impossible to trust other people ('them') unless you understand the concept of self-esteem (eliminating fear) and the concept of self-responsibility (eliminating blame), for yourself and for the people employed by your organisation. Trust starts with building personal self-esteem, then interpersonal one-on-one development, then the team, and then the organisation. Customers ultimately 'smell' this intangible extra.

The PITOC™ formula again!

High trust organisations are 'empowered' organisations where risk, purpose, direction, energy, drive and enthusiasm are alive and well and apparent to all concerned. High trust organisations form stronger value-adding partnerships with other organisations which is the 'way of the business world' right now. High trust and strong relationships go hand in hand at the Personal(P), the Interpersonal (I), the Team(T), the Organisational(O) and Customer (C) levels (PITOC™).

As an entrepreneurial manager, you should constantly use the LOQVE formula to encourage people to work for the organisation and not against it. People rarely work consciously against the organisation. But unconsciously, they may have many different behaviours, attitudes and actions to show that they are not in harmony with management. Although it is doubtful that you will totally eradicate mistrust, you can slowly build trust and confidence among most people. This is the process of 'bottling' that intellectual capital. It's an investment, but an investment that takes a long time to pay off.

4 TO ENSURE THAT INTELLIGENT DECISION-MAKING TAKES PLACE.

Your primary role as an entrepreneurial manager is to creatively solve problems by making intelligent decisions.

A major choke point in decision-making is lack of accurate information or blocked channels of communication. Formal and informal information is transmitted upwards, downwards and across the organisation in a poor, ineffective or irregular way. 'Nobody told me' or 'It's the first I've heard of it' are oft-used responses by staff and by management. Sometimes there's truth in these responses, sometimes they are used as a convenient cloak – the miscommunication has happened so many times that everyone now accepts such responses as acceptable and standard. As much as 80% of the problems will probably be found in the process flow but remember people manage the process.

You realise that the best solutions to local problems come from the people closest to operating the tasks in question. These people are your local experts. The skills of LOQVE are vital in intelligence-gathering within the organisation. Your organisation has the solutions to most of your problems under your own feet, but somehow the transmission and the receiving gets clogged up between the local experts and the decision-makers.

One of the best ways of gathering information is by walking the shop floor and having impromptu LOQVE sessions. Another way is to conduct annual structured surveys within the organisation. Yet another way is to channel information upwards through feedback sessions which would be facilitated by internal champions such as line managers.

BECOME A MASTER

Everyone is a communicator. The only question is: 'How good are you at it?' Everyone scores 10 out of 10 on some interactions. Everyone scores 0 out of 10 sometimes. The key question is: Do you average 4, 5, 6 out of 10, or 7, 8, 9 out of 10? You are being voted on daily. Your present state (emotional, professional, career, financial) is more a result of these votes than almost any other factor. You have a choice to ignore everything in this chapter and go your merry way like 80% of the population, or you can become a master communicator by carefully learning their application over time. Remember that all choices lead to consequences. Decide.

APPLICATION EXERCISE

1 Think about the application of LOQVE in all your personal communication interactions whether they are selling situations, or giving or receiving feedback at meetings. Your ability to diagnose why certain interactions have been successful or unsuccessful is a key entrepreneurial management skill. Write out 10 areas for improvement.

2 Think about a recent meeting, interview or negotiation that you have had and reflect on your non-verbal behaviour. Remember that there are 20,000 non-verbal signals. Work on improving two areas immediately.

3 Practise tone of voice variations, especially on the telephone. Test run different tones and monitor the reactions to them.

4 Set up small group feedback sessions to listen to the expression of the feelings and thoughts of your staff. Write on a flip-chart: 'What are the issues around here that, if we resolve them, would really make this a better place in which to work?' You just Listen, Observe, Question. Don't defend. Don't Attack or Justify. Rather Verify and Explain.

5 Pick your top five customers or significant influencers in your business and think out how you could communicate better with them on a face-to-face basis. Set up a meeting or have lunch together.

PITOC™ COMMUNICATION

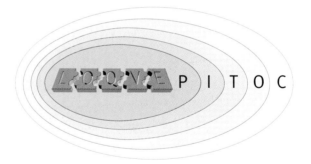

Your challenge is to maximise communications at all five PITOC™ levels. This is one of the biggest challenges in creating personal and business advantage. To the amateur, communication looks simple. To the true professional, it is an extremely complex process made easy.

5

MASTERING STRATEGIC THINKING AND PLANNING

'If you don't stand and fight when you have a chance to win, ONE DAY, you may be asked to go and fight when you have no chance to win'

—Winston Churchill

Your ability to develop a clear strategic thinking and planning process is likely to be your single most important entrepreneurial management issue for the next five years. How do you get every single stakeholder in your business working towards a shared strategy?

The management of strategy development is described typically in terms of planning and analytical systems. Strategic thinking, however, is equally important but less well developed.

In this chapter, I will provide a total framework that synergistically combines the discipline of strategic thinking with the science of strategic planning.

The very essence of entrepreneurial management is the creation of strategic advantage. Entrepreneurial managers must go through the challenges of planning, thinking, experiencing, responding, defining, measuring, developing, implementing and changing, every day of their lives.

Become an avid student of the art of strategy. Make a decision to study strategy, to understand strategy and, ultimately, to implement strategy. Strategy as a subject has been complicated almost beyond recognition by academics, consultants and authors as they strive to make the subject meaningful to the ordinary manager. They have mystified the subject. As a result, most managers feel daunted by the study of strategy and by its operation as a management success tool.

You realise that strategy is an essential thinking tool and a powerful planning process to gain the individual, team or organisational competitive edge. You use the thinking tools and the technical tools of strategy much like a carpenter would use his brain power and tools to make a table or chair.

The purpose of this chapter on Strategic Thinking and Planning is to:

1 Trace the history and development of the science of strategy with the purpose of gaining an insight into its importance and capability. You are introduced to some strategic thinkers to enable you to better understand the subject. Understanding is important to mastery.

2 Give you a total overview of the subject so that you can start to apply the techniques of strategic thinking and planning.

The DIY home-maker has a toolbox that is similar to the toolbox used by the professional tradesman. He doesn't need to study every tool forever before trying it out. Similarly, the tools and techniques of good strategy can be applied immediately.

3 Give you a practical model (The STP Model) on how to set realistic, simple, accessible and powerful business strategy for your own business unit or organisation.

My overall goal is to give you a crystal-clear understanding of the concepts of strategy. These concepts are accessible, realistic, practical and highly applicable. More importantly, you can use them at the sharp end of business on an operational day-to-day level. Strategy techniques, applied actively, are powerful tools for building your organisation.

Strategy has been used and abused by corporate and bureaucratic organisations. Massive documents on strategy, that cost fortunes to develop, gather dust in government and corporate organisations. These documents have been given no sense of ownership by many of the organisations that commissioned them, and they have not been acted on.

Part of the reason is that strategy has been misunderstood and that it has been shrouded in mystery and techniques. You need to realise at this point that there is a wide gap between the 'thinking' part of strategy and the 'planning part'. When the thinking part and the planning part synchronise, then we have a force – a twin force of practicality and emotion. 'Emotional strategy' and 'analytical strategy' when combined with clear executions are unrivalled.

HOW STRATEGY BECOMES A SCIENCE

Strategy is as old as the hills or, at least, as old as human conflict. Military examples and imagery have always played a key role in business development, probably because of a host of similarities. Who is the enemy/competitor? Where is the battlefield/market? What resources are deployed? How do we engage?

The Art of War written in 500BC by Sun Tzu, a Chinese military general, is a classic, then and now, because it challenges the assumptions that many people have about strategy. It is probably where the art of strategy was first encountered. Strategy is not mere theory. Sun Tzu challenges fundamentals. Why engage in battle when you can win by other means? Why not attack your enemy's (competitor's) strategy (rather than blindly pursue your own)? Or his alliances? Or next best, his soldiers?

Sun Tzu has no room for sentiment. He says: 'Deploy forces to defend the strategic points: exercise vigilance in preparation, do not be indolent. Deeply investigate the true situation, secretly await their laxity. Wait until they leave their strongholds, then seize what they love.'

The word strategy itself comes from the Greek word *strategia* which means the art or science of being a (military) general. The Greek and Roman generals knew that wars were won by a careful management of politics, logistics, planning tactics and taking action, but the parallels between military and business strategy can be made throughout all periods of history right up to the 1990 Gulf War. Day-to-day business is like a series of battles in a war. If the overall strategy is correct (and it is usually correct if a systems thinking approach is taken) a number of tactical errors can be made without hindering the achievement of the overall objective.

SCRIPTING STRATEGY

Although good managers down through history have plotted grand strategies, it is only since World War II that management scholars have seriously started to script the methodologies and science of strategy.

In modern times, the first identifiable phases of a strategic thinking approach was in the 1950's and in the early 1960's. Businesses were developing from simple single-product organisations into more complex multi-product organisations, and there was an attempt to implement day-to-day rules that put boundaries around what a functional area could or could not do.

Alfred Chandler, one of the intellectuals of the 1950's and author of

Strategy and Structure in 1962, defined strategy as 'the setting of long term goals and objectives, the determination of courses of action and allocation of resources to achieving the objectives.' He argued that new challenges (size, complexity) give rise to new structures. His thesis wasn't just that structure follows strategy. Among the earlier entrepreneurial leaders who were pioneers of the strategy movement was Alfred Sloan, who in the 1920's wrote *My Years with General Motors*.

In 1960, Theodore Levitt's article, 'Marketing Myopia', in the *Harvard Business Review*, became a catalyst for strategic thinking in marketing and management. He was one of the first to take a broad perspective and a radical look at the overall purpose of strategy. This article was a landmark and opened the doors to a new way of thinking about strategy and more importantly, implementing it in business.

In 1965, H Igor Ansoff wrote the monumental book, *Corporate Strategy*. In the decade between 1965 and 1975, this book became the bible of strategic planning as managers struggled to cope with rapid changes in organisations and the rapid growth in size, shape and complexities of modern business. Though Ansoff's approach may appear to be very structured and analytical, he created a new language and processes that allowed fundamental concepts to be developed. These included the product-market matrix, competency profiling, synergy and corporate advantage.

Probably the two most powerful techniques in the history of strategy were The Experience Curve and The Growth-Share Matrix, developed by the Boston Consulting Group (BCG) which was founded in 1964 by Bruce Henderson. The 60's and early 70's were the 'golden years' of strategy and probably fitted with the economic, cultural, social and political developments in Ireland such as the Lemass Era, in which Sean Lemass, as Taoiseach, implemented the recommendations of the Whitaker Report on Economic Expansion.

In the 1970's, two other important books were *The Nature of Managerial Work,* by Henry Mintzberg in 1973 and *Strategic Management,* by H Igor Ansoff in 1979.

Mintzberg wrote another book in 1994 called *The Rise and Fall of Strategic Planning* in which he declared strategic planning to be 'dead.' He argue that strategic planning itself does not produce a strategy. This makes my point exactly – that creative strategic systems thinking is the key. I believe that blood, sweat, tears, commitment, involvement, guts, nerve and time spent selling the compelling vision is the secret. Strategy is primarily an emotional issue. The old school liked hard data, certainty and structure. The new school of strategists incorporate the 'soft' intellectual capital issues, deal with change and discontinuity and the freedom to be flexible – what I call Emotional Strategy.

However, the star of corporate strategy world-wide is probably Michael Porter, a Harvard Business School professor and consultant and probably second only to Tom Peters as the highest paid lecturer in the world. He wrote *Competitive Strategy: Techniques for Analysing Industries and Competitors* (1980), and *Competitive Advantage* (1985). In both books, Porter proposes three generic strategies or viable approaches dealing with competitive forces. For Porter, strategy is distilled down to how to compete.

The first competitive strategy is differentiation. This means competing on the basis of value added to customers through, for example: extra quality, extra service, easier to handle, fun to see, status value or other features so that the customer will pay more to cover the higher costs. The second competitive strategy is cost-based leadership. Quality and service are not unimportant however because the third strategy is a clear focus to perform excellently.

Using his Five Competitive Forces model, Porter places an organisation in the context of its industry and identifies the organisation's own value chain systematically. The industry rules are set by these five forces:

1 New competitor demands or responses which use up resources and therefore lower profits.
2 Substitutes can affect prices.
3 Buyers will use any bargaining power to reduce costs.
4 Suppliers will leverage advantage over you if they can.
5 Rivalry leads to investment in Research and Development and innovation marketing and this reduces profit.

Porter has some insightful thoughts on these issues:

– Seek out the most demanding buyers because they will set the standards for your people.

– Seek buyers with the most difficult needs because they will force you to continually research and develop your products/services.

– Seek out the industry's toughest regulations and set these as your norms.

– Treat employees as permanent partners.

– Use your outstanding competitors as motivators.

In a nutshell, Porter's Competitive Strategy is about creating business advantage – gaining a winning edge. He suggests that you look at your competitor in four different ways:

1 Future goals: What are they trying to achieve in terms of market leadership and technology?

2 Assumptions: What assumptions are they making towards the industry and their competitors?

3 Current strategy: What is the current reality and their current sales and marketing approach?

4 Opportunities: Where do they think they are going?

'Customer-based strategies are the basis of all strategy', wrote Kenichi Ohmae in his brilliant book *The Mind of the Strategist*. This book is compulsory reading for the entrepreneurial manager because it explains how strategy is most effective when it combines analysis, intuition and will-power in the pursuit of that winning edge.

In 1990, Ohmae wrote *The Borderless World*, where he writes about nothing being 'overseas' any longer and where the multinationals see themselves as being 'equidistant from all customers'. He suggests that the secret of success in the borderless world is knowledge of their key markets.

The study of Japanese organisations, such as Honda, Toyota, and Mitsubishi in the 1980's, who were totally obsessed with market leadership, beating their competitors and satisfying customers, is essential for the entrepreneurial strategic manager.

Influential strategic thinkers and writers of our own time are Charles Handy, Rosabeth Moss Kanter, Tom Peters and, of course, Peter Drucker.

Tom Peters was probably the world's foremost management thinker/shaper of the 80's. His views on change and excellence, strategy and management development are heeded throughout the Western world. He and Bob Waterman co-authored the best-selling, *In Search of Excellence*, published in 1982. Today the book has sold more than eight million copies – exceptional sales for a business book. Peters continues to sell his ideas to audiences all over the world in personal appearances and through his books, videos and audio-cassettes.

In Search of Excellence was an outstanding book in that it placed the customer at the centre of strategy. Despite the fact that about 30 of the 43 companies that he described as 'excellent' were in trouble by the end of the 80's, the message and the lessons were still clear. In his follow-up book in 1987, *Thriving On Chaos*, Peters' first line, 'there are no excellent companies', seemed to contradict the message from his earlier best-seller.

However, I believe his statement demonstrates his acknowledgement of the nature of today's business world of constant change, discontinuity, and shock, where even good companies will fail if they are not entrepreneurial and strategic in attitude. Constant renewal is the name of the game today.

In *Liberation Management* (1992), Peters makes five major points:

1 All business is becoming fashion.

2 Create mini strategic business units everywhere.

3 Organise everything and everyone around projects.

4 Destroy functional departments.

5 Use partners outside the formal organisation.

He suggests that to create sustainable business advantage, very little can happen unless the structures and strategies of current organisations are changed.

Charles Handy, a native of County Kildare in Ireland, is one of the more futuristic management writers of today. Handy's main thesis is that the nature of work and the type of organisations needed today is changing very fast.

The best place to get an understanding of Handy's work is *The Age of Unreason*, published in 1989. He writes that the future firm will have a shamrock shape made up of core internal workers, a network of suppliers or contractors and a high percentage of the workforce being temporary or part-time hired help. Handy has developed a thought-provoking equation of $1/2$ x 2 x 3 = P, which means that the organisation of the future will employ half as many people, paid twice as well, producing three times as much.

In *The Empty Raincoat* (1994), he suggests that governments shouldn't be surprised that as a productivity and economic boom sets in, there will be no corresponding reduction in unemployment rates. He suggests that the reason is simple: 'Organisations have learned that it is possible to grow their businesses sometimes exponentially without growing the labour force. The "knowledge worker" has arrived'.

Rosabeth Moss Kanter, a Harvard Business lecturer, believes that empowerment should be the driving force behind the change management strategy. She has written three important books, all worth reading. *Men and Women of the Corporation* (1977) looks at how bureaucratic structures paralyse the individual, the team and the organisation. *The Change Masters* (1983) continues the theme of unlocking the potential of the individual to maximise the potential of the team within a framework of common organisational purpose.

In *When Giants Learn to Dance* (1989) she stresses that the attributes of the entrepreneur such as flexibility, responsiveness and personal initiative could greatly empower the larger organisation to reach its potential. The importance of discipline and vision go a long way towards developing a synergy throughout the organisation. She talks about 'the power of the elephant with the agility of a dancer.'

She also developed the acronym PAL, which means 'Pool resources with others, Ally to exploit an opportunity and Link systems in a partnership.' The wise organisation becomes partners with customers, suppliers, contractors and even competitors of all kinds.

Many other leaders in management thinking deserve to be studied and read to develop a broader picture of business and strategic development. It would be useful to study how Deming, Juran and Crosby influenced the Quality movement and how Peter Drucker's thinking and writing will dominate management development well into the 21st century.

The trend in recent years has been to get the individual, the team and the organisation to get all their resources working in formation towards the objective of winning and keeping customers. The objective of smart organisations is to establish competitive advantage over competitors by business focus, market segmentation, specialising, by attaining a favourable cost position and by having a better product or service.

Many of the techniques of strategy applied by business leaders and military generals for hundreds of years are applicable today. Nothing has changed, yet paradoxically in another sense, everything has changed.

TOWARDS A SHARED STRATEGY

I am asked continually by managers: 'Who should be involved in developing strategy.' Implicit in their question is: 'It's not for everyone.' It's as though the development of strategy should be conducted secretly. Unfortunately, this response is part of the legacy of corporate strategic thinkers of the 60's and 70's in particular. Many managers feel that they are inadequate to carry out a strategic thinking and planning exercise. However, the entrepreneurial manager decides that strategy will be a key weapon in creating competitive advantage. He also decides to learn how to do it.

WHO SHOULD BE INVOLVED?

Everyone who is involved in the operational supervisory day-to-day affairs of the business should be involved in setting strategy. This includes functional heads, senior managers, but most importantly, the managing directors and chief executives. If the leader of the organisation is not involved, it becomes a less-than-effective exercise.

Is it possible to involve the majority of stakeholders in creating a shared strategy? Yes it is. Involving the whole system, (internal and external customers) in developing a new culture or change, or inputting into strategy requires delicate handling by an expert facilitator. People will support what they help create and the concept of shared strategy is more likely to get implemented across the board. Involving a critical mass of people in developing a shared strategy massively increases ownership, commitment, alignment and speed. The people who are closest to the problems really appreciate this opportunity to give feedback and engage in creativity and innovation.

However, expert handling is key. I have seen one disaster where a CEO decided to do this himself – it took his company three years to recover from the lambasting he got. The problem was that he was part of the problem.

To carry out the exercise of setting strategy, heed the advice, 'the person who acts as his own lawyer has a fool for a client.' It's essential that you hire a professional expert who has the capability to be a facilitator to your group for the important exercise of setting business strategy.

Later in this chapter, I will explain how I work with organisations in developing a strategic thinking process and setting business strategy.

WHAT IS STRATEGY?

Part of the 'problem' with developing strategy as a thinking tool is the answering of the question 'What is Strategy?' There are many definitions and interpretations, and of course, this just adds to the challenge of de-mystifying strategy and developing a simple and practiced system that every manager, and the entrepreneurial manager in particular, can use.

The Concise Oxford Dictionary defines strategy in militaristic terms: *'generalship, the art of war: management of an army or armies in a campaign, art of so moving or disposing troops or ships or aircraft as to impose upon the enemy the place and time and conditions for fighting preferred by oneself.'*

To the lay person, strategy is a plan. It's a clearly set out way of dealing with a certain kind of situation. For example, a child has a 'strategy' to organise a birthday party. A business has a strategy to enter a new market. A sports team has a strategy to win a match or a championship. A political party has a strategy to win an election.

According to this interpretation, strategies have two essential characteristics: (1) they are made in advance of the actions to which they apply, and (2) they are developed consciously and purposefully.

I believe that the cause of much of the confusion and mystification about strategy is that, in sport, in the military, and in management, strategy has been interpreted as being just a plan of doing things.

STRATEGY IS A WAY OF THINKING

The key to becoming an effective strategist is the realisation that strategy is much more than just planning. Strategic planning is relatively easy. Strategic thinking is what separates the amateurs from the professionals. Strategic thinking is visioning in action. To becoming a strategic thinker, it is essential to know that:

– Strategy is a manoeuvre. Sometimes you will hear people in a sports context say 'that was a good strategy,' or 'he has an excellent strategy to outwit his opponent.' In this sense strategy can be used as a ploy or a threat to outwit rivals and gain the competitive edge.

– Strategy is a sequence of actions. Strategy is also about the pattern of behaviour which individuals, teams and organisations have in achieving their objective.

A friend of mine's objective was to build a new house within one year. His sequence of actions was save money, identify and buy a site, get a mortgage, work with the architect on design, get a reliable builder, subcontract as much as possible, move in, landscape the garden.

– Strategy is positioning. How individuals, teams or organisations position themselves within their internal environment and within the external environment is essential to good strategy. If you are in sales, do you position yourself as a mere seller of products or as a doctor with solutions to customer problems? The former just sells. The latter consults, listens, matches needs, offers solutions and befriends his customer.

– Strategy is a way of thinking. It is a mindset which must be continuously worked at. If you don't use it, you lose it. The culture and ideologies of some organisations have developed from the influence of one person, then spread to the team, and eventually the whole organisation. Hewlett Packard have developed The HP Way. It started with two founders, Bill Hewlett and David Packard, working in a garage building testing equipment. The consistency of the MacDonald's product in 25,000 outlets world-wide is derived from its thinking about Q S C and V – 'quality, service, cleanliness and value'.

The Superquinn strategy is derived from the approach of Feargal Quinn who eats, sleeps and drinks customer service. He is the personification of Ralph Waldo Emerson's statement that: 'every organisation is the length and shadow of one man.'

Strategy is a perspective, a focused way of seeing the world. In this respect, strategy is to the organisation what personality is to the individual. It contains a sum of the grand strategy, the driving force, the culture, and the world-view of the organisation.

Development of strategic thinking means developing a shared vision and collective consciousness and learning of the organisation. It is identifying and leading with these core competencies. This development is one of the major challenges for the entrepreneurial manager within himself in the first instance, and within the individuals, teams, and, eventually, his total organisation.

CLARIFYING MISCONCEPTIONS ABOUT STRATEGY

Strategic Thinking and Planning encompasses all of the above perspectives on strategy. I have developed and implemented this model out of frustration with more complicated models.

It gathers, integrates and co-ordinates the emotional, mental, physical and even spiritual qualities of the person and the team. Many brilliant technical strategies, I believe, fail because they fail to connect on all these four levels.

A question that managers frequently ask me is: 'What is the difference between strategy and tactics?' I explain that tactics are more concerned with the practical plans for implementing strategic goals. Responsibility for implementing and developing tactics often lies with executives who are not, themselves, concerned with overall strategic formulation.

Another regular question is: 'Can you transfer strategy models to a personal situation?' Personal leadership strategy can, of course, be completed privately, but don't underestimate the amount of time it will take. To do a serious strategic overview of your personal situation could initially take as long as 20 hours of thinking, writing, researching and restructuring. But this is only the start – thereafter, it must be continuously updated and improved upon.

The STP model outlined in the next pages is perfectly transportable to the family situation. Your spouse/partner and yourself could take a long weekend in some quiet hotel or guest house and lock yourselves away to force the project to completion. Peace and quiet, a deadline and a reward at the end will induce your creative juices towards providing solutions. 'What about separate teams or branches?' Business unit (team) strategy, can be created within a smaller team at a departmental or functional level. The amount of time for this creation should not be underestimated.

At senior management level, any serious attempt to develop a strategic thinking process and planning should initially take a minimum of three days. Furthermore, proper groundwork preparation and regular reviews are imperative. Of course, every operational management meeting, (held monthly in many organisations), is linked (directly or indirectly) with the overall strategy.

WHERE SHOULD YOU SET STRATEGY?

Strategy formulation meetings should be conducted at an overnight venue to allow for discussion and team building. Being away from the work environment, the office or the factory floor, propels the team into focusing on the job at hand.

Strategic business development meetings should never be held in the boardroom or a meeting room situated close to the work environment. Participants cannot be objective when they're beside the administration office or the production line. There's simply too much of a tendency to nip out at the coffee breaks or at lunch time to deal with day-to-day operational issues. Reviews, follow-up and action meetings should be held off-site also.

The venue for a strategic business meeting should be a quiet location that is remote from the office. I recommend that the venues be good hotels in secluded rural areas. People will 'associate' the whole strategic development with that place, and will, for many years afterwards, refer to the conversations, the discussions and the goals that were set there. The meeting could become known as 'the Mount Juliet Summit.'

It's important to pick a venue or a large room that is quiet, fresh, and provides an ambience and a relaxing environment conducive to creativity and systems thinking and planning. This is a very absorbing and tiring process and people go from exhilarating 'highs' to washed-out, brain-dead 'lows.' Focused concentration is important and a good environment is key to productive concentration. Strategic thinking requires total focus on the job in hand over an extended period of time.

WHY SET STRATEGY?

Rather than set strategies, some organisations prefer to 'respond' to situations. They rationalise this by saying that all plans and forecasts are inaccurate anyway. There is too much change in the internal and external environment and the costs, time and inconvenience spent in such reflection and planning is frustrating and pointless.

Many other organisations only resort to strategy when a disaster, such as loss of a major customer contract strikes. They then rush to establish strategies and get their thinking processes in order. All too often, it's too late. This is emphasised when we consider that 58% of all new Irish businesses fail within five years of start-up. The European average for such failure is 46%. Regular, constant, vigilance and crisis anticipation is an important management skill.

THE STRATEGIC THINKING AND PLANNING (STP) APPROACH:

- will discipline you to look at your internal weaknesses, strengths, and core competencies and how to maximise them. It will also discipline you to explore the external opportunities and threats to your business. This process alone shows up distinctive advantages and choke points on a grand and local scale.
- will provide you with a framework against which your organisation's progress can be assessed over time.
- will help you assess important long term decisions and discuss options without the crisis-management approach.
- will provide a focus and direction for your organisation's energies. The future can be influenced towards a compelling shared strategy.
- will enhance co-ordination and co-operation between departments, business units and other divisions within a multi-business organisation.
- will generate a better return on your investments and equity, sales and net profit.
- will help re-deploy hitherto under-utilised resources and reposition you in the market place.
- will help you ultimately to take decisive action. All good strategy is goal-oriented. Managers avoid goal commitment like the plague – even those who attended goal setting courses.

'Success must be summoned: it will not come unbidden and unplanned, and to succeed you must cultivate the habits of thinking strategically,' says Kenichi Ohmae, master strategist and leader of McKinsey & Co, Tokyo.

HOW TO SET STRATEGY USING THE STP MODEL

When you have the right people involved, all well prepared, with an understanding of what strategy is about, and you are prepared to give it the necessary time, in a proper location, and you are clear in your thinking about the ultimate reasons for setting strategy, you are then at the strategy formulation stage.

The STP model is simple, practical, accessible and powerful. Above all, it gets fantastic results. It is equally applicable to your personal situation, your team/department set-up, and it can provide a framework for setting overall organisational strategy.

I have developed this model to keep everyone involved, and focused on achieving a successful outcome. It is very easy to get side-tracked, and fail to complete the process. This consequently leaves a vacuum. Such a vacuum can be filled with cynicism and scepticism. Completion of the total strategy exercise is critically important. Completion means the production of a 30-50 page document that pulls all the elements of the process together.

Time is the great enemy of this strategic thinking and planning approach. The independent expert facilitator's job in conducting a strategy exercise is to achieve balance between pushing the process and giving enough time for discussion and dialogue to viewpoints as they arise. The amount of discussion and dialogue will be directly proportional to the amount of ownership and commitment to the final product.

When the process starts it is mostly a communications, creativity and team exercise because most organisations already have the answers to their own challenges within their own capability and knowledge base.

THE SEVEN STEPS OF THE STRATEGIC THINKING AND PLANNING(STP) MODEL

The STP model has seven distinctive steps. It starts with an examination of your current reality – the current situation analysis (Step 1). Then it takes a quick step back into looking at the history and the development of your business (Step 2). This is followed by an examination of Values (Step 3) and the creation of a Mission Statement (Step 4). From this comes a Vision Statement (Step 5). Then we get more focused as we develop Strategic Goals (Step 6) and Tactical Plans (Step 7).

The Strategic Thinking and Planning (STP)Model

Strategic Thinking and Planning is a learned practice. The management of strategy development is typically described in terms of strategic planning and analytical systems. Strategic thinking, however, is equally important. Getting to grips with a strategic thinking and planning process is central to creating business advantage and mastering the strategy challenge.

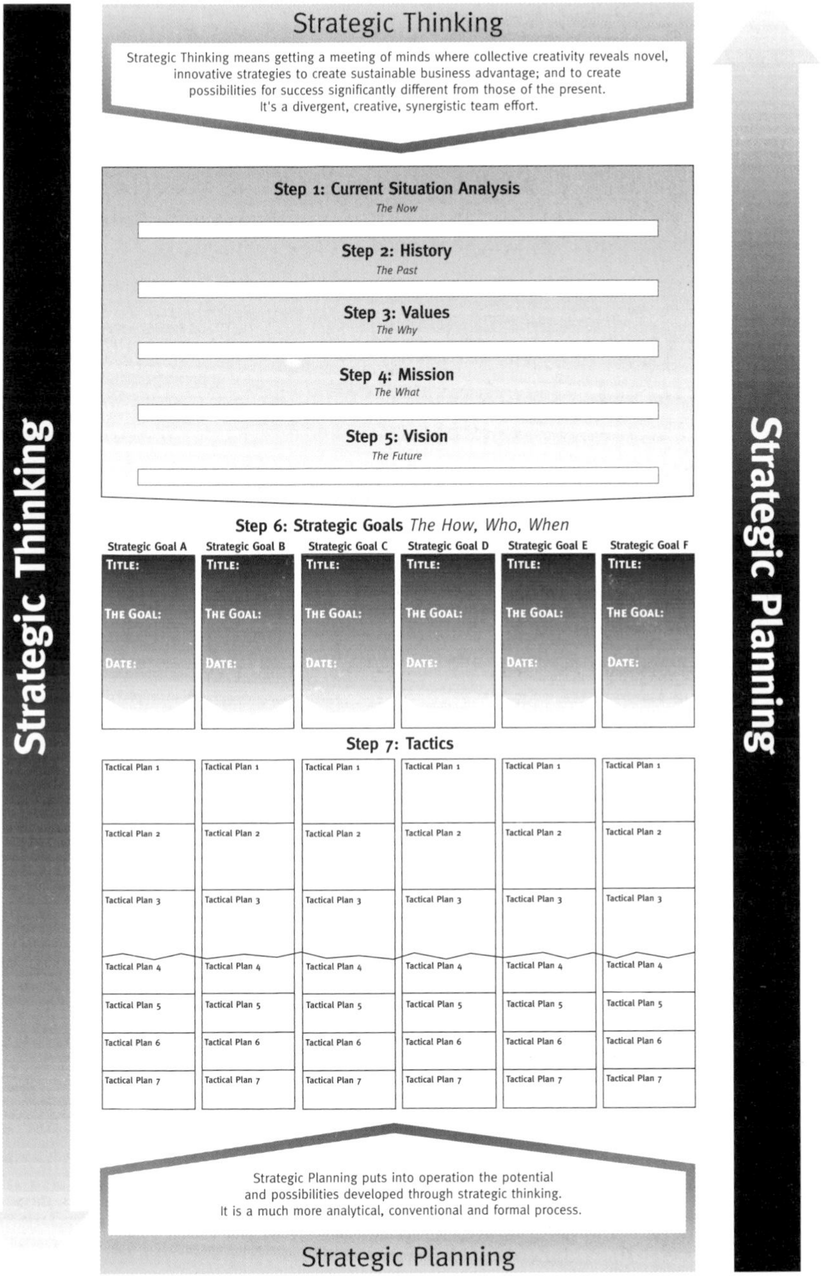

Strategic Thinking

Strategic Thinking means getting a meeting of minds where collective creativity reveals novel, innovative strategies to create sustainable business advantage; and to create possibilities for success significantly different from those of the present. It's a divergent, creative, synergistic team effort.

Strategic Thinking (vertical, left margin)

Strategic Planning (vertical, right margin)

Step 1: Current Situation Analysis
The Now

Step 2: History
The Past

Step 3: Values
The Why

Step 4: Mission
The What

Step 5: Vision
The Future

Step 6: Strategic Goals *The How, Who, When*

Strategic Goal A	Strategic Goal B	Strategic Goal C	Strategic Goal D	Strategic Goal E	Strategic Goal F
TITLE:	TITLE:	TITLE:	TITLE:	TITLE:	TITLE:
THE GOAL:	THE GOAL:	THE GOAL:	THE GOAL:	THE GOAL:	THE GOAL:
DATE:	DATE:	DATE:	DATE:	DATE:	DATE:

Step 7: Tactics

Tactical Plan 1	Tactical Plan 1	Tactical Plan 1	Tactical Plan 1	Tactical Plan 1	Tactical Plan 1
Tactical Plan 2	Tactical Plan 2	Tactical Plan 2	Tactical Plan 2	Tactical Plan 2	Tactical Plan 2
Tactical Plan 3	Tactical Plan 3	Tactical Plan 3	Tactical Plan 3	Tactical Plan 3	Tactical Plan 3
Tactical Plan 4	Tactical Plan 4	Tactical Plan 4	Tactical Plan 4	Tactical Plan 4	Tactical Plan 4
Tactical Plan 5	Tactical Plan 5	Tactical Plan 5	Tactical Plan 5	Tactical Plan 5	Tactical Plan 5
Tactical Plan 6	Tactical Plan 6	Tactical Plan 6	Tactical Plan 6	Tactical Plan 6	Tactical Plan 6
Tactical Plan 7	Tactical Plan 7	Tactical Plan 7	Tactical Plan 7	Tactical Plan 7	Tactical Plan 7

Strategic Planning puts into operation the potential and possibilities developed through strategic thinking. It is a much more analytical, conventional and formal process.

Strategic Planning

Let's look at how we progress through each stage:

STEP 1 CURRENT SITUATION ANALYSIS (THE 'NOW')

The best method of starting the Strategic Thinking and Planning (STP) process is with a Current Situation Analysis.

What is your current reality? This is a snapshot of the current 'state of affairs' within your business – turnover, sales, costs, profit, trends, outlook, products/services, quality, people, customers, suppliers, physical resources, intangible resources, challenges, key issues, potential, communication, structure, technology, distribution, competition analysis, the market.

A re-assessment of 'What business we are in and how do we excel?' and 'Who is my customer?' are always useful. What is your critical success factor (CSF)? What are your core competencies? What competencies will you need in three years time? Use basic business practices.

You can start with a SWOT analysis. SWOT is an acronym for Strengths, Weaknesses, Opportunities and Threats. It allows everyone in your team to get involved in the process at an early stage. It is especially good for newcomers to strategic thinking and talking. More to the point, everyone has plenty of ideas about the strengths, weaknesses, opportunities and threats within your business. This allows them to verbalise and formalise each idea.

The simplest approach to completing your SWOT analysis is to start by listing your strengths and weaknesses on a flipchart. Keep in mind that strengths and weaknesses exist internally within your organisation and are relative to your competitors. Opportunities and threats exist externally to your organisation. They probably face all players in your industry or markets.

STRENGTHS AND WEAKNESSES

The strengths and weaknesses of your organisation can relate to:

Customer Care levels: What are the service performance indicators that you measure? What do your customers like about you? What would cause them to go elsewhere? You must be specific in your answers to the questions.

Processes, functions, roles: Are your processes clear? Eighty per cent of your problems – errors, reworks, delays, non-conformance to quality – will originate in your processes. Does everyone know their critical KRA (Key Result Area) and job definitions?

Competencies: What are the task and personality factors that you should be leveraging off? Or are they holding you back because they are weaknesses? How do you define, measure and develop leadership, system thinking, relationships building, specific skill areas, action orientation, emotional intelligence?

Skills: Have you distinguished your skill requirements for each person and job area? What about the hard skills such as computer literacy, financials, production and marketing? What about the soft skills such as change management, coaching/mentoring, communication, negotiation, selling, problem solving, creativity and team building?

Knowledge: We live in the Information Age. Knowledge is the product of that Age. Do you really know what you know? How are your information systems with regard to marketing/sales, business acumen, finance (cashflow), technology, strategic thinking and planning, networking and knowledge management?

Innovation: Your ability to introduce new ways of doing things is vital. Do you individually or collectively resist change in your products, processes or resources? Innovation, change, and marketing go hand in hand. How flexible are you relative to your industry?

Physical resources: How modern or how obsolete are your vehicles, premises, and equipment?

Inventory and stock control: The storage and assessment of the movement of stock has become a science. How good are you at storage of stock, matching it to markets and movement: and Just-In-Time and Kaizen? What about Efficient Consumer Response (ECR), Distribution, Warehousing, Delivery, Stock Control?

Corporate identity and image: Are you sending out the kind of messages that you want your stakeholders to pick up? Are your sales people consistent in delivering what you promise and how you promise it? How about your literature, letterheads and brochures? Is the appearance, colour, and design of your office or plant (inside and outside) consistent with the image you wish to convey? What about the quality, service, price, packaging of your product?

Quality control: What is the non-conformance level? Wastage?

Internal communications: Openness, honesty or blaming? Is the grapevine or underground transmission service to the fore? Have you ever measured key factors in this area such as trust, commitment, contribution? How much are your processes and systems contributing to poor internal communication? How much is poor communication 'really' costing in terms of delays, lost customers, and low morale?

Production: Can you improve throughput and quality? Can you reduce waste? Relative to your competition, how are you doing? Are you setting your benchmark against the Best?

Customer type ('Who is my customer?'): Are you selling to the right customers? Have you done a Pareto Analysis? Are you getting enough 'good' business, or do you take whatever comes your way? Who is getting the profitable, easy business in your industry?

Identification of critical success factors: What do you need to be really good at to create business advantage? Does everyone else know these factors? Does each person have their own critical success factor? Do they know them?

Identification of Choke Points: What is your biggest weakness right now? If you eliminated this, would it free up your whole system? (see Chapter 2).

EXPLOIT YOUR STRENGTHS, ELIMINATE YOUR WEAKNESSES

How your strengths and weaknesses compare with those of your competitors is a key issue. Your task is to build on your strengths and compensate for your weaknesses. Avoid trying to link up strengths directly with opportunities, and weaknesses with threats. As a group, take your five major strengths and discuss why they are strengths.

EXPLOIT EACH STRENGTH

CLEARLY STATE THE STRENGTH _

ORIGIN OF STRENGTH	WHAT CONTRIBUTION DOES IT MAKE?	HOW CAN WE ADD FURTHER VALUE TO IT?	WHAT RESOURCES SHOULD BE DEPLOYED?	WHAT ARE THE DANGERS TO IT?
1	1	1	1	1
2	2	2	2	2
3	3	3	3	3

Likewise, expose each weakness with a deeper critical analysis that each one deserves – causes, effects, and remedies.

ELIMINATE EACH WEAKNESS

CLEARLY STATE THE WEAKNESS _
_ _

CAUSES OF WEAKNESS	EFFECTS ON THE COMPANY	ACTION TO REMEDY	COST OF REMEDY	WHAT HELP IS NEEDED? IS IT CURABLE AT ALL? OTHER COMMENT
1	1	1	1	1
2	2	2	2	2
3	3	3	3	3

OPPORTUNITIES AND THREATS

The opportunities and threats to your business are external factors. Opportunities and threats usually come from:

- Competitors and industry trends
- The economy – local or global
- Market factors (changing trade patterns/needs)
- New Product Development
- Regulation or Deregulation
- Technological Development
- Globalisation
- New Trends and Consumer expectations.

You can classify the opportunities and threats to your business according to their level of seriousness and probability of occurrence. In the appropriate quadrant on The Opportunity/Threats Matrix here, rate each opportunity or threat on a scale of 0 to 10. For example, you might rate the opportunity of a competitor opening a depot in Cork to have a high chance of occurrence at 7, and the level of seriousness of the impact to be not very serious at 4. In this way, write in your assessment of each threat and opportunity in the appropriate quadrant.

MAPPING YOUR OPPORTUNITIES AND THREATS

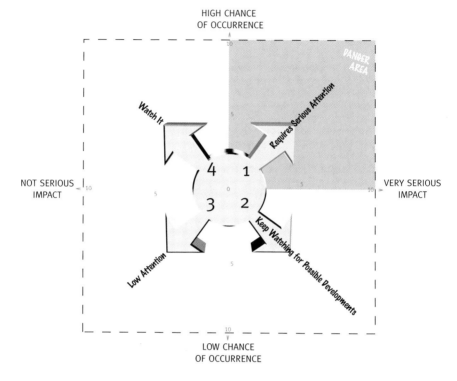

Your ability to exploit your opportunities and prepare or make contingency plans for your threats is helped by mapping them on the Opportunities/Threats Matrix. Threats and opportunities that have a low chance of occurrence and do not have serious impact can be mapped in quadrant 3. Give serious attention of course to threats and opportunities that have a serious impact and a high chance of occurrence(quadrant 1). Watch too for threats that have a high chance of occurrence and do not have serious impact.

When you have completed this exercise, focus first on quadrant 1 to rate your opportunities. These can become the basis for your strategic goals. Contingency planning and scenario 'what ifs' can also be conducted to rate your threats.

Identifying your, say, six opportunities and six threats can provide a very graphic and poignant message. I worked with one company that had two threats in the 8x8 intersection of quadrant 1. No member of the management team had previously given much thought or planning to these threats. Management spent five hours that very evening talking and scenario planning. Within three days, they came up with a ready-for-action document. One of the threats was the 'arrival' of the British multiple retail stores to trade in the Irish marketplace. Eight months later the threat did happen but they were ready. From their previous planning exercise they were able to offset much of the downside.

FORMULATING CURRENT THINKING

When you have completed the SWOT analysis you can use a number of other strategic tools to move the STP process along depending on the group and situation. At the end of many first-time meetings on SWOT analysis, I have watched managers emerge with sufficient clarity to double turnover and performance. They replaced complexity and disarray with clarity and clear focus. They had used an often disparaged but, from my experience, one of the most powerful tools of management.

Once you have completed the SWOT analysis, ask the group members to answer the following three questions:

1 What business are we in?

2 What business should we be in?

3 What do we have to do to get to where we want to be?

1 WHAT BUSINESS ARE WE IN?

The question 'What business are we in?' seems at first sight to have answers that are simple and obvious. Invariably, however, groups tend to give many different perspectives in answering the question.

I worked with an organisation where there was a major debate on the question as to whether they were a transport company, a distribution company or a logistics company. Clear thinking at this point was central to how they would set their long term vision and strategic goals. They began to realise why there was conflict, mistrust, low morale and frustration throughout the organisation. They had fundamentally different views about their business. Wrong assumptions or wrong interpretations are the cause of most problems.

Failure to clarify 'What business are we in?' is given in the classic example of the owners of the American railways at the turn of the 20th century. They considered themselves to be in the train business rather than the transportation industry. They therefore missed out on capturing new customers as the railroads became used less frequently as road/air transport became more popular.

I have a client who is in the office communications business, has a range of products and services (including mobile phones) that is greater than the more narrowly focused stationery shop that she used manage. Is her customer someone who buys stationery? Or, is her customer someone who needs total office communications?

When I set up my own company in 1989, I was in the management training business and my customer was the small and medium business owner. Now, however, the answer to 'What business are we in?' and 'Who are our customers?' has changed considerably. We are now in the performance improvement, consulting and organisation development business. We provide strategic change management solutions. We provide systems, techniques and know-how to solve business problems. Our corporate slogan is *Creating Business Advantage*. We provide long-term solutions to a wide range of business problems rather than attempting short-term fixes. Consequently, our customer profile has changed.

Rather than be 'ships in the night' with a three day solution, we become long term partners-in-profit, mentors and business consultants to our clients. In three years' time, we will provide solutions to *creating business advantage* in a different way.

If your business supplies just one product, ask yourself how sensitive are its sales to changes in fashion, reduced customer incomes, sudden increases in the cost of raw materials or other input prices, changes in interest rates, currency changes, government policy and import/export controls?

During the 1996 BSE beef crisis, one of my clients in the beef business suffered as prices and demand dropped overnight. He set a strategy in place to broaden the company's exports to more than one product. The company now supplies pork and chicken products and is gradually gaining back its sales and profit level. Another of my clients had major purchase penalties from Great Britain as sterling plummeted. It really helped him to focus on his business and whether he should be in it or not.

2 WHAT BUSINESS SHOULD WE BE IN?

Some companies/organisations become so busy coping with current customer demands and supplying customer needs that they fail to invest thinking time and other resources into exploring possibilities in allied areas. Where do you see your products in three years' time, in five years' time? What are the trends in the market place? How are your competitors doing? How easy is it to enter a new market? How are you placed relative to your market, your products and your competitors? When is a new idea the latest fad or the start of a new trend? Are you keeping up to date? Knowledge management is more important than ever to keep a winning edge.

PRODUCT/MARKET MATRIX

The Product/Market expansion matrix is a simple yet effective way to look at possibilities for developing your business. There are two variables to consider: one is your products and the other is your markets. One variable is: Do you stay in the same market or seek out new markets? The other variable is: Do you sell/market more of your current product or develop new products? Plotted together, on a four quadrant matrix, you can see where you are at present and where you could be.

BUSINESS EXPANSION: GROWTH STRATEGIES

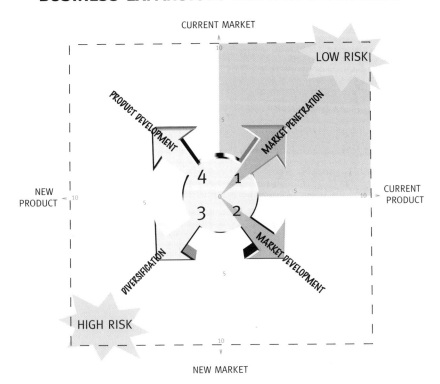

You have a choice of four ways in which to expand your business. You can choose the high risk way of diversification into a new market with a new product . You can go for market penetration (Low risk) with your current product or service in your current market. You can go for product development of a new product in your current market or you can go for market development of the current product in a new market. Whichever way you choose requires a different strategy and each strategy has different consequences for your business.

Let's examine the Product Market Expansion Matrix more closely by examining each quadrant.

Quadrant 1 – Market Penetration: Has the lowest risk factor because you are familiar with both variables – your current products and your current markets. To expand, it means more sales and a more aggressive approach to penetrating your market with your current products.

There are only three ways to grow your current business: (1) increase the number of your customers, (2) increase the average amount that customers buy and (3) increase your customers' frequency of purchase.

Salesmanship, marketing, advertising, widening your product appeal, information and data management and utilisation and all the other methods and support mechanisms contribute to increasing this market quadrant. By simply brainstorming 20 ideas for improving sales you will come up with an improved performance. (See Chapter 7).

There are about 20 ways in which to sell a product. However, most businesses just use one or two of these ways. Why not explore other possibilities? Just one more way could dramatically improve your business.

Quadrant 2 – Market Development: Means that you will expand into a new market with your current product range, but at least one variable (your current product) is familiar to you. Or it involves bringing your current products to an export market.

What is your strategy in this regard? Does it require investigation, research, and, above all, time, to seek out new market. Are you watching the trends internationally? Are you surfing the Net? Are you reading the trade magazines? Attending the trade shows? It's not urgent but it's always important.

An example is a hardware client who decided to sell and hire building equipment to the local domestic market rather than just building contractors.

Quadrant 3 – Diversification: Is high risk because you are developing new products in new markets. Putting products you know nothing about into a market you know nothing about can be like the 'blind leading the blind'. It is often a disastrous approach for small and medium business owners, but not always. Enter with care, caution and the necessary resources. (See Chapter 2).

Virgin, whose boss is Richard Branson, is a perfect example of a varied business organisation with multiple products. A good example in Ireland is where the cigarette giants Carrolls went into the fish farming business: it was a new product in a new market. It failed.

Quadrant 4 – Product Development: This is where you take a new product into your current market or sell into your current industry sector. Obviously, the task of creating new products, even with your established customers, takes time and energy and the correct deployment of your current resources.

Answering the question: 'What business should we be in?' and 'Who is my customer?' can open up all kinds of potential for discussion and dialogue. This is strategy in action and it's where the entrepreneurial manager is most productive.

Every hour spent pondering and talking about these strategic questions will save you up to 50 hours of wasted time, loss of resources and heartache down the road. The natural inclination of all managers is to launch, to do something now. It takes discipline to wait and think and strategise. Be aware of this in yourself and your team. Napoleon said: 'Time spent on reconnaissance is seldom wasted.'

3 What we have to do to get to where we want to Be

The whole strategic thinking and planning exercise is ultimately about answering the question: 'What do we have to do to get to where we want to be?' Asking the right question is central to Strategic Planning and successful completion of the STP model. The answers are relatively easy. As the process develops, Values, Mission, Vision, Strategic Goals and Tactical Plans are formulated. The answer to the question grows and evolves in the minds and hearts of the people involved. Ultimately, this is the essence of Strategy: where are you now? How are you going to get to where you want to be?

Many other techniques can be applied at this current situation analysis stage, but this gets everyone thinking and talking openly about core issues and sets the scene for the rest of the process. Other available techniques to obtain your organisation's 'vital signs' include environment scans, competency maps, competition and industry analyses.

Step 2: History (The 'Past')

At this stage in the strategy formulation process, I usually get the group to do a quick analysis of the history, development and structure of the organisation from the time the organisation was set up. It should cover its significant moments, traditions, successful strategic moves and the major reasons for the current situation.

Questions include: 'As the development path progressed what were the obstacles?', 'How has the business grown and expanded?' Without understanding who you have been and what it has meant, it is difficult to focus on where you are going or ought to go. Your history is a key part of 'Who you are' – your culture. This highlights the difference between thinkers and planners of strategy.

Planners look at the past to find data points that allow them to uncover and plot trend lines. Thinkers look back to uncover plot lines in order to decipher the moral of the story. Planners mine the past for data. Thinkers mine the past for stories, which help to link current reality with its past soul.

This part of the exercise can be completed quickly. It gives a breathing space from the Current Situation Analysis. It also serves to put the overall process in context and it serves to achieve clarity. So don't overlook it.

In many cases, newer members of the team have never heard the story of the organisation and its past processes and problems. By understanding the past, they get a better sense of the present and the future. In my experience, teams who really delve into the first two stages of the STP process look twice as far into the future as those who do not.

STEP 3: VALUES (THE 'WHY')

Values are at the heart and foundation of what makes a person or individual, a team or organisation work. Most individuals, teams and organisations don't have the inclination or the time to have a meaningful discussion on the core beliefs and the value system of their organisation.

Of course, individual values affect team values, and team values affect the organisation's values. The organisational culture is, in effect, a combination of the mind-set of every person working in the organisation. Your culture is 'How we do things around here' and you sense it from a mile away. It's the 'fuel' of the fire of achievement.

SO WHAT ARE VALUES?

A personal value can be described as a statement of what is important and significant to you as an individual. A team, business or organisation value, therefore, describes what is important and significant to your group. It's your belief system. It's the perception of the organisation held by the majority of your stakeholders.

Your values are your primary control system because they are the only set of procedures that do not depend on fear to operate.

Rules, laws and procedures manuals are imbued with boundary lines such as: 'If you break this rule you will be penalised' or, 'You're in trouble'. This breeds fear and inhibitions and it takes a lot of time to police.

Every organisation has a value system whether it's good or bad, clear or unclear to all concerned. Values provide a framework for decision-making. They provide a basis for action and they help everyone to live with the results of actions taken. Values are at the heart of personal and business strategy. They are your unifying principles and core beliefs. All improvements in your personal or business development begin by clarifying and ordering your true values, and then committing yourself to living consistently by them.

So what are your business values? What is your attitude to risk, to achieving high performance? What about growth? What about resources deployment? Independence? Contribution? People? Teamwork? Profit? Freedom of Action? Communication? Quality? Health and Safety? Remuneration? Innovation? Learning? Ethical standards? The environment?

THE VALUES EXERCISE

I have found from my experience of working with groups that there is an initial reluctance to even start a value exercise. To many people it seems a little bit soft, abstract or irrelevant to their situation. However, once they participate in the exercise, they quickly find that value assessment is central to all the challenges and problems they have within their organisation. They begin to love the exercise itself.

The mechanics of the value exercise are simple. Get everyone to brainstorm key words and phrases that constitute their personal and organisational values. Alternatively, you can get groups to answer the questions: 'What does our company stand for?' 'What do we do that gives everyone the most pride?' or 'What is really satisfying about what we do?'

The next part of the exercise is to graph the key words and phrases into Value Statements. This can be really difficult. But it's where emotional strategy really works.

I worked with a client who proclaimed that his first value was honesty and integrity. However, this raised a major debate because his staff knew that in their effort to save costs they were putting a sub-standard raw material into their finished product. They were living a lie. They were stressed.

The whole organisation sensed that the customer and the regulatory officials would find out sooner or later. The staff worked under a cloud of unease. They had to resolve a mental conflict of lying to the customer and to themselves. In this case, during The STP process, they made a decision to purchase the correct standard of raw material, even though it cost them considerably more money. They sought alternative savings elsewhere, and, of course, they found them. They also realised that from a legal point of view the whole operation could have been jeopardised because of their previous shortcuts.

I encouraged the group to craft or fashion a final set of values and rank them in order of priority, starting with the headline 'Our Core Values are ...'

This exercise has a cleansing effect and everybody feels fired-up to get on with the next stage of the process. But it is difficult and demonstrates to themselves just how unclear they have been on core principles and ways of doing things. To facilitate the meeting requires total focused concentration for many hours.

I have frequently had to stay with the group for up to five hours on this searching exercise alone. Completing this exercise gives everyone a real sense of achievement and encouragement to get stuck into the next step. It also demonstrates the importance and value of getting away from the work environment.

STEP 4: MISSION (THE 'WHAT')

There has been much confusion and many conflicting opinions about the difference between a Mission and a Vision. A friend of mine says: 'It's OK for scientists to disagree.' However, when following The STP model, it's important that everyone be clear on the same definition.

In my view, a Mission should evolve from the Values Statement. The Mission Statement of your organisation is a broadly-based enduring statement of purpose that distinguishes your organisation from others of its type. It is the reason for the long term existence of your business. It crystallises and articulates the values, dreams, behaviours and culture of your organisation. It is about how you aspire to do things. It's your operational, ethical and fundamental guiding light.

Developing 'a sense of mission' is often times more important than a formal mission statement if employees are to believe in their organisation. They have to think that your company is there to achieve something. You must constantly live it. And constantly talk about it.

For example, the mission of NASA (the US Space Agency), after World War II, was to explore Space for the betterment of mankind. An organisation's Mission Statement comprises the answers to the questions: 'What?' 'Who?' 'How?' and encapsulates the driving forces of the organisation.

Crafting the Mission Statement from a mixed bag of descriptive words and phrases and distilling these words into one cogent sentence is, in itself, often a soul-searching, and painstaking but rewarding exercise. When the group has agreed the final Mission Statement, everyone feels a sense of commitment, ownership and exhilaration. This is the very essence of strategic thinking and planning.

I have seen groups spend hours arguing over words and phrases that best represent what they are about. They realise that the causes of many of their troubles and weaknesses lie with the different and diverse assumptions and beliefs of each individual and group.

The importance of developing your Mission Statement is challenged by many sceptics who say that the production of Mission Statements is pointless, because they are soon forgotten, misunderstood or impossible to aspire to. Many otherwise excellent managers miss the point. Entrepreneurial managers know that involvement has a 1:1 ratio with commitment and that good Mission Statements repeated at every opportunity will inspire people towards this ratio of involvement and commitment.

The problem has more to do with involving more people in the loop, giving and receiving feedback, and then selling-on or explaining the tone and intent of the finished version.

In our company, we talk about Value Statements and Mission Statements at every opportunity. We give a copy of both statements to all new staff and we explain the common sense application of our number one value of conducting our business with 'energy', 'integrity' and 'professionalism.' I can talk non-stop for two hours on this value alone.

Recently I saw a parcel for posting in our reception area that was packed in a sloppy way. All I had to ask was: 'Do you think that looks professional?' The answer was obvious. Everyone on our staff can spend any amount of extra money they need in order to present us in a professional way.

Shakespeare said integrity means 'to thine own self be true.' Imagine the questions this would unearth regarding honest contribution and performance: 'Are you happy with your own contribution?' Integrity means Trust! That is why I say that Value Statements and Mission Statements are the best regulatory strategies in the world. But they're not for framing in reception areas. They're for living. By everyone.

STEP 5: VISION (THE 'FUTURE')

One of my clients who has a turnover of €15m wrote a Vision statement several years ago for his company: 'To be the best in our industry.' His colleagues thought it was a great statement. In reality is was meaningless. It can't really be realised. Every competitor today tells their customers: 'We are the best' in some way or other. It's not time bounded. It's not specific. It had no meaning or fire power. By the time the company had completed The STP process, their vision was 'To grow our company to €30m with a net profit of 8% by opening four new branches, developing our staff to 75 people by 30th December 2003.' Everyone was excited about this. Apprehensive? Yes. Sceptical? Sure! All kinds of potential opportunity beckoned. Focused team work prevailed.

WRITING AN STP VISION STATEMENT

A vision is a clear description of a desired state of affairs at a particular moment in the future. A Vision Statement should :

(1) focus on operations;

(2) have clear measurable objectives/ results/outcomes;

(3) change the basis on which you compete in the market place.

A Vision Statement is a yardstick – 'Look around, are we there yet?' – And it's a rallying cry – 'It will be great when we get there, so let's …'

A good example of a vision that was fulfilled was President John F Kennedy's pledge in 1961 of 'achieving the goal, before this decade is out, of landing a man on the Moon and returning him safely to Earth.' The best visions evolve from everyone's input in the organisation, but the management team must play a central role in creating the Vision Statement and in bringing it to fruition.

A Vision Statement today should have a three to five year time frame. It should be Specific, Measurable, Achievable, Realistic and Time-bounded (SMART). I find that teams get to the Vision Statement relatively quickly. They get to it more quickly when they have to dig deep on the earlier parts of the STP process.

Your primary job as the entrepreneurial manager is to focus on the values, mission and vision of your team or organisation. It may be up to others to take responsibility for the implementation of the strategic goals and tactical plans which I'll explain now.

Before taking a decision on significant operational issues, you should ask yourself two questions:

1 'How is this action consistent with our values and mission?' and

2 'Is the action helping us move forward to realise our vision?'

There is nothing like a vision to unite a team, if it is clear, specific, time bounded and realistic. It is only for internal eyes. Everything however is dependent on execution. A vision without execution is just a dream.

STEP 6: SETTING STRATEGIC GOALS (THE 'HOW' AND THE 'WHO')

Your ability to set and achieve your definite goals is the ultimate purpose of entrepreneurial management. Your vision is your BIG goal. Your strategic goals give operational purpose to your values and mission.

I have been amazed at senior managers who have been on Goal-Setting courses and can give lectures on 'How to set Goals.' But they fudge and prevaricate on setting and implementing this strategic thinking and planning process. Ultimately, success is the progressive realisation of predetermined goals.

Every business or organisation should have at least six strategic goals. Each strategic goal should be achievable within six to 24 months.

Each goal should be SMART, that is Specific, Measurable, Achievable, Realistic and Time-bounded. You must be able to say 'Yes' or 'No', 'I did' or 'I did not' achieve the goal at the end of the period. No fluff. It must be measurable. You can measure time, money, and production levels but not sentiments.

This is the execution stage of strategy. Implementation has been taking place from the very start of the process. An excellent overall strategy, executed badly at this stage, will fail. An average strategy, executed well, can achieve outstanding success.

Your six strategic goals become the focus for your actions throughout the year. When you ask the question 'What is the best use of my time right now?', the answer, invariably, should be: 'Concentrate on moving forward on one of my strategic goals.'

Another focus question that you can engrave on your desk is: 'Is what I am doing right now helping to push forward one of my strategic goals?' If the answer is 'No', you need to rethink. Your ability to 'stay strategic' over an extended period of time is a mental discipline that few managers have mastered. Some find it difficult to 'stay strategic' even for a few hours. Some can't stay focused for even 30 minutes.

Strategic goals are important, but rarely urgent. They may involve delegation, research and development, outsourcing, arranging finance or personnel.

They may involve re-deploying some of your six resources (see Chapter 2) or a re-engineering of your processes.

Your six strategic goals should incorporate your driving forces (your real advantage in the market place), and your core competencies. These are the collective knowledge and skills that your organisation has learned and that make you different. What are you really good at that is different from your competitor? Could this know-how (intellectual property) be used in another market? Does it make a sufficient difference to customers?

Each of your six strategic goals should have one executive who takes overall responsibility for its implementation. I endeavour to get as many names as possible written into the final STP document.

When you get down to it, people know what they have to do to achieve their mission and vision. I have found managers freewheel through this section provided the time and conditions are right.

The following areas may be guidelines for strategic goals:

Measuring improvement of financial and profit performance
Production
Marketing
Service
Re-structuring, Re-engineering, Re-inventing …
Distribution
Safety
Location, Site, Situation
Technology, Knowledge Management
The Environment
Partnering
Professional Development
Leadership and Succession Planning
Innovation and Research
Sales (turnover, number of customers, type of customer)

Developing (buying) or exploiting other distinctive capabilities
for competitive advantage
Re-deploying resources involving other stakeholders
The Market and Products
Improving the Reputation, Image and Profile
Globalisation: Exporting/Importing.
Mergers and Acquisitions

Here is an example of the company I mentioned earlier whose vision is to grow from €15m to over €30m over four years.

The company management developed six strategic goals as follows:

1 To invest 5% of payroll over the following 12 months in developing everyone to cross sell at the front counter; to develop a sales culture and increase sales by 20% from counter sales.

2 To invest €300,000 on upgrading their technology friendliness.

3 To increase indigenous sales by 15% over the next 12 months by introducing three distinct sales strategies: (1)setting up a call centre, (2)hiring four new sales representatives and (3)carrying out one-day monthly training sessions for the current sales team.

4 To appoint an Export Sales Manager with responsibility to set up ten agents in Europe, each contributing on average €60,000 sales within 18 months.

5 To open three new branches each contributing €1m within 24 months.

6 To totally change the visual image, logo and culture of the business over 18 months.

Notice that each goal is just a SMART statement of a desired future state. The details come later. The natural tendency to 'argue' with how each goal can or cannot be achieved must be resisted at this point. Just set them down for now and you'll be amazed at how much 'How Power' you have. And creativity. And innovation. And team spirit. And focus. But now you have a thinking process and a planning framework to make sense of it. Emotional strategy in action. The tactics, at last, give that real 'hands-on' feel.

STEP 7: TACTICAL PLANS (THE 'WHO' AND THE 'WHEN')

Tactical Plans are the operational, day-to-day plans and objectives that are necessary to carry out each strategic goal. They are, in effect, short term goals. They must be specific, measurable, achievable, realistic and time-bounded. Otherwise they are just nice ideas.

Different people may take responsibility for each different Tactical Plan, reporting to someone with overall executive responsibility for the Strategic Goal and for its successful implementation within the set time limit. 'Who does it?' and 'By When?' are key questions in tactical planning. These key result areas become time management priorities but, as you can see now, they are priorities with a purpose. Everything works towards achievement of the vision while being consistent with the values and mission of the company.

At the end of the year, you should review and upgrade your strategic goals, re-focus on your vision, your mission and core values. Your values and mission should not change in any significant way over time. Your vision statements will change over the years but your strategic goals should be upgraded every twelve to twenty four months, or even more regularly. Tactical plans should be constantly changed, upgraded, completed or eliminated. They are a 'living thing.'

General George Patton (1885-1945), one of the colourful American Generals of World War II, said: 'No plan ever survives contact with the enemy.' In business, the plan will change similarly. So be flexible. Make a mess of this STP document. I have seen tattered well-inked STP documents two to four years later. I have seen executives hold on to their copy like a child holds a favourite toy. A messy well-worked document is surely better than a beautifully produced unused plan!

A CHECKING SYSTEM TO EVALUATE YOUR STRATEGIC THINKING AND PLANNING (STP) PROCESS

Before you put the final touches to completing your strategic thinking and planning process, run a check using the OOMMEEES screening system. This system comprises the basic ingredients of all good strategy. As I outlined at the beginning of this chapter, all good business strategy has parallels in military strategy. Each of the OOMMEEES elements can be present to a greater or lesser degree. It should be used like a filtering system to establish the overall strength of your strategic framework.

Each letter in The OOMMEEES formula represents a key strategic ingredient:

OBJECTIVE

All good strategy must have a well-defined, clear objective. Setting the objective requires clear thinking, particularly among the leadership team, on the values, the mission and the vision of your organisation. Is everybody clear about your overall purpose? Is everyone committed to the strategic goals? Will they take responsibility for implementation of the tactical plans to achieve the strategic goals? Commitment and clarity about the overall STP process is an essential step towards achieving the clear objective. You must sell the overall objective! You must explain what you have created and give insights into the How. If your troops have enough reasons (Know-Why), they will overcome any How.

OFFENSIVE

An essential ingredient of all good strategy is the act of taking the offensive and moving forward. Napoleon said: 'It's impossible to be too strong at the decisive point.' The question you have to ask yourself and your team is: 'What new initiatives does your strategic framework take?' More importantly, 'Is your offensive moving in the right direction?'

You must deploy the next three variables of mass, manoeuvre and economy efficiently and effectively.

MASS

When considering mass, questions you must ask are: 'How do you bring about superior scale in critical resource areas at the right time, in the right place, with the right impact?' 'How do you mass your resources with your thinking and planning process/framework to gain a decisive edge?' Lack of concentration and focus are major human failings. Distraction is everywhere. Discipline fades. Persistence withers. You must do what you committed to do with the right force to create strategic advantage. Teamwork and clear communication are critical factors in massing the troops!

MANOEUVRE

You know that you must have the ability to be flexible and mobile with your resources so that you may deal with any threats and exploit emerging opportunities. Change dictates this. How flexible and how quickly can you react to changes that may be required in your strategic goals in particular? Could you move the necessary resources into place and re-deploy hitherto under-utilised resources to exploit opportunities? Can you Manoeuvre?

In military terms, deviation, deception or the indirect approach are regarded as excellent tactics. What manoeuvres are you/should you be scheming? How will you manage time, equipment, raw materials and money to achieve your overall objective? How good is your intelligence gathering?

The critical variable with mobility is people. How will you deploy your brain power? If unfounded or false expectations are raised it can often lead to a cynical back-lash to the overall strategic process. The resource that will cause you the most problems will be the people resource. Manage people extra carefully.

Scenario planning has become a whole new methodology in the last 10 years. Are you using it? How could you use it?

ECONOMY

We would all have a better chance to achieve our strategic goals if we had limitless resources. The secret of good strategy, however, is to use your resources sparingly and to secure your position so as to protect your resources from counter moves or for the 'rainy day.' Crisis anticipation is important here. One of the reasons that Wellington won the Battle of Waterloo was because he held back 17,000 troops for a 'what if' scenario. His decision was central to winning the battle.

How much will this cost you across the six resources? (See Chapter 2). Of course, you can make great things happen if you invest a small fortune in it. But always be thinking: 'How can I deploy my resources and implement my strategy at the least cost?' Many of the best strategic initiatives cost very little money, but they require an investment cost of thinking time. For example, expanding your business by applying superior sales and sales management skills to your current product range is far cheaper in most cases than launching a new product or entering a new market. Be prudent. Be wise.

EXECUTION

Many a poor plan has been rescued by superb execution. Everything depends on execution. Having a vision is not the solution on its own. More importantly, many (theoretically) brilliant plans have been wrecked because some key resource (or person) was not put in place or because the plans were too complicated for everyone to understand, or because a competitor was allowed the opportunity to manoeuvre and take a counter-offensive. The central theme of this book is action-orientation and execution.

EXPLOITATION

When you've got a clear direction and you are focused on the outcome, your next vital step is to implement and exploit all the opportunities in the marketplace. The fear of taking risks, self-limiting beliefs, procrastination, lack of focus and direction will be your main internal causes of failure of strategy. You should strike at your competitors' 'Achilles Heel' to exploit opportunities. Focus on your strong points and their weak points for success.

SURPRISE

How much originality, added-value and uniqueness can you bring to your strategic plans? When, where, why and how you kick off your strategic initiatives can add greatly to the overall impact. In military battles and in sport, a new approach or surprise methodology can be the secret of a successful outcome. The Execution, Exploitation and the Surprise steps are keys to the successful implementation of strategy.

In the 1990 Gulf War, when Saddam Hussein's army attacked Kuwait, the Allied forces, led by the Americans, used many of the variables in the OOMMEEES acronym. The Objective was clear from the outset – to drive Saddam Hussein's troops out of Kuwait. There was unity of leadership among the Americans, British, French and Saudi Arabian troops and the Offensive action was quick and decisive. The initiative was taken straight away. The critical advantage of the Allied Forces was the superior strength (Mass) of the American Airforce. They used this resource efficiently and with minimum waste (Economy).

There was plenty of opportunity to use other resources with sea power and land troops (500,000 men and women massed on the Iraqi border). The American Airforce pounded the Iraqi Home Guard (Execution), and once they were knocked out, they Exploited the opportunity to move forward.

The Iraqis weren't expecting such an onslaught (Surprise), nor so quickly and certainly not the massive counter move into Iraq which devastated thousands of Iraqi tanks and planes, and sadly, human life. Overall, there were relatively few fatalities of troops (Economy) for a war of this scale and, of course, Kuwaiti oil reserves (Economy) were saved.

In contrast, an examination of the war in Vietnam in the 60's would show many ingredients of this strategic formula to be missing. What was the overall direction and objective of American involvement in Vietnam? Politically?

Militarily? Economically? What was the Humanitarian cost? How were resources deployed? How did the length of the war affect the costs? Should they have cut their losses and got out earlier when the exploitation and surprise elements were neutralised?

OOMMEEES STRATEGY TEST

Before you Rubber Stamp your strategy, do this Strategy Test, rating your answers on a scale of 1-7:

OBJECTIVE

Will the implementation of your strategy differentiate you from your competition? Is there 100% clarity, cohesiveness and 'collective power' from start to finish? Does everyone know why you are doing this?

Very Poor	Poor	Neutral	Good	Excellent
1	2	3	4	5	6	7

OFFENSIVE

Will the implementation of this strategy give you the competitive edge over your competition? Is it an action-oriented strategy?

Very Poor	Poor	Neutral	Good	Excellent
1	2	3	4	5	6	7

MASS

Are you satisfied that the deployment of your resources is sufficient and focused on achieving your (critical early win) strategic goals? Is there a concentration of effort, time, money, etc?

Very Poor	Poor	Neutral	Good	Excellent
1	2	3	4	5	6	7

MANOEUVRE

Are you and your team aware and flexible enough to re-allocate resources to exploit success or reduce vulnerability? Is your 'intelligence' or feedback (control) system capable of giving early warning signals?

Very Poor	Poor	Neutral	Good	Excellent
1	2	3	4	5	6	7

ECONOMY

Have you costed and budgeted your plans (cash flow projection, etc.)? Have you budgeted to achieve the objectives with minimum expenditure? What about security? What defence have you to protect against a competitor attack?

Very Poor	Poor	Neutral		Good		Excellent
1	2	3	4	5	6	7

EXECUTION

Who will lead the implementation process? Is this person a capable project manager? What are the immediate KRAs? Can he/she think 'big picture' and orchestrate operationally?

Very Poor	Poor	Neutral		Good		Excellent
1	2	3	4	5	6	7

EXPLOITATION

Are you researching and watching out for new trends and emerging opportunities in your industry and gearing up to exploit them if they are consistent with your overall strategic thrust? Do these trends or opportunities build on or complement your strengths?

Very Poor	Poor	Neutral		Good		Excellent
1	2	3	4	5	6	7

SURPRISE

Have you thought out the launch time, place and style of any new initiatives? Will your approach be direct or indirect? Who knows about it? Who needs to know about it? What advantage can be gained by keeping it a surprise?

Very Poor	Poor	Neutral		Good		Excellent
1	2	3	4	5	6	7

CREATING STRATEGIC ADVANTAGE: SUMMARY

Strategic thinking and strategic planning is the very essence of creating business advantage and entrepreneurial management. Strategic thinking is more creative, divergent, process-focused. It is top-down and the starting point of the STP model. Not everyone is ready for it or capable of plugging into it with a prepared mind.

Strategic planning is more analytical, formal, structure-oriented. It puts into operation and shapes the plans that were developed in the thinking stages. There is a natural human tendency to get planning quickly. The STP model helps to synchronise the two processes together. Strategy has for too long lacked the emotion and the human feel. Here now is emotional strategy.

APPLICATION EXERCISES

1 Complete a personal or family strategy analysis using the STP model.

2 How could you apply Strategic Thinking and Planning to your business? What help do you need? Who could help? Where do you start?

3 Brainstorm 10 immediate things you need to do to get going. The secret of success in this area is massive and immediate action.

4 Embrace Strategic Thinking and Planning for your organisation. Get Help. Take a three to five year perspective on it.

PITOC™ STRATEGY

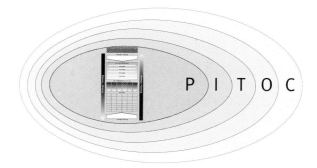

Every technique and element of the strategy process can be applied at the personal mastery, interpersonal, team, organisation and customer levels. Continually applying them at every opportunity, at every level, is the best way to master strategic thinking and planning.

6

MANAGING OUTSTANDING
CUSTOMER CARE

Peter Drucker, the most futuristic and probably the most respected of 20th century management thinkers, says: 'There is only one valid definition of business purpose: to create and keep a customer.' The result of creating the customer and keeping the customer, of course, is a profit.

What he says is profound. Profits may go up and down, price/earning ratios may rocket, turnover may increase and decrease, staff may leave, salaries may increase, world markets may change, premises may be inadequate, cashflow may go up and down, but the business cannot succeed in the long term without the customer. Customers are the Kings and Queens of the business jungle.

Having defined the purpose of a business, Peter Drucker then logically puts marketing in context and gives a perspective to it that every entrepreneurial manager should internalise. It is this:

'Markets are not created by God, nature or economic forces, but by businessmen. The want they satisfy may have been felt by the customer before he was offered the means of satisfying it. It may, indeed, like the want of food in a famine, have dominated the customer's life and filled all his waking moments. But it was a theoretical want before: only when the action of businessmen makes it an effective demand is there a customer, a market.'

There are many examples of markets being created. Sony developed the Walkman despite the customer research that showed no indication that such a product was needed. Compact discs (CDs) have replaced audiocassettes to fulfil the need for a better quality and wider range of music.

All of Drucker's books should be basic reading for every entrepreneurial manager. He puts the philosophy of business and marketing in a succinct sentence: 'Because it is its purpose to create a customer, any business enterprise has two, and only these two, basic functions: marketing and innovation. They are the entrepreneurial functions. Marketing is the distinguishing, the unique function of the business.'

Business people have described increased profit as the purest motive of all. The ordinary manager reads this philosophy passively and puts it away into the NOT JUST NOW file. The entrepreneurial manager reads it, repeats it like a mantra, puts framed copies of it beside his mission and customer care statement on his office wall and on his factory wall. Then he invites all his sales people, all his staff, and all the workers in the enterprise to turn Drucker's words into action.

Thousands of books, articles, videos, training and degree courses, and seminars have been written and conducted on marketing. Most of them are excellent. Some are rubbish. But read them. Do the courses, take the classes, and attend the seminars, read the books over years to become a master of marketing and innovation. If you are to stay in business in the 21st century, it is vital that you engage in a continuous life-long learning process focusing in particular on the marketing philosophy and the marketing process.

To me, marketing is simply the exercise of working with markets. Markets equal segmented bundles of customers of different likes and dislikes, whose needs, wants and demands should be matched with products and services that will satisfy those needs, wants and demands precisely at a maximum possible profit.

Here are some definitions of marketing that have been devised by academics:

- 'Marketing is the delivery of customer satisfaction at a profit'
– Kotler and Armstrong.
- 'The central idea of marketing is of a matching between a company's capabilities and the wants of customers in order to achieve the goals of the firm'
– Malcolm HB McDonald.
- 'The marketing concept says that a firm should focus all of its efforts on satisfying its customers at a profit'
– E. Jerome McCarthy.
- 'The aim of marketing is to make selling superfluous' – (that is the product sells itself or the customer buys it)
– Peter Drucker.
- 'The performance of business activities that direct the flow of goods and services from producer to consumer or user'

– American Marketing Association.

• 'Getting the right goods, to the right people, in the right place, at the right time, at the right price, with the right level of communication and at a profit'

– Chartered Institute of Marketing (UK).

Boil them all down – I'm a practical person – and they all mean basically the same: 'What do customers want now and in the future?' But giving it to them with goods is no longer good enough. To gain strategic advantage, you must give exceptional, outstanding customer care.

Like many management subjects, demystifying the subject helps in implementing it. Theodore L Levitt says: 'Marketing is a subject uncommonly related with uncontrolled uncontrollables, unstandardisable and unpredictable hazards. Like politics and sex, marketing is a squishy subject'. So beware.

For the benefit of the student and the entrepreneurial manager, I am in this chapter setting out control steps that, if applied with commitment, will take you along the road to excellence in marketing and towards at least a 100% improvement in your present situation.

These steps are based on practical experiences good and bad, on intensive and extensive reading of the best and the worst books. Most importantly, they are based on their application in my life as a sales person, as a sales and marketing manager, as a company chief executive, as an entrepreneur, and as an adviser to hundreds of national and international firms and organisations. I believe that every manager doing anything worthwhile gets marketing wrong. But excellent entrepreneurial managers keep on trying to get it right.

The stages of the marketing process are:

STEP 1 GET A GOOD PHILOSOPHY – EVERYONE IS IN MARKETING

The basis of every management activity, indeed every good human action, is a good philosophy. It's like the operating system for a computer. You can't go anywhere without it. I suggest that your first important step as the entrepreneurial marketing manager in the new process is to internalise Drucker's profound philosophical words … 'any business enterprise has two, and only two, basic functions: marketing and innovation'.

This crystallises the importance of marketing and the importance of being futuristic in a fast changing world. Now you and your staff have the starting point of a basic philosophy that can be incorporated into your business culture. Marketing is no longer the function of the marketing department, the sales manager, the advertising agency or the consultant. It's a function of everybody. Everybody is in marketing. Everybody has a role in helping to turn wants and needs into demand, and demand into revenue. Everyone in your business should be contributing to your marketing effort.

STEP 2 TEST QUANTITATIVELY AND QUALITATIVELY

Your second step is to set up a quantitative and qualitative testing system which will indicate where you are situated in the marketplace, and what your present and potential customers' needs and wants are. You should segment the market. Your strategic thinking and planning analysis will guide you.

If you don't know where you are now, how will you know the distance and the action to take so that you will reach your destination? If you don't know what your customers' real wants, needs and demands are, how can you satisfy them? If you don't check the trends, the fashions and the fads in the marketplace, how do you know that your product or service will be in demand in a year from now?

You should check your position using this qualitative and quantitative system at regular intervals from now on to measure your progress and to check if you are heading in the direction of your overall shared strategy. If necessary get the specialists to help.

STEP 3 DEVELOP AN OUTSTANDING CUSTOMER CARE (OCC) CULTURE

Focus all of your attention on developing an Outstanding Customer Care (OCC) culture. You, as entrepreneurial manager, will already know that very few of today's customers are loyal. They are fickle, whimsical, impatient, choosy and disloyal. They already expect quality products and excellent service as minimum standards.

A small paragraph in a newspaper, a tiny piece of a feature on television, a recommendation by a friend, a slight economic upturn or downturn, a small increase in interest rates, a small change in your corporate identity. Add to this the greeting of your front office receptionist or sales people, a bad word from a customer in a pub, in the supermarket, in the shop or on the street. Any or all of these actions can turn customers towards or from your product, your service or business. It's tough. Running a business can be like running a gauntlet of contrary, awkward customers.

Your challenge is to go beyond excellence and develop an outstanding customer care culture. It is no longer sufficient to focus so much of your resources just to *create* a customer. Your challenge is to *keep* the customer, forever, by developing and managing an outstanding customer care culture. Customer retention is the key to best practice marketing.

Your marketing ethos and philosophy must permeate the entire organisation, from the managing director to the directors and shareholders, to the receptionist on the front desk and the backroom staff on the production line, out to the sales force and the after-sales service department. Remember that everybody is in marketing. It takes everybody to develop an OCC culture.

The sales representative or the advertising director may not be working under the control of the marketing manager. The role of the marketing manager today must be to keep the customer care culture fresh and well and alive throughout the organisation. His role now is to direct the marketing effort, and the objective of the marketing effort must be to infuse the entire staff and organisation with an attitude of 'We would not be in business, we would not be employed but for our customers. Our business, our conditions, our salaries, our career advancement is in direct proportion to our standards of provision of outstanding customer care.' No longer does he just pore over demographic trends, sales force attitudes, regional sales figures.

In the ideal business, all sales and office staff, all administrators, all production line workers are marketers and they know, understand and can predict trends. They get worried and upset when the customer gets upset. It is less expensive to invest in keeping customers than in trying to create new customers. A satisfied customer may tell only ten people, but a dissatisfied customer will tell a hundred.

Feargal Quinn in *Crowning the Customer – How to Become Customer Driven*, says: 'All too often the real energy on the marketing front goes into attracting new customers while the ultimately more important task of nourishing the existing customer base gets a lower glamour rating.' Exactly.

Now let us step outside the office to meet the customer. You as the entrepreneurial manager should study your customers and, like a chess player, attempt to predict their next moves. You should develop an appropriate marketing mix that will attract them, interest them, whet their desires and spur them into the action of purchases and repeat purchases. Don't get complacent with this. I am amazed at how many senior executives 'lose touch' with their customers on a personal basis - sometimes for years. Set a goal to do lunch with your best customers two or three times per year at a minimum. A member of the audience asked Peter Drucker at a conference (September 1998) I attended in London; 'What should be the key activities of the 21st century executive?' He gave a succinct and threefold reply:

1 Continue to learn and re-learn

2 Ask for help

3 Get out of your office and meet your customers.

CONTROL THE CONTROLLABLES

In the 1950,s, Dr E Jerome McCarthy identified four major classifications in the marketing mix – Product, Place, Promotion and Price. They are called the 4 Ps. They are the controllable variables that marketers can control in the quest for markets, customers and growth. The 4 Ps are often extended to 6 in a new mix to include Profit and People.

All other variables are uncontrollable in the sense that you have little influence or control over the elements of change, such as the political climate, legislation changes, social values, climatic cycles of prosperity and recession, technology, demographic and medical developments. You should pay little attention to the uncontrollables and focus on the 6Ps that you can control. Often added to the 6Ps (content) are the 6Rs (process) of Research, Recruitment, Relationships, Recovery, Retention and Retirement. Let's look at each of the 6 Ps in turn:

1 PRODUCT

As the entrepreneurial manager, you will forever be trying new ways and means to develop existing products and create new products to satisfy changing customer wants, needs and demands. Innovate, Innovate, and Innovate. Sometimes reinvention produces a better product than the original product as Gillian Bowler, founder of Budget Travel, writes in *Executive Excellence* (August 1998). She cites Baileys Irish Cream as an example of a mix of whiskey and cream to produce a world class winner. She says the musical *Riverdance* is another example of blending together – traditional Irish dancing and music being revitalised with new life and energy to produce a smash hit.

2 PLACE

Convenience, availability, speed, delivery, ambience, cleanliness, freshness, site location, and distribution are factors of place. Where do your customers buy your products and services? What impressions are you signalling? Sometimes you may get so close to your own place that you can't see the wood for the trees. Your own place becomes too personal. You must control the visuals as well as the efficiency of your place.

3 PROMOTION

Consumers today are promotion sensitive. They will interpret signals from advertisements on your web site, on television, on radio, in the press and magazines and they will be influenced by tastefully produced or tackily produced pieces of communication. Layout and Design may be the new winning edge variables in the 21st century.

4 PRICE

From the consumers' point of view, price sends signals of value-for-money, cheapness or lack of quality. The starting point for establishment of a price is what the market will bear and what the market perceives to be an appropriate price. It is, of course, good to do a break-even analysis and to manage fixed costs and variable costs.

5 PEOPLE

Your people ultimately create the ideas and translate them into action steps. Combining freedom of action to deliver personal relationship marketing while keeping control of the process and other variables is the major people challenge.

6 PROFIT

The result of marketing should be a sufficient profit to make it all worthwhile. You must respect profit. Irish people don't pay sufficient attention to this key variable. They love the sale and the cut and thrust of business but what's the point if you lose the game and are taken out of the marketplace. What's the point of a magnificent marketing campaign – with bells and whistles – that makes you bankrupt? Remember that 58% of all start-ups fail within five years of start-up.

So you need to control those six factors in the marketing mix. Of course you may soon find that the marketing mix may be good for today but perhaps not so good for tomorrow. Innovate to cope with change.

DEVELOPING AN OUTSTANDING CUSTOMER CARE CULTURE

The core of this chapter is about creating business advantage and gaining the winning competitive edge by developing an Outstanding Customer Care (OCC) culture. Developing an OCC culture is a system and toolkit for doing just that, but it must be applied rigorously, systematically and over time. The system can be positioned under five main headings as follows:

1 IDENTIFY HOW TO EXCEED EXISTING AND POTENTIAL CUSTOMERS' NEEDS AND EXPECTATIONS

As an entrepreneurial manager you focus on the achievements of strategic business goals through meeting and exceeding customer needs and expectations better than the competition. As customer expectations are increasing everlastingly, this is central to understanding the philosophy of OCC. Mediocrity will not do. Good enough, seldom is. Not all products come in boxes. A service can be a product. So can an idea. Or a product can be a combination of hard goods, services and ideas.

For example, a hospital's primary purpose can be patient care (a service). A hospital may offer services like x-rays or cat scans. It may also contain an idea – for example, the idea may be that the hospital is a 'wellness centre for preventative medicine'.

Even when a product is tangible, it may possess intangible qualities. The product may be a brand item. The retailer selling it may have a reputation for the ultimate quality or for value at low price. The product may carry a warranty that is real or implied. The manufacturer's reputation may also be part of the product. But all products have one vital common denominator – they satisfy a real or perceived want or need by the customer. And the customer has quality and service expectations built around that need.

2 DECIDE WHAT IS THE BEST STRATEGY TO TAKE IN DEVELOPING AN OUTSTANDING CUSTOMER CARE CULTURE.

Later, in this chapter, we will look at the five pieces in the jigsaw that help deliver a product or service that exceeds customer wants, or needs and expectations. Every product has an obvious benefit, but there are also other benefits such as responsiveness, brand name, packaging, quality, guarantees, after-sales service, delivery, credit terms and so on.

3 DEVELOP PROCEDURES AND DISTRIBUTION SYSTEMS FOR MORE EFFECTIVE
DELIVERY OF YOUR PRODUCT OR SERVICE.

How you get the goods out of the woods is often more important than the product itself. Logistics is inextricably linked with marketing and customer care. Logistics management is the process of strategically managing the procurement, movement, storage of materials, parts and finished inventory and related information-flows through the organisation and its marketing channels in such a way that current and future profitability are optimised through the cost effective fulfilment of orders. Globalisation, time compressions and demands for OCC are driving this revolution in logistics. Distribution channels or retail/wholesale outlets will have a big bearing on the measure of marketing penetration of the product.

4 COMMUNICATE CONTINUOUSLY WITH CUSTOMERS

Informing and persuading customers – selling, public relations, and advertising – is a key activity of marketing. Akio Morito, chairman of Sony, once said: 'Communications is the most important form of marketing.'

There are many methods of informing and persuading customers to buy your products. The methods include face-to-face selling, direct or telemarketing, advertising and sales promotion. However, the key points of influence that build loyalty are the 'moments of impression' that customers experience with your product or organisation on an ongoing basis.

5 MANAGING OCC AFTER THE SALE

An OCC system provides a framework for you as a manager to lead your people and organisation beyond excellence in customer care. It will give you the opportunity to think through your organisation's future and re-establish your organisation's mission, strategies and systems for the 21st century. Getting the sale is relatively simple – to manage the ongoing long-term process is the challenge.

HOW AN OCC CULTURE HELPS

Developing an OCC culture will make an important contribution to your sales and marketing strategies in the following ways:
- It will help gain long-term customer loyalty
- It will help open new sales channels
- It will help to create sustainable competitive advantage

- You can use the Managing Outstanding Customer Care (MOCC) model as a tool for shaping a truly customer-driven organisation. It's a 'culture' thing.

Everyone today is talking about customer care. It is seen as a key driving force in business success, and it may be the critical factor in sustaining your competitive advantage. The great paradox is that the majority of customers are still unhappy about the service they receive.

Through this system, you learn a set of techniques that enable you to manage the customer's experience with your organisation effectively. It's at the very front end of successful marketing. Even so, many managers are inclined to let the interactions with the customer 'just happen' rather than manage them. Customer focus depends on consistently outstanding customer service over a long period of time.

Owners, managers, supervisors and employees at all levels in an organisation should start to think about their jobs as Customer Service jobs. The bottom line of managing your customer's experience is this: 'If you, as a manager, are not directly dealing with the customer yourself, your job is to support and provide back-up to the person who is serving the customer.'

MOMENTS OF IMPRESSION ON THE JOURNEY OF SERVICE

Service is the first thing a new customer notices when he or she comes into contact with your organisation. Before he or she has had a chance to see your product or even to inquire about the price, the potential prospect has probably encountered a salesperson, a receptionist, a telephonist or some other 'presentable' of your organisation. This initial contact can turn out to be a Moment of Impression.

A Moment of Impression, then, happens every time a customer comes in contact with any aspect or person in your business, directly or indirectly, and has the opportunity to form an impression (positive or negative). A relatively simple encounter like leaving your car in the garage for a service exemplifies the interaction for things to go very well or very badly.

The question is this: At what point do you the customer say 'Enough is Enough' and simply take your business elsewhere. Furthermore, it's doubtful if you tell the 'offending' business that you are leaving or why. So they continue in blissful ignorance – creating and losing customers. Have you named the critical Moments of Impression on the Journey of Service in your business?

THE JOURNEY OF SERVICE

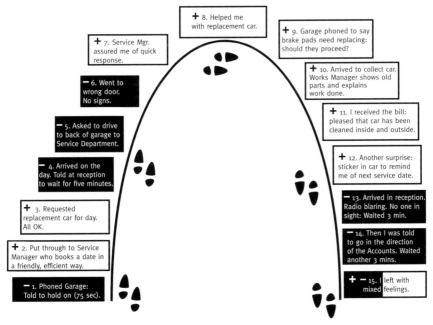

+ 8. Helped me with replacement car.

+ 9. Garage phoned to say brake pads need replacing: should they proceed?

+ 7. Service Mgr. assured me of quick response.

− 6. Went to wrong door. No signs.

+ 10. Arrived to collect car. Works Manager shows old parts and explains work done.

− 5. Asked to drive to back of garage to Service Department.

+ 11. I received the bill: pleased that car has been cleaned inside and outside.

− 4. Arrived on the day. Told at reception to wait for five minutes.

+ 12. Another surprise: sticker in car to remind me of next service date.

+ 3. Requested replacement car for day. All OK.

− 13. Arrived in reception. Radio blaring. No one in sight: Waited 3 min.

+ 2. Put through to Service Manager who books a date in a friendly, efficient way.

− 14. Then I was told to go in the direction of the Accounts. Waited another 3 mins.

− 1. Phoned Garage: Told to hold on (75 sec).

+ − 15. I left with mixed feelings.

I left my car in for a service. Here are some of my positive and negative Moments of Impression. Follow my steps from the moment I entered the garage (Moment 1) to the moment I left (Moment 15) and you will see why I left that garage with mixed feelings. Everyone counts on the Journey of Service. It takes six positive Moments of Impression to make up for one negative point of contact. One negative experience can potentially destroy the complete journey.
− = NEGATIVE   + = POSITIVE

Such points of contact often determine whether or not this customer will ever do business with your organisation again. These Moments of Impression are part of the cycle of service that customers encounter as they do business.

Outstanding Customer Care (OCC) is a product in its own right. Its production, quality and delivery must be managed just as other aspects of an organisation are managed effectively and efficiently.

MANAGEMENT EMPOWERMENT

There is a vital link between the achievement of an OCC culture and organisational development. Many management groups have attempted to improve customer relations without considering their organisation's ability to deal with the necessary change. They need to learn a whole new way of thinking about the customer and how that thinking fits in with their strategic purpose.

One 20 minute jog will never make you fit – in fact it will only make you sore and stiff. However, a daily 20-minute run over a long period of time will make you fit. Similarly, one short stab at the process will not create this new culture. In fact, often times, it creates scepticism and cynicism as to how it does not work. Proceed with caution.

Gearing the whole operation to work towards an outstanding customer care culture requires as much management thinking and planning as any other important business initiative.

TOTAL ORGANISATION COMMITMENT

To really succeed, the pursuit of an outstanding customer care culture must become an undying obsession. It requires every single person in your organisation to focus his or her energies and enthusiasm on not just getting it right, but on constantly improving it. Customer care therefore becomes a dominating theme throughout your organisation – it is continually debated, continually reviewed, continually challenged – and its successes are continually celebrated.

This obsession must be top-down and bottom-up. The commitment must be visible and tangible and real. If it is not, the resulting customer care will be, at best, mediocre.

Everyone in the organisation needs to be fully trained so that outstanding customer care techniques are visible to the internal and external customer. Such training should be seen not as a series of events, but as an organisational development effort that requires both individual and organisational changes. It must fit into your strategic thinking and planning process. (See Chapter 5).

In practice, the development of an OCC culture can be driven by internal champions and a customer care team who must absorb the achievement of their goal and become obsessed with 'all things customer.'

Any training workshop contains many important concepts and skills, but they should be only part of the whole. Other customer-related activities such as on-the-job training and one-to-one coaching are required to keep this fire of customer care alive. In the Age of Excellence, rapid growth and change, continuous improvement, quality, high standards and empowerment, an outstanding customer care culture can become the differentiating factor for your businesses. The success of this customer care initiative depends on how seriously it is carried out by management and staff. It requires a new mind-set and lots of hard work. You, as the entrepreneurial manager must embrace it, understand it and, above all, live it.

THE OCC MANAGEMENT MODEL

Managing Outstanding Customer Care provides a framework with which to achieve exceptional and consistent customer care. OCC occurs when the expectations of the customer are surpassed by their experience. It represents the sum total of the customer's experience.

There are five elements in the OCC Management Model:
1 The Customer
2 The Service Culture
3 The People
4 The Product
5 The Procedures and System

THE CUSTOMER MANAGEMENT MODEL

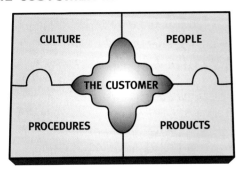

To manage outstanding customer care, you must develop a philosophy of how you conduct business internally and externally – all of the time. Your organisation's culture, products, procedures and people must be aligned to serve your Customers in an exceptional manner. An outstanding customer care culture will differentiate your organisation from your competitors. More than any other factor, it takes dedicated effort and a long period of time to develop. This culture is difficult to create and develop, but virtually impossible to replicate or copy.

You can steal away my people, you can steal my products, but you will find it virtually impossible to copy my culture.

The customer's ultimate decision to do business with your organisation is consciously or unconsciously dependent on the combination of these factors.

You recruit, train and support competent people, you have quality products that are promoted effectively, you have procedures and systems that ensure best practice customer care. Ultimately, your customer decides on the combination of factors appropriate to him or her.

The Managing Outstanding Customer (MOCC) model provides a framework with which you can view the sum total of your customer's experiences.

1 THE CUSTOMER

Understanding customers' needs and buying motivation is the central piece in the OCC Management model. This means finding out what the customers really want by listening, observing, questioning, verifying, and collating market research. From this, you develop a customer care mindset. You must supply what customers need and expect in the first instance, not what you think they need. You see your customers not just as a sale for short-term gain but as a long-term investment. This is the essential mindset of OCC.

Recognise that a lost customer is not just a few pounds in income, but rather the backend loss of thousands or tens of thousands of pounds over a period of many years. Good customer care will not do this but outstanding (exceptional) customer care enhances the chance of success.

The psychological cost of customer tension on employees can lead to stress, job dissatisfaction, absenteeism and poor productivity and performance.

Changing employee behaviour takes time. Changing customer perceptions takes even longer. You need to understand that an initial resistance to change or discovery of problem areas can appear to indicate that things are worse, rather than better, in the early stages of this customer care journey.

The UK Institute of Customer Service surveyed over 200 companies and found only 40% had detailed information on the annual profitability of each customer segment. How well do you know the expectations and contribution of your customers? Could you be ignoring net profit customers? Are your biggest customers your most profitable? Do you know?

THE CUSTOMER CARE ICEBERG

The front-line Moments of Impression are often just the tip of the iceberg for most organisations. What goes on behind the scenes (below the waterline) will to a large extent determine the ongoing quality of the customer's experience on their Journey of Service.

Supporting the front line troops psychologically and technologically is important to delivering outstanding customer care. The processes, the systems, the structures, and the culture are also relevant. The causes of most negative moments of impression can be found in these below-the-surface, places.

THE ICEBERG MODEL

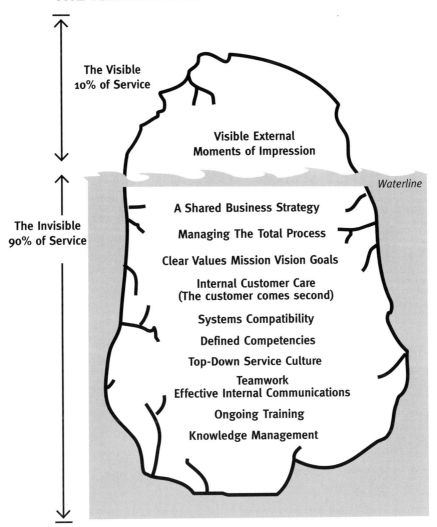

The Visible 10% of Service

Visible External Moments of Impression

Waterline

The Invisible 90% of Service

A Shared Business Strategy

Managing The Total Process

Clear Values Mission Vision Goals

Internal Customer Care
(The customer comes second)

Systems Compatibility

Defined Competencies

Top-Down Service Culture

Teamwork
Effective Internal Communications

Ongoing Training

Knowledge Management

The front-line Moments of Impression are often the 10% tip of the Customer Care Iceberg. Ninety per cent (90%) of the causes of your customer problems are invisible to your external customer. What goes on below the waterline (behind the scenes) will determine the ongoing quality of your customer's experience on his/her journey of service.

MANAGING ASSUMPTIONS, PERCEPTIONS AND EXPECTATIONS

A hotel in Dublin was very customer focused. Many large businesses used their facilities to hold important conferences there. The hotel conference manager felt that they needed to improve the quality of their coffee breaks. She gathered the members of her staff and asked them to outline what they thought were the key things to which they should give special attention during the guest's coffee breaks.

This is what the staff said:

1 Hot tea and coffee

2 Biscuits or pastries

3 Fine china

4 Good service.

Now, based on this information, would she have improved the quality of the coffee breaks for her customers? Before making any changes, she decided to ask the same questions of her customers, who were managers from various high-ranking businesses.

This is what her customers said they wanted from coffee breaks:

1 Easy access to a telephone

2 No queuing in the toilets

3 Time and space to chat to others

4 Hot coffee.

As you see, the conference manager learned that what the hotel staff value and what customers value are completely different. Put yourself in the other person's shoes when considering what he or she values. In other words, ask your customer.

The questions for your business are:

'How often do you presume what the customer wants?'

'How often do your sales people, customer service contact people, managers and employees make assumptions about what either the internal or external customer may want?'

We are prisoners of our perceptions. In delivering outstanding customer care, perception is often times more important than the reality.

CUSTOMER FOCUS GROUPS

By creating Customer Focus groups, you can tune in to the customer's expectations on an ongoing basis. They will allow you to keep your ear to the ground and win long-term customer loyalty.

Here's how to start. Select a cross-section of approximately 20 customers. Arrange a meeting with them (max. 60-90 minutes long) to look at ways to improve customer service. Formally invite them by letter and with a follow-up phone call. Offer them a gift to attract them. Expect 20-30% not to turn up.

Have an experienced facilitator present at the meeting and attempt to create an open, friendly atmosphere. Use their first name. Encourage critical feedback. Observe and listen attentively. Use eye contact and be open to their needs, wants and criticisms. Do not justify or defend, especially in the beginning.

Ask open questions: 'How can we better serve your needs?' or 'What are your expectations now?' or 'How have they changed?' Tape-record the proceedings and write up a report. (watch out for key words and underlying sentiments). Thank them verbally on the night and repeat this courtesy with a follow-up note. After the meeting, keep in touch by writing or telephone your customer just to say 'Thank you' or 'Is everything all right?' Treat your customers as guests.

Listen to their needs, wants and criticisms on an ongoing basis and learn their preferences. Compliment and reassure them. Be a friend. Feargal Quinn wrote in *Executive Excellence* (October 1998) that it's the simple things like *'using a person's first name'* that contribute to that OCC feeling.

DIMENSIONS OF CUSTOMER CARE

To create business advantage and gain the competitive edge and to create perceptions of unique added value in your customer's mind, more emphasis is needed on the intangible or soft dimension of customer care. An environment needs to be created where the internal and external customers have positive Moments of Impression.

MEASURING OUTSTANDING CUSTOMER CARE

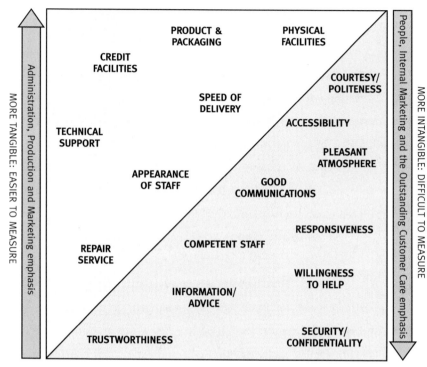

To gain competitive advantage and to create perceptions of unique added value in your customer's mind, you must place more emphasis on the intangible or soft dimension of customer care. You must help to create an environment where the internal customer and the external customer have positive moments of impression.
You need to consider measuring hard and soft elements of customer care. The tangible (hard) elements are easier to quantify than the more intangible (soft) elements and they are relatively more difficult to identify and measure.

MANAGING THE CUSTOMER'S EXPERIENCE

Here are some challenges for you to consider for managing outstanding customer care:

• Are you 100% sure that what you are selling is totally compatible with what the customer wants to buy? Again, look at both your product and your service. Ask your customers. Listen.

• Service can only be a competitive weapon if it's outstanding. Good service is just not good enough anymore.

• Recognise and manage the Moments of Impression where your internal and external customers meet each other.

• Every person in your organisation should be directly or indirectly working towards helping to serve the customer. In other words, everyone has customer. Your customers are people who depend on you to get their job done.

- Visible management has to come from the top with managers at every level practising what they preach.

Research has shown that customers leave the average business primarily for the 'softer' reasons as follows:

1% Die

3% Move from the locality

5% Develop Other Relationships

9% Competitor Reasons

14% Product Dissatisfaction

68% Employee indifference – Lack of OCC.

Delivering OCC is a product and a service in itself. A service, however, is produced at the point of delivery. Unlike other products, it cannot be stock-piled in advance, or held in readiness.

If improperly performed, a service cannot be 'recalled' and 'repaired' or 'replaced'. If it cannot be repeated, then apologies are the only means of recourse for customer satisfaction.

The person receiving the service is merely left with a feeling. The value of the service is internal with his or her personal experience.

Managing the customer's experience with the organisation then is managing the Moments of Impression on the Journey of Outstanding Customer Care.

The entrepreneurial manager realises that most businesses focus nearly all their efforts on the first part of the business equation – creating a customer – but they are usually bad at the second half of the purpose of the business equation – keeping that customer. Exceeding customer expectation – 'loving them to death' is at the heart and soul of outstanding customer care.

Database management and sales and customer automation is central to after-care service and it is the major choke point for most organisations. Could it be your choke point?

At this stage of reading this book on entrepreneurial management, you know the importance of letting one little factor affect all your other activities and resources. Ripple effects always have causes.

How does the entrepreneurial manager create additional business advantage through managing OCC?

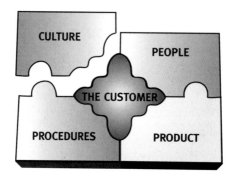

2 THE SERVICE CULTURE

Your company should stand out from the competition because of its service philosophy (rooted in your values), mission or culture. Do not try to be all things to all people. Your culture should determine what you want, not how you are going to achieve it. It should motivate and develop people through an image of a desired state of affairs that inspires action. It should focus on everyone flying in formation.

A culture is a set of values, attitudes and ways of doing things that are acceptable to everyone. It defines a behaviour that everyone lives by. It cannot be put in place – it develops over time.

You need to develop a culture service theme that states what your organisation is about. Furthermore, everyone needs to buy into it from the start. Your culture should be a clear, short values statement that also describes your uniqueness.

How do you go about it? First, decide to do it. Then commit to work on the process. Gather ideas from customers: Ask them 'What three things do you want us to do very well for you as a customer?' Ask for a spontaneous response, which is usually the most truthful.

Gather ideas from staff. Brainstorm the top five things you need to do to delight the customer and exceed their expectations. Listen carefully to the language that is used. Some words and phrases may be used over and over again. Then keep in mind that involvement and participation from internal and external customers are very important for the culture to work long term. You'll need to write and rewrite several themes over time. Aim for at least ten words. Superquinn uses the following very successfully: 'Come for the prices and you'll stay for the service'. Coca Cola has the line 'Coke is it' and Avis Rent-A-Car say 'we try harder'. The Bank of Ireland asks: 'Now, what can we do for you?' Every employee must know and feel ownership of the 'What we are about' statement. The process of involvement can be more important than the statement itself. Patience is essential. Don't push too hard.

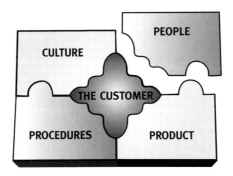

3 DEVELOPING CUSTOMER FRIENDLY PEOPLE

Customer-oriented, front-line people should be empowered to deal with the customer as they see fit. Managing individual Moments of Impression are beyond the immediate control of most managers. Peak performing, front-line people should be rewarded for giving good service – not just for processing customers.

Certain social types (See Chapter 2) are more at home serving customers than others. Your job as a manager is to make sure that you match the person and the job correctly. One hotel manager said aptly: 'We don't hire people and train them to be nice. We hire nice people'. People quickly forget ideas taught to them in a training session. Training should therefore be ongoing and of different varieties: one-to-one coaching, small group activities, on-the-job training and more formal sessions. These help reinforce the basics and show that you are committed to the service culture.

Why not have your best people invest ten minutes per day in training other people? Items to cover could be product knowledge, handling difficult customer situations, or changes occurring within the company or industry. Teachers – your supervisors – grow in stature and confidence as they teach more. Teach them to teach.

Training builds confidence and competence. Reward staff for outstanding customer services with:
- Prizes and awards
- Promotions and job enrichment – What about job rotation?
- Work flexibility
- Pins and badges
- Employee of the month awards
- 'Thank you' letters

- Newsletter write-ups
- Surprise celebratory parties.

Brainstorm certain 'Thou shalt nots' for your organisation. These are actions that customer service people should avoid. Keep asking your management team: 'How else can we support our front-line people?' Dealing with customers can be emotionally draining. Do you have an adequate work-break system for customer service people? Remember: 'Fatigue makes cowards (and grouches) of us all!'

Encourage people to 'go over and above' for the customer. These people could be recognised as Customer Service champions. Catch them doing the right things right and let them know. Nothing is as motivational as verbal reinforcement given appropriately and in a timely manner.

The great motivators for employees are:

- Appreciation of work well done.
- Feeling of being 'in' on things.
- Help with personal problems.

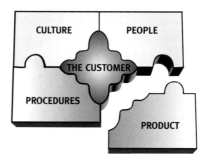

4 THE PRODUCT

In any overall service package, the product has to be right. It's a basic requirement and causes the most argument. Customers are 100% emotional. They just launch their own arguments from a logical standpoint. Service is probably the first thing that the customer will question when things go wrong. In the last two or three decades, we concentrated on getting production right. Today we expect, and increasingly get, a good quality product. Remember that the service is part of the product.

If your product is substandard today, rest assured that you'll be out of business very quickly because the 'word' travels fast. And customers are far more sophisticated in terms of their rights to return a product, their mobility, their choices and options. I asked the owner of a business which went bankrupt after four years trading, 'What happened?' His instinctive answer was ' The product wouldn't sell anymore'. Of course. But, why were five of his competitors selling virtually the same product and doing great business? Poor product sales was the effect of other causes.

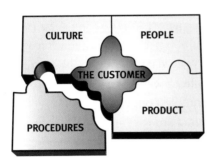

5 THE PROCEDURES AND SYSTEMS

Procedures and systems should be designed to make things easy for your customer. Your procedures should be based on your values and mission, or culture, and should help your people deliver your product to the customer in a better, faster, cheaper, easier, different way. Are your processes really putting the customer first? Consider such things as car parking, signs, payment systems, sales methods, ordering and delivery systems, responsiveness and speed etc. Sometimes, you can be so busy selling your product that you haven't time to ask 'Is there a better way of doing this?' or 'Why are we doing it this way?' Often the answer can be 'We've always done it this way!' Your objective should not be to be perceived as just the best, but to be perceived as the 'only one.'

When organisations develop new products, they often change the way they do things. They train those involved on product knowledge, but they fail to update the support processes, and systems are not updated. You, as an entre-preneurial manager, should innovate, innovate, and innovate in every aspect of your processes. Rip out old ways!

Look at the simplest places for improvement – the telephone system, the computer back-up, how you pass messages, product information, office supplies, invoicing, delivering, order processing. What are your Top 10 regular mistakes or errors? Why do they occur and reoccur? Zone in on eliminating them. Remember that 80% of your errors, delays and frustrations will occur in the process.

Make sure that systems and processes have an empowering effect on the management and staff. For instance, what happens when a customer wants to return a product? Can your staff authorise a small discount or some other form of compensation? The best procedural system in your company will be your values – if you use them and if everybody understands them. Common sense is not common practice; it must be worked on all the time.

Why not do marketing audits? A marketing audit is a comprehensive, systematic, independent examination of your environment, objectives, strategies and activities with a view to determining problem areas and opportunities. Philip Kotler, the US professor who invented the concept of marketing audits, says the most common problems uncovered are:

1 Lack of information about customers' behaviours and attitudes

2 Failure to segment the market in the most advantageous way

3 Price cutting rather than improvement in value

4 No real clarity regarding their strengths, weaknesses, opportunities and threats

5 A tendency to see advertising and promotion as marketing

6 No future investment for Human Resource Development (HRD) and branding.

To maximise the benefit of an outstanding customer care programme, tangible observations should be made over time.

For example, you could measure:

• Average scores on customers' surveys

• Number of customer complaints received/handled

• Number of company follow-up calls to customers to assess satisfaction

• Regular management surveys of employee behaviour towards customers such as eye contact, smile, friendly expression, helpful attitude, courtesy, etc.

• Service performance customer research.

GROWING YOUR BUSINESS

The whole purpose of using a philosophy and a system like the MOCC toolkit is to keep lifetime loyal customers, gain a winning edge and create a profitable business advantage. Just by having a process and methodology can give you that extra advantage. But what practical steps can you take to grow your business?

You have three obvious ways to grow your current business.

GROWING YOUR BUSINESS

1 Increase your customer base – get more customers.

2 Increase the average transaction value per customer – get customers to buy more of your products and services.

3 Increase the frequency of purchases by customers. Increase the number of times that a customer purchases your products or services.

1 INCREASE YOUR CUSTOMER BASE

Here are 11 ways to increase your customer base:

(1) DEVELOP WORD OF MOUTH POWER

Develop a system to keep in touch with and continually communicate with current and past customers. This will help you to develop residual business. A key part in the purpose of a business definition is keeping customers. This is a blind spot for many organisations. Contact your customers directly by telephone, by post, by E-mail or by personal visits. Keep giving them compelling reasons to do business with you. Don't be naïve. Your competitors are constantly selling their ideas too. Loyalty must be earned and re-earned.

Direct contact communication should encourage your customers to make an immediate response. Direct response communication is salesmanship in print or over the airways. The secret is not to make assumptions for your old or present customers. Explain continually the 'reasons why' your distinctive capability or unique selling proposition is important to them. What is the net result of OCC? It's word-of-mouth marketing which is still the best promotional technique in the world.

(II) BE CLEAR ABOUT YOUR UNIQUENESS

Every moment of impression is an opportunity to resell your uniqueness. Your uniqueness is made up of the features that distinguish your business or products from your competitor.

I regularly ask business owners and managers: 'What is your unique selling proposition?' or 'What is it that differentiates you from your competitors?' Their different array of answers says everything. In most organisations, no one is clear of the order of the number 1, the number 2 or the number 3 selling proposition.

Clarity is vitally important at this point. Otherwise you cannot consciously promote, encourage and educate your customer systematically and consistently over time to understand the reasons why he or she should do business with you. A professional uses systematic, consistent answers. The amateur makes it up as he goes along.

Put another way: 'What are your unique strengths?' 'How can you exploit those strengths to create business advantage?'

Some unique distinctive capabilities could centre on your broad selection of products, your better purchase price or lower price, your added service approach, or the extra comfort and prestige involved.

(III) MAKE MORE SALES CALLS

To increase your sales in business-to-business markets, your obvious first step is to knock on more doors (cold calling). This is good up to a point, but it is a hard slog and it involves hard selling and desperation sometimes. Sales people need to be very well trained and totally professional to maximise this approach. In consumer markets, companies give customers and prospective customers the opportunities to touch and taste the product. They offer free samples at home, major promotions and product launches and media advertising.

(IV) ASK FOR REFERRALS

In business-to-business markets, ask for referrals. This is probably the best way to get introductions to new potential customers. Yet, surprisingly few sales people employ this methodology on a systematic basis.

It really only works well when there is a good relationship between buyer and seller, total trust and respect for both the product and the service and the individuals. It costs very little to ask 'Who else do you think would be interested in talking to me about my product?' or 'I am expanding my business and I would appreciate your help.'

(V) TAKE AWAY THE RISK

Human beings have been conditioned to be fearful – to have a fear of loss. Some are even more risk-averse than others. They are afraid of making mistakes no matter how small. They fear making a wrong choice because they may look silly. Therefore, taking away risk by giving a free trial, delayed payment or 100% guarantee can take away that initial resistance and buyer's remorse. A good customer relations person will identify the risk-sensitive or risk-averse customer in the bat of an eyelid.

(VI) FORM VALUE ADDING PARTNERSHIPS

Value adding partnerships are an effective and an interesting way to develop contacts and new customers. Many non-competitors with the same customer base use their combined resources to mutually benefit each other.

I was at a presentation last year where a bank, an auctioneering firm and an accounting firm hosted a presentation to business leaders on the tax and financial implications of property purchasing. The bank invited the 200 guests from their client list. The auctioneering and accounting firms obviously gained from the exposure and introduction. Six months later, there was a reciprocal arrangement.

(VII) USE ADVERTISING

Advertising is one of the most widely used marketing communication techniques. It undoubtedly plays a more important role in consumer markets than in business to business products.

Advertising requires a systematic approach. Advertising campaigns and advertising headlines and responses are tested and checked at each stage of their development for impact, effectiveness and value for money. Direct response/reply advertising can be measured and therefore form a basis for future campaigns. You can make a direct comparison with the bottom line results.

Lord Leverhulme, founder of Unilever, said that half of the money spent on advertising is wasted, but he did not know which half. Using today's rapid computerised testing and research techniques, organisations can plan their advertising effectiveness leaving minimum wastage.

Advertising can allow you to get your message quickly and cost effectively to both prospects and customers whether by mass marketing advertisements or by more precise, targeted advertising. If advertising is part of an integrated marketing campaign, it can, of course, greatly reinforce the effectiveness of all marketing activities.

(VIII) DO DIRECT MARKETING

Provided your objectives are clear, direct marketing can be one of the most versatile and precise customer communications methods in either business-to-business or consumer markets. It can be used in its own right or as part of an overall integrated marketing campaign.

Effective database management is the key to success. It helps to build more detailed profiles of markets, market segments and individual customers. Because it is more targeted, it can be extremely cost effective and, of course, precisely measured.

As part of an integrated relationship marketing campaign, it really adds value and strengthens the role of advertising, public relations, direct mail, mail order, telemarketing and personal selling. This is because of its one-to-one precision, immediate impact/action, and measurability.

Direct marketing has become a science, yet it is deceptively simple. You should creatively figure out how to use it for maximum benefit. Then just do it. Most small and medium companies use far too few marketing and sales approaches.

Here are the benefits of direct marketing:
• high response and conversion
• high customer retention and loyalty
• opportunity to cross-sell and sell up
• cost effective
• better segmentation
• measurable
• links in with or supports an integrated marketing campaign.

(IX) DO TELEMARKETING

Telemarketing is becoming the new way to do business nationally and internationally. The boom in telemarketing is set to continue. It is deceptively simple to operate. Yet the secret is a disciplined, systematic, long-term approach. Telemarketing can take two forms:

1 Inbound, where the prospect, or customer, calls the company in response to an offer or to get further information, and

2 Outbound, where you take the initiative to make direct contact over the telephone as part of an integrated campaign to:

Follow up sales leads

Sell directly

Carry out market research

Support the sales force.

It can be selective, precise, flexible, fast response and measurable.

After doing a mailing to a past, present or prospective customer, a low pressure, information-orientated telemarketing follow-up can increase results by 300 to 1,000 %. It's a difficult job because there is a natural resistance to it from customers. Telemarketing operators need high social skills, and analytical skills. They must also exercise high levels of discipline.

Telemarketing can also be used to great effect as a follow-up service call to make sure everything is in order with the original purchase. You can then use the 'By the way Mr Jones, do you know that ...' to create more sales.

Calling current customers is even easier and more successful. Keeping in touch, educating and informing your customers on the telephone is personalised marketing in action. Don't make assumptions. Errant assumptions are a major reason for loss of customers.

(X) BECOME AN EXPERT ... EDUCATE YOUR CUSTOMERS

A great way to establish yourself as being different and an expert in your industry is to conduct special events, executive briefings or send free worthwhile information to your prospects or customers. People like to feel safe in what they are buying and with whom they are buying it. Buying is primarily emotional but if you can add safety, credibility and information to your basic proposition (desire for gain), then it not only helps get that initial sale but also long term residual business. That's keeping the customer!

Virtually every business has opportunities to educate customers and give them valuable free information. Don't assume that your customers are not interested. Special events, briefings and extra services increase the perceived value of your service through better customer understanding and education. This can allow you to increase your margins.

First do your homework. Read everything about your product that you can, and identify and keep abreast of trends and forecasts. Write articles for trade journals that you can give to customers and prospects. Give seminars in your market area or team up with others. Get on local radio and in the press. Write a book.

Everything adds up. Just do it. You probably have more knowledge and expertise lying dormant in your brain than you appreciate. Sell it. Use it.

(XI) DEVELOP IMAGE PERCEPTION REALITY

Whether you like it or not, you have an image in your customer's mind. This may be good or bad, justified or unjustified. The perception is the reality, however, from the customer's perspective and your job is to create perceptions of your unique added value in comparison to your competitor. If the combination of your public relations, advertising, marketing, moments of impression are that the customer believes that you are actually better than you are, this is the reality. If, despite all your efforts, or your non-efforts, the customer believes the opposite, then this is also the reality.

The secret to keeping those customers is to exceed customer expectations through mastering outstanding customer care and by communicating frequently with your customers so that your product and business are top of their mind. I believe that customers are hoping, wanting, even praying for you to live up to or go beyond their expectations. So become an OCC fanatic. It is a constant nurturing process.

2 INCREASE THE AVERAGE TRANSACTION VALUE

The second way to increase business is to increase the average transaction value per customer. To do this you can focus on improving professional selling skills, integrated relationship marketing and MOCC. How do you increase your sales to the benefit of your customer with very little effort? Here's how.

(I) SELL TO PEOPLE IN THE BUYING MOOD

Have everyone in the organisation focus on the importance and implications of up-selling, cross-selling and selling complementary and ancillary products.

I recently went into a camera shop to buy a cassette for my camcorder. It should have cost me about €12. However, I left the shop having spent €60, feeling very good about my purchases, but on reflection realising that a real professional had just sold me €48 more than I had anticipated. He used the listening, questioning techniques of LOQVE.

My favourite clothes shop always sells me extra ties, shirts, shoes, and socks when I am buying suits from them. At sales time, they have a coffee dock where you pour yourself a drink. At Christmas, they even have alcohol. They're so nice, you feel (almost) obliged to buy something.

Here's an example of a lost opportunity. I went into a hardware store to buy some paint to decorate a bedroom. When I got home, I found that I had no paintbrushes. Had the sales assistant suggested other odds and ends that an obvious DIY enthusiast might need, I would probably have bought paint-brushes and a paint scraper and perhaps a roll of masking tape. Lost sales. I borrowed the paintbrushes and a scraper from my neighbour.

When your customer is in the buying mood, it is always easier to add complementary and ancillary products than try to resell these products at even a much lower price product at a later point.

By packaging complementary products and services together you can create a higher perceived value. Through this method you can employ an important negotiating tactic of giving something of high value to the customer, but of relatively low value/cost to yourself.

To gain long term credibility, be sure that the add-on is of legitimate value and benefit to your customer. Car dealers are masters at up-selling – from providing servicing, to selling spare parts, to selling accessories, to selling finance. Banks are cross-selling additional products and services all the time. What about hotels? Airlines? Restaurants?

The basic concept of a quarterly, half-yearly or annual consulting or service contract can be applied to virtually any business. It keeps you in touch and keeps your customer. Keep thinking of ways of keeping customers for sustainable competitive advantage.

(II) Increase Prices

A very simple way to increase your average transaction value is to increase your prices and hence your margins. Many businesses are obsessed about how their price is set relative to the price charged by their competition. This is nonsense. If you differentiate yourself by employing the techniques outlined in this book, you can actually gain credibility and stature by charging higher prices.

You have bought products from as simple as a writing pen to as significant as family holidays, because of who you were buying them from, where you were buying them and the prestige value or branding associated with them.

Your job as an entrepreneurial manager is to create business advantage by the winning edge formula of gaining small incremental advantages in a wide range of activities within your organisation. The sum total of these efforts means that people will pay more for your product and service. Therefore you will increase your average transaction value, sales, income and profit.

We pay extra for professional advice, service and products all the time. Stop reading for a moment and look at what you are wearing or using within eyeshot right now! Is there anything there that you could have bought for a lower price? Of course there is. So stop being sensitive to price. And apologising for it. Or being fearful of it. Concentrate on improving the value that you are offering. Focus on differentiating your offering.

Your challenge is to always be seeking ways to brand yourself, your product, your business as better, faster, different, easier and as more pleasant to do business with. In a nutshell, you want people to say that they always get a professional team performance from interacting with your business. Your job is to get everybody thinking, talking, acting and behaving in a professional way. The OCC way!

A brand is not just a label – it's your trademark with your customers and it must be protected, nurtured and used carefully with deliberate targeted purpose.

(III) Lock in to long term relationships

Another method of increasing the average transaction value of your product or service is to offer larger units of purchase over extended periods of time. Think about 'locking in' your customers to just do business with you. Magazine subscription companies are constantly trying to get you to pay up front for two and three year subscriptions rather than buy it on a monthly, quarterly or even yearly basis. Virtually every business has some opportunity to do this. A hairdresser offers the fifth visit to her salon free of charge. Capital equipment sellers realise the service contract is what makes the 'life-time' possibility possible – the second and subsequent sales cost relatively less time and effort. The objective is to keep the customer coming back and giving them a professional service so that they will stay long term.

3 INCREASE THE FREQUENCY OF PURCHASES BY CUSTOMERS

The third way to grow your business is by increasing the frequency of purchase – get your customer buying on a more regular basis.

To increase transaction frequency you can focus on continually innovating, reinventing and researching and developing new products and services that can add value to the original products you sold them. Or simply offer customers a new range of products.

'How do people know that you are striving to be the best in your field, and that you want to keep them continually doing business with you, and that you are offering above and beyond the average selling proposition of your competitor?' The answer is simple. You tell them, you educate them, you inform them. You develop systems to keep in touch. People are not telepathic, they don't care and think about you as much as you think they do. Just don't make assumptions.

Think about four possible levels at which you might increase the number of customer interactions, whether it is business to business, retail or direct to the consumer. It is possible that you may be conducting business at all four levels. However, it may be possible to flexibly position your offering to increase the quality, quantity and frequency of purchases.

The four levels are:

Level 1 Transactions
Level 2 Product Solution
Level 3 Business Solution and
Level 4 Partnerships.

LEVEL 1: SIMPLE BUY/SELL TRANSACTIONS

In simple buy/sell transactions the customer has no intention of being loyal and factors such as convenience may be more important than quality. You have a headache, you buy a pain-killer. This is a simple purchase for a simple sale. Your objective should be to make these transactions better, faster, cheaper, easier and above all, more convenient.

LEVEL 2: PRODUCT SOLUTION

In the product solution level you establish the needs of your customer by listening, observing, and questioning. From the range of possibilities ascertained through needs establishment, you provide your product as a solution. You may even fine-tune or customise your products for your customer. You get to know your customer much better but you still focus on delivering your product as a solution to their problem. Using the doctor/patient analogy it is equivalent to the doctor examining, diagnosing and prescribing medicine as your cure.

FLEXIBLE POSITIONING

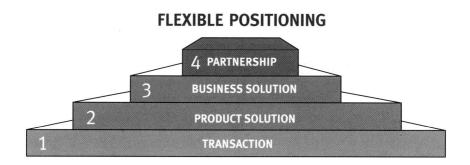

You can position yourself in four different ways. You can be in the business of simple trans-
actions. You can provide a product solution.
A business solution is all-encompassing. There's more involved. A partnership is a close
working relationship where the buyer and the seller work towards a mutually successful
outcome.

LEVEL 3: THE BUSINESS SOLUTION

At the business solution level you listen carefully for causes of the problems and their effects. You listen at a deeper level to the sources of the problems and the answer to the question, 'Where does it really hurt?' It's the equivalent of the doctor doing a full medical check-up including tests, scans and x-rays. Often times your customer is unsure of their problem. As a business doctor, you explore the situation thoroughly, identify the problem and recommend an agreed solution.

LEVEL 4: PARTNERSHIP

At the partnership level the old buyer-seller game fades away. Partnerships are based on total trust and the clear understanding that both parties can work together to the resolution of a problem. Partnerships take time to develop. Positive relationships are critical to their success.

The development of this partnership-type relationship is like the development of the time-honoured 'boy meets girl' scenario. When a boy and girl meet for the first time, do they decide immediately to become partners, get engaged or get married? No! At best they decide to have another date! Then another and so on. After a period of time when they both like and respect one another they may decide to get engaged and then formalise their arrangement into a long-term partnership called marriage.

In a business context you form a contract and agree to take responsibility for the totality of that relationship. 'If it's not right for you, it's not right for me.' It's a win/win game – not a win/lose game. Like marriage, this is, of course, a more demanding relationship, but it is ultimately what you are endeavouring to achieve – to cement a relationship and therefore increase the quality, quantity and frequency of purchases.

In my own business I have all four of these relationships with my clients. My objective is to nurture them from simple transactions to providing product solutions to business solutions and partnerships. One division of our business, the Learning Resource Centre, supplies audiotapes, books, videos, CD-ROMs and personality/career profile reports. The supply and sale of these are simple transactions conducted over the telephone, by direct mail or at briefings and seminars that we conduct around the country. Many of our best clients started off their relationship with us by such simple transactions.

We recently supplied a product solution to a client who had bought an audiotape three years earlier and rang us up with a sales problem. He was about to enter his five months busy period and needed something to kick-start his 12 sales representatives who were cruising along in their comfort zones.

Having discussed the situation with him for several hours, we identified two choke points in the sales team. One was poor time management skill and the second was a total inability to prospect for new customers. They believed they had no time to get new customers. We customised a product solution for this client and his return on investment was repaid within one month because each sales representative went wild with prospecting, getting referrals and prioritising their sales calls.

However, our company is really geared towards providing business solutions where the diagnosis is not always so clear cut. A business owner of a substantial medium sized business came to me several years ago and outlined a range of performance problems. He had already tried several improvement initiatives but new problems and challenges seemed to develop as fast as he sorted out an old problem. He explained that he was demoralised and fed-up putting a first aid dressing on a problem that obviously needed major surgery. He was working up to 70 and 80 hours a week, was very stressed and was having major difficulties in his family life.

We analysed his situation and we diagnosed a total business solution across the processes, structures and resources within his business. The business had outgrown the one man band stage and the business solution lay in strengthening and the redeployment of key resources, installing procedures and management structures for a more mature organisation. Over the last two years this business has developed a five strong management team and the business owner has learned the secret of letting other people be the heroes.

Our ultimate objective (level 4) – partnership – is to help our clients create sustainable business advantage by working in close partnership with them. Our mission statement is: 'to partner with our clients, to create business advantage by energising individuals, teams and organisations to maximise their full potential.' At a partnership level we are interested in where the ship is going, not so much with the state of play on board the ship.

This is a leadership and strategic change management role. It involves everything from forming long term mentoring relationships with key executives to auditing and monitoring the customer and staff climates. Trust and commitment are the essence of a good partnership. It's a learning process for both sides. You bring your experience, expertise and resources and then it's a judgement call with regard to being subjective and objective. If you get too involved, too hands-on, you in effect become a temporary manager. If you stay too objective and somewhat uncommitted, the 'marriage' bond may have difficulties.

Your challenge as the entrepreneurial manager is to develop more and more of these high calibre relationships using all the techniques and ideas outlined in this book. You will develop lifelong loyal customers if you endeavour to work at this partnership level.

Efficient Consumer Response (ECR) is a practical example of partnerships in action. ECR was launched in Europe in 1994 as a strategy to remove unnecessary costs from the grocery supply chain and to make the sector as a whole more responsive to consumer demand. It involves a continuous flow of information requiring manufacturers and retailers to work together in joint planning and forecasting.

The mission statement of ECR Europe offers the best definition of this global initiative: 'Working together to fulfil consumer wishes better, faster, and at less cost'. Embedded in this simple statement are the two fundamental principles that guide all ECR efforts:

1 **Focus on Consumers.** A commitment to the belief that sustained business success stems only from providing consumers with products and services that consistently meet or surpass their expectations.

2 Working together. Recognition that the greatest consumer value can be offered only when trading partners work together, both within their own company and with their trading partners. What is new about ECR is the integrated manner in which it looks at the entire supply chain. The retailers and suppliers are now focusing on the efficiency of the total grocery chain, working towards ultimate consumer satisfaction. Partnerships are not only working between suppliers and customers but between competitors and non-competitors. You should explore this approach to doing business no matter what business you are in.

NETWORKING

Think about networking as a proactive way of developing longer relationships and better quality relationships with your customers. Think creatively. Ask yourself: 'Who could I work with where we could collectively create a business advantage and add value for our customers and ourselves?' Think about becoming the central hub of the network. Two other good questions are: 'What are your dreams and how could we dream together?' 'How could we create mutual benefits?'

Look at all of your customers' requirements, especially all those non-competing products and services which they are supplied with. Good partnerships are built on solid relationships and trust. Take the initiative and deliver some value to your network partners – before they expect a return. Give a new partner leads and referrals as soon as possible after you form an alliance. Do them a 'good turn'.

Once you have started the initiative, ask them for referrals and leads. If, over time, it becomes clear that the flow with your new partner is all one way, replace them with someone else. Always send a 'Thank You' card and an update on an introduction or how an introduced relationship is developing. If you become an outstanding networker, you will surpass any formal marketing techniques.

Provided you are still exceeding customer expectations, and satisfying customer requirements, the single best way to increase the number of transactions and the amount of repeat business a customer will have with you, over time, is to communicate with them personally, on the telephone or by letter. Do it in as unique a way as possible.

My clothes shop supplier sends me a sock in the post announcing a new range of suits or an upcoming sale. On another occasion, he sent a white handkerchief with the details of an upcoming sale printed on it. No paper. But it was very memorable and you could use the handkerchief.

Make the effort to treat your customer as special by inviting him to off-time briefings or get-togethers, closed-door sales or seminars.

Price reductions, easy payment plans, special customer programmes, and so on can gain customer commitment to do business with you over an extended period of time.

CREATING AND KEEPING CUSTOMER ADVANTAGE

Developing an outstanding customer care culture and implementing successful marketing communication techniques is about increasing sales and profits from the same quantity of marketing expenditure and efforts that you are already making. It is the simple things, consistently, systematically applied, that produce tremendous profits. Be smart and do the simple things well. Don't confuse big spending with successful results. Think about sales and marketing not as skills, functions, arts or sciences but as attitudes. Think of an OCC culture as a core competency and an attitude to create and keep customers.

Use a combination of follow-up methods over time to move your customer to ever-increasing levels of decisive action. Once you start the communication process with customers, keep contacting them, because people's circumstances and needs keep changing. My best friends/clients have taken up to seven 'contacts' such as attending information briefings or mini-seminars, making small purchases before they give us the green light to go ahead on major improvement initiatives (Partnerships).

Always telephone new customers within a week to ten days of initial purchase and you will be astonished at the effect it has in keeping them long term. It shows that you are concerned and it helps to reduce any buyer's remorse that they may have. It also makes them more receptive to your next offer and you can get referrals or other points of information. My company runs a leadership development programme of between six and ten days spread over one year, but we always telephone after Day One to get the executives' input and listen to any concerns they may have.

Keep in touch with old customers, prospects, employers, employees, and suppliers. You never know when or where they will re-surface as an influencer or as a customer. It's a small world. So make every effort to make last impressions as good as first impressions. Endeavour to never burn your bridges with anyone – the cost could be great and the opportunity too lucrative.

APPLICATION EXERCISES

1 Do a staff (internal customer) and an external customer satisfaction audit to determine the temperature of your business.

2 Build in to everyone's job description a primary or, at least, a secondary responsibility for OCC, sales and marketing. They should be given a specific, practical role in this area.

3 Sharpen up on all the basics. Everything counts. Every detail is either adding-to or taking-from your credibility and perception. Brainstorm 100 low cost, simple things that you could improve on over the next 30 days. Be sure to write them down.

4 Have six friends act as customers to your business. Lead them through your full sales cycle. Give them criteria to give you feedback on and listen to their own emotional read out. You'll learn more from doing this exercise than from a very expensive research campaign.

5 At your company get-together, ask everyone to write down on separate 2x4 cards the answers to the following three questions:

(i) What is our unique selling proposition (USP)? You'll be astonished at the array of answers. Through discussion, agree on the number one best USP.

(ii) Why am I on the payroll?
a.How many staff members feel that they are customer contributors?
b.How many see business development as part of their job?

(ii) What three things could we do in the next 24 hours to achieve OCC?Agree on a certain number that give the early win feeling. Agree a reporting back time to the group. Then ask for some more actions to develop OCC.

CONSIDER THESE QUESTIONS

Q.1 Does management have a clear vision of the future of your company? Has that vision been clearly communicated to everyone in the organisation? Is it customer or organisation focused?

Q.2 Are your management team members taking the necessary steps to lead your industry and market place or is there a tendency to 'wait and see?'

Q.3 Are distinctive competencies of your organisation well understood by all employees. Is there a plan in place to ensure that customer core competencies are being constantly enhanced?

Q.4 Is top management bogged down in operational issues or is it investing the time and intellectual energy necessary in understanding the future of the industry?

Q.5 Is your company pursuing growth and new business development with as much passion as it is pursuing operational efficiencies?

PITOC™ CUSTOMER CARE

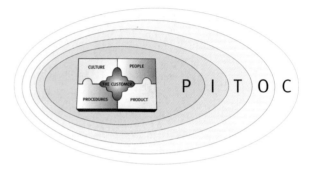

The principles of marketing are universal and can be applied at all five PITOC™ levels. To master marketing, master PITOC™. Both are inextricably linked to create personal and business advantage.

7

TURNING CREATIVE THINKING INTO INNOVATION

Why do some people achieve more than others on a personal and professional level? Why do some businesses outperform others in similar markets and with similar resources?

Your brainpower is an intangible asset. It is probably an infinite resource because idea generation is limitless. Everyone can learn to think more creatively. Your challenge is to systematically capture your own and everybody else's best ideas to create business advantage.

The ordinary manager rarely thinks about thinking. He thinks that thinking is a natural, God-given ability. You, the entrepreneurial manager, realise that creative advanced-level thinking is a learnable skill and that this skill is fundamental to creating business advantage and maximising your resources and distinctive competencies. It also helps determine your happiness and success in business and in your personal life.

You must distinguish between paying wages to people and investing in their thinking power. To unlock the potential of the human capital that is already resident, but probably dormant, within your organisation you must first create the environment for it. Human capital can be your most valuable resource. To get the most from this resource, invest in it. By doing so, you are also investing in innovation – the catalyst for all development.

Why don't more businesses do this? It's because innovation is intangible and takes a leap of faith. Buying capital equipment is easy – you can see it perform. Buying land or property is easy – you can walk on it, touch it and see it.

Thinking is different from intelligence. Intelligence is like the hardware in a computer. Thinking is like the software that maximises the potential of that computer. In his book, *Maximum Achievement*, Brian Tracy says: 'Intelligence is a way of acting.' He also says that there are several forms of intelligence and methods of thinking. I agree. Common sense is not always common practice.

I have met many highly intelligent people – by IQ test and education standards – who are poor thinkers. They get caught in the intelligence trap thinking they know all that they need to know. I have met many less 'intelligent' people who are streetwise and are excellent thinkers and high achievers. Universities don't fully credit experience as knowledge. In my opinion, to know and not to do is not yet to know.

Peter Drucker said that a business enterprise has two, and only two, basic functions – marketing and innovation. Marketing has received a lot of attention over the last three or four decades and most companies have a marketing policy or strategy in place. But innovation gets much less recognition and even less application.

Like marketing, strategy, identity, and IT, there is some confusion about the definitions of creativity and innovation. And where does research and development fit in? I see creativity as the starting point of innovation. Creativity is the ideas generation stage – it's the free-flow of 'possibilities.' Later in this chapter we will look at ways to unlock this creativity.

Innovation is the implementation of creative practical ideas into products and projects that are commercially viable. Innovativeness is therefore a core competency that helps facilitate change and growth. It is the engine room used to secure your future sales and earnings.

WHY CREATIVE IDEAS FAIL TO BECOME INNOVATIONS

So why do so many creative ideas not become innovations? Why are so many great ideas not turned into money? Here are six general reasons:

1 COMFORT ZONE EXCUSES

Creativity takes time and space and most managers prefer what is safe and logical (the status quo) to what is new and even crazy. They have a comfort zone to protect and they protect it consciously or unconsciously. They have fear of failure and rejection, false assumptions and other misconceptions. They use lame excuses ('we've already tried that').

As the innovative entrepreneurial manager you must view the situation differently. You must use every technique outlined in this book to unlock your own creativity and the creative potential of your team.

2 IDEA SOLD BADLY

Selling a creative idea is as important as the creative process itself. It never becomes an innovation unless you persuade other people of its value. Many ideas die at this stage. Remember that there is a natural human resistance to change. You must be aware of this and be prepared for it. Keep in mind the two basic motivators. One is positive – the desire for gain and improvement. The other is negative – the fear of loss (of money, status, power). You should ensure that the benefits outweigh the risks as perceived by others.

How can you legitimise it and make it more credible? One way is to put it in writing. Enthusiasm is strong but a well-presented proposal is even stronger.

I remember being part of a sales team many years ago and everyone being asked to submit ideas for improvement. I produced a very comprehensive, well thought out submission while everyone else submitted some hand-written ideas. Not only were my ideas being used for 12 months afterwards but I tripled my income in that company over the next three years. Do you think there was a connection between my written ideas and my income?

3 LACK OF FOCUS

Another reason why creative ideas die is lack of overall focus and direction within the organisation. You must get your strategic thinking and planning exercise completed. Otherwise good ideas don't get implemented. They have nowhere to fit into the overall scheme of things. Lack of empowerment and negativity just swamps them out. As the entrepreneurial manager you make a strategic decision to out-think and out-perform your competitors.

4 THE VICIOUS CIRCLE

Managers don't realise that creative thinking, decision making, being innovative and being an excellent problem solver are learnable skills. They don't realise how important these skills are in today's business world. They don't realise that there is a vast pool of creativity procedures that can be applied to virtually any problem. The feeling that 'there is no solution to my problem' has a consequent draining effect on operational and strategic direction.

Most of the causes of creativity block are mental. They are therefore solvable in most cases. Be aware of them in yourself.

– Fixed beliefs – 'blind spots'. *It's a great idea, but!'*
– Your background conditioning. *'I don't believe ...'*
– The right/wrong, yes/no absolutes approach.
– Fear of success and failure.

– The Comfort Zone (status quo). *'I've always been like this ...'*

– Inferiority complexes. *'I'm no good at ...'*

– The 'business is serious' ethos.

– Not loving mistakes.

Many managers are trapped in a vicious circle because of this lack of realisation. This has a consequent draining effect on attitude levels, commitment, perseverance, clarity and often leads to paralysis, a feeling of being out of control and high stress levels.

This, in turn, leads to an acceleration of personal doubts, fears and a secret questioning of their own capabilities and competencies. This in turn leads to cover-ups, blaming and a 'work faster' mentality. Being busy is confused with business activity. Activity is confused with progress. And so the vicious circle continues.

5 THE INTELLIGENCE TRAP

Most managers do not know how to approach problem solving, creativity or innovation. How to identify and where to identify the constraints seems unclear. But there are only six general areas in which to identify constraints: (1) Systems, (2) Structure, (3) Strategic direction, (4) Processes, (5) People and (6) Culture. The ability to name the constraint area goes a long way towards sorting out the block. If you can't name it, you do not know it.

Most managers are further confused about the nature of management. They have the worst form of learning disease – the intelligence trap. They simply don't know that they don't know and the flip side of that coin is they think they know all there is to know. Their heads are so full of old knowledge that there is no room for new input. They don't know that there are tried and tested techniques to solve virtually every business problem that has ever been heard of.

During a 'Learning for Life Conference' which I was addressing, a fellow speaker, Professor Brendan Kennelly of Trinity College, Dublin, said: 'A lot of learning is unlearning.' This is a profound statement, with a profound message for most managers. Learning to forget is a 21st century mindset.

6 THE PERSONAL MASTERY BLOCK

The sixth major block to creative thinking and innovation is a lack of personal mastery skills. If these are lacking, there is an outgoing ripple effect on interpersonal, team and organisational capabilities. Customers sense this and so the downward spiral continues. Because as Ralph Waldo Emerson said:

'Every organisation is the length and shadow of one man', there is a consequent low level of creativity, problem solving and innovation in the immediate team and probably throughout the organisation. Stress levels rise which lead to poorer communication, lower morale and bad time management. The concept of learning our way out of difficulties or into a better situation has not even been considered.

I have worked with hundreds of organisations – small, medium and large – of which in my view, very few are restricted by a lack of resources, core competencies or market opportunities. 'We have met the enemy and they are us' is a statement that was never more applicable than to this situation. For example, the potential for you to cut costs and increase revenues is enormous. Your 'secret' is to focus on solving the ongoing problems, generating creative ideas and implementation of innovative solutions. Use all the possibilities within your control.

THE APPLICATION OF CREATIVITY AND INNOVATION

Your creativity therefore is not inborn, but developed, practised and applied in a systematic way over time. It is said that like genius, creativity is 1% inspiration and 99% perspiration.

Creativity and innovative approaches can be used to:

– Do more with less. How about doing a value analysis of overheads? 'Why am I on the payroll?' 'What does my job contribute?' 'And for whom?' Then ask your boss or colleague to compare.

– Reorganise, reengineer, and restructure your organisation. What costs could you cut out? How could you increase sales by 20%?

– Boost the morale of your already excellent staff to give even more outstanding customer service. 'Your customer comes second' seems like an odd statement. But your staff deliver outstanding customer care. They therefore, come first. When ideas come from the staff (the grassroots), they have twice the chance of 'catching on' or germinating.

– Improve your product and service delivery. No matter how

good you think your product or service is, someone, somewhere, right now is seeking to do it differently. Distribution methods and logistics are, for instance, becoming a science just like other defined management functions.

– Anticipate your trends in the marketplace and capitalise (better, faster, cheaper, and easier) on new developments for growth and expansion. Remember that innovation and marketing are bedfellows, and that all other functions are costs.

NEW THINKING REQUIRED

Today, innovation and marketing are the most important building blocks of competitive advantage. At school, you were taught to think in a linear, one-dimensional fashion. Your personality make-up tends to lead you to tackle problems and situations from your knowledge base and from your experience base. This type of thinking is useful and logical and works to a certain degree. However, continuously innovating and creating business advantage in a time of accelerated change requires you to step out of your normal experience, your normal space and past knowledge, and use non-traditional thinking methods.

The purpose of 'systems thinking' is to help you achieve your personal, professional and business goals in a better, faster, cheaper, easier, newer, different way. Your natural and developed competencies are, of course, the guiding light in your creative thinking process. By learning, practising and developing new thinking methods and technologies, you will be better equipped to achieve your objectives.

In this chapter I give a number of reasons why creative thinking is an essential skill for today's business environment. I outline three reasons why managers have a block or blind spot in their thinking capabilities. I also outline several techniques that you can use on a personal, interpersonal, team and organisational level in your business to enable you to be an excellent problem solver, achieve above average success in your decision-making, and continually come up with innovative solutions for market and organisational problems.

The ultimate goal is to help you achieve personal mastery, improve all your person-to-person interactions, improve teamwork, productivity, and bottom line profit and create and keep more customers.

When I speak to groups of managers at business events, I ask them to raise their hands to the question: 'How many of you here feel that you are creative?' The response is that usually less than 20% of the attendance feel that they are creative. Most are sceptical about learning to be creative. Most associate creativity with people who are good with their physical intelligences such as artists or an exceptional sports player or an entertainer. This is the same tendency that equates intelligence with educational results. It's flawed thinking.

Real managers have proved all of the ideas presented here in real situations, creatively solving problems and bringing about innovative solutions that they hitherto believed impossible. Because the ideas appear to be simple, many people dismiss or ignore them as possible avenues for improvement.

One of your secrets as the entrepreneurial manager will be your ability to find solutions and solve problems at a higher level than those around you. Your ability to continuously implement one of the many 'creativity procedures' available to generate new and useful ideas is what will distinguish you from the rest. You must learn a whole range of creative thinking skills rather than staying stuck in the old traditional linear thinking process.

The 'Brainstorming' technique was invented over 50 years ago, when the Model A Ford motorcar was in use. But using only the Brainstorming technique is like getting around in a Model A Ford today. Failure to use up-to-date creativity procedures is like ignoring computers, wireless communication, Internet and the freedom that modern electronic technology can give. Even those companies that can afford a permanent Research and Development and Innovation (R and D, and I) department – and most cannot – find it difficult to come up with enough commercial ideas to make it viable. Innovation is the lifeblood of a changing organisation. Undoubtedly the best ideas come from the culture and attitude of its people.

WHY CREATIVE THINKING SKILLS AND INNOVATION ARE MORE IMPORTANT NOW THAN EVER BEFORE

The main reasons why creative thinking skills and innovation are more important today than in the past has to do with the accelerated pace of change, and the new positioning of knowledge as a power resource. The speed with which you solve problems and create better solutions is a critical success factor.

Everyone in your organisation should have just one job title – Problem Solver. Of course your ability to reach the best possible solution is also important. To maintain your winning edge capability of being better, faster, cheaper, easier, newer, different, you must implement the most up-to-date creative thinking techniques.

The information age and instant communication technologies mean that innovation, research and development must be 10-100 times faster than in the past. All new products, fads and fashions start out as creative ideas. Creative thinking techniques accelerate this process and enable you to keep up to speed with the pace of change.

It continues to amaze me why sensible, apparently intelligent managers continue to surrender themselves to non-solutions. They stubbornly fossilise in their present positions without attempting the mastery of time management skills or developing new sales and marketing projects. The sad aspect of this is that because they get overwhelmed by a host of smaller problems, they therefore rarely apply their thinking prowess to developing strategic goals and being innovative. An awareness of these blocks may be the first step to understanding why more managers don't apply creative thinking skills.

HOW TO APPLY CREATIVE THINKING TECHNIQUES

Most people know what to be creative on. They also know why great ideas don't get turned into products or successful ventures. Their challenge is to find a systematic approach.

Here is a problem solving sequence that works well to produce creative solutions for innovation:

STEP I CLARIFY THE PROBLEMS

Ask yourself: 'What is the problem?' 'Is there a problem?' 'What are its effects?' Define several problem statements as clearly as possible. This is key. Preparation is important here. Gather the facts. Decide which creative thinking techniques you will use. Resist the temptation to go for an early solution.

STEPS TO INNOVATION

step 1
CLARIFY THE PROBLEMS.
What is the core problem?
What are the effects?

step 7
AGREE REPORTING AND
FEEDBACK PROCEDURE
By When?

step 2
IDENTIFY THE CAUSES
All the causes

THE INNOVATION
PROCESS

step 6
ASSIGN RESPONSIBILITY
FOR THE OUTCOME.
Who will do it?

step 3
GENERATE POSSIBLE SOLUTIONS
All the solutions

step 4
SELECT THE BEST SOLUTION
By agreement

step 5
IMPLEMENT DECISIONS.
Actions to be taken

Starting with identification and clarification of the problems and their effects in your organisation, work carefully through the seven steps of the innovation process to achieve desirable change. A systems approach is key to innovation success.

Start your problem statements with the words 'How to ...' eg:
How to increase ...
How to change ...
How to fix ...
How to enhance ...
How to cope with ...
How to do away with ...
How to deliver ...
How to make best use of ...
How to control ...
How to begin, plan ...
How to sell ...
How to commence ...
How to establish ...
How to inspire ...
How to create ...
How to distribute ...
How to substitute ...
How to move forward ...

During this stage you bring to bear all your personal competencies, experiences, expertise, training, travelling and so on. What you dwell upon grows. Keep a focus on the problem over time. The alternative principle of indirect effort also helps. Ease back on the eagerness to find a solution. Take time out. Do other things. Let your subconscious work it out in a relaxed way. Many genius solutions just 'pop up' in this way.

As much as 80% of the solution will come from a clear definition of the problem, so spend time at this stage clearly establishing the following:

What assumptions are being made? Whose problem is it? Who understands the problem, really? What is the nature of the problem (financial, marketing, administration, distribution, or personnel)? All this will help you with the final problem statement.

Kenichi Ohmae in his book *Mind of a Strategist* uses a stalemate breaking technique. Instead of brainstorming solutions, he gets groups to brainstorm assumptions. He has them then make a complete list of ways to overturn those assumptions.

A key aspect at this stage is to outline the effects of the problem. What are the present effects? What are the long-term effects? How does the problem affect the 'Big Picture?' How much does it cost?

Another way to get a fresh prospective is, having written the problem, view it as if you were a martian, a child or an animal. Seems a bit crazy, but try it and see.

Sometimes just changing the format of the words can transform a 'How to' problem statement. For example, you can transform 'How to get rid of that slow selling product' into 'How to increase the sales of …' It's the optimist's approach. Optimism is a key to creativity.

STEP II IDENTIFY THE CAUSES OF THE PROBLEM

To understand and solve the problem it is critically important to understand the cause. The principle of cause and effect comes into play here. Sometimes the problem can be solved at the source. A cause and effect or fishbone diagram (it resembles the skeleton of a fish when completed) is a visual technique to help categorise a large number of ideas and issues into more manageable groups.

The first step is to define the problem clearly and write it in a box at the right-hand side of the page or on a flipchart. Then draw a fishbone structure with six bones.

THE FISHBONE CAUSE AND EFFECT FRAMEWORK

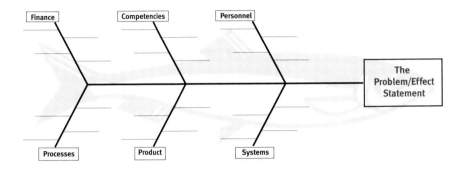

The Fishbone provides an excellent means through which you can identify the causes and effects of a problem. Your ability to see the total problem in graphic detail with the causes of the problem clearly identified is critical to creativity and innovation.

You can use Post-It stickers to place issues on particular fish bones. It's a great technique to categorise and get a visual overview. It clearly shows the possible relationships between causes and the problems and helps the freeflow of ideas. You can approach it in two ways. First you develop categories (bones), then brainstorm ideas and fit them to the categories. Second, you can brainstorm first. Then group the ideas/causes into categories.

Once you have identified the causes, you will need to dig deeper before jumping to solutions/conclusions. Be factual here. Get figures. Never assume. Trace back to the root causes or choke points that seem to be repeated. Get expert help with this stage. Ask questions, listen to all concerned. What are the causes of the effects in the workplace? You will find that most of the more easily measured effects (wastage, quality problems, breakdowns etc) have psychological (soft) causes. Unfortunately, most managers tend to fix the wrong problem. This may give temporary relief but rarely solves the long term problem (causes). Your focus should be on identifying and remedying the *real* causes.

CAUSES AND EFFECTS IN THE WORKPLACE

Soft Causes
Possible psychological/mental

Hard Conditions
Problem Effects

LOW SELF-ESTEEM
- LACK OF RESPONSIBILITY
- AN AVOIDANCE CULTURE
- LACKS OWNERSHIP OF PROBLEM
- POOR INTERNAL COMMUNICATIONS
- THE BLAME GAME
- LOW SELF ESTEEM

WASTE
- DEFECTIVE PRODUCTION
- OVER PRODUCTION
- INVENTORIES
- MOTION/WAITING
- PROCESSES
- TRANSPORT

VERY LOW · LOW · NEUTRAL · HIGH · VERY HIGH
0 1 2 3 4 5

UNCLEAR STRATEGY
- LOW BUY-IN TO COMPANY VALUES
- LACK OF INTEREST
- OWNERSHIP LACKING
- PROBLEM - SOLVING SKILLS LOW
- TQM IS A 'BOLT ON' ACTIVITY

QUALITY PROBLEMS
- HIGHER COSTS
- COST OF DOING IT AGAIN
- LOST SALES
- TARNISHED/IMAGE
- LEAD TIME TOO LONG

VERY LOW · LOW · NEUTRAL · HIGH · VERY HIGH
0 1 2 3 4 5

POOR ATTITUDES
- 'IT'S NOT MY FAULT'
- LOW ATTENTION TO DETAIL
- LOW INITIATIVE/OWNERSHIP SKILLS
- POOR TIME CONTROL

BREAKDOWNS
- BOTTLENECKS/DELAYS
- CUSTOMER COMPLAINTS
- EXTRA COSTS
- CRISIS MANAGEMENT

VERY LOW · LOW · NEUTRAL · HIGH · VERY HIGH
0 1 2 3 4 5

DEMOTIVATION
- FEELING OF OWNERSHIP LOW
- POOR INVOLVEMENT
- HIGH STRESS
- DISSATISFACTION
- COMMUNICATION PROBLEM
- NO SENSE OF TEAM

ABSENTEEISM
- LOWER PRODUCTION
- LOWER QUALITY
- PRESSURE ON SYSTEM
- CUSTOMER DELAYS
- COSTS OF TEMPORARIES
- PRODUCTIVITY DOWN

VERY LOW · LOW · NEUTRAL · HIGH · VERY HIGH
0 1 2 3 4 5

NEGATIVE CULTURE
- VALUES, STRATEGIES, GOALS FUZZY
- FEARS AND INSECURITIES ABOUND
- LACK OF MOTIVATION/INVOLVEMENT
- POOR COMMUNICATION
- NO PERSONAL TRAINING

STAFF TURNOVER
- COSTS OF RETRAINING
- RECRUITMENT COSTS (TIME/EXPENSES)
- QUALITY SUFFERS
- CUSTOMER SERVICE SUFFERS
- STRAIN ON THE TEAM

VERY LOW · LOW · NEUTRAL · HIGH · VERY HIGH
0 1 2 3 4 5

LOOSE CONTROLS
- BOREDOM/FATIGUE/STRESS
- POOR TRAINING – TECHNICAL
- POOR TRAINING – ATTITUDE

ACCIDENTS
- INSURANCE CLAIMS
- TIME LOST
- PRODUCTIVITY PROBLEMS

VERY LOW · LOW · NEUTRAL · HIGH · VERY HIGH
0 1 2 3 4 5

ATTITUDE FACTORS
- POOR QUALITY PRODUCT
- LOW CUSTOMER CARE SKILLS
- POOR COMMUNICATION SKILLS
- POOR CUSTOMER APPRECIATION

CUSTOMER COMPLAINTS
- COSTS OF RETURNS
- BAD FEELINGS/POOR PUBLIC RELATIONS
- LOST SALES/CUSTOMERS
- TIME WASTED

VERY LOW · LOW · NEUTRAL · HIGH · VERY HIGH
0 1 2 3 4 5

INFERIOR PRESENTION
- PRODUCTS INFERIOR
- SELLING METHODS NOT GOOD
- POOR SALES TRAINING
- SALES MANAGEMENT INEFFECTIVE
- PROSPECTING NEGLIBILITY

LOW SALES
- TURNOVER POTENTIAL LOW
- CALL RATIO NOT PROFITABLE
- WRONG CUSTOMER PORTFOLIO
- PROFIT/ROI PROBLEMS
- ROI RATIO LOW
- SALES/STAFF RATIO LOW

VERY LOW · LOW · NEUTRAL · HIGH · VERY HIGH
0 1 2 3 4 5

Score the effects (problems) for your business on the right hand side.
Then look at the possible causes on the left hand side.
Are the effects (the actual conditions) directly related to the causes?
Are you struggling with the effects and not giving enough consideration to the causes?
Consider this:
'All costs walk on two feet. Most causes are Mental. Conditions are effects'.

How you label the fish bones is important. Some will overlap as main issues emerge. For instance in manufacturing, the 4M's have been traditionally used: Men, Machines, Methods and Materials. An example of how the basic six fish bones can be developed is outlined below using an example of a small company with a 'low sales problem'. At this stage it begins to look like a Mind Map.

Total clarity around the nature of the problem is critical at this stage. Give it time to emerge. But stay focused on identifying it. Most people are so easily diverted. Some people just can't concentrate for three minutes, let alone 30 minutes, or three hours. Eighty per cent of the solution will come from clearly identifying and writing up the problem effect statement.

IDENTIFYING SALES PROBLEMS: CAUSES AND EFFECTS

This company has a sales problem. Identifying the causes of the poor sales was easy when using the Fishbone diagram.
The marketing manager identified six major causes of the sales problem. These were poor marketing, inadequate deployment of key resources, increase in competitor activity, inadequate sales training, lack of attention to key accounts and inadequate personnel management systems.

STEP III GENERATE POSSIBLE SOLUTIONS

Most undisciplined individuals and teams come to the possible solutions stage far too quickly. There is absolutely no guarantee however that you will come up with a magical solution. But if your preparation and thinking and mental expectation are properly tuned and you use the creative thinking techniques outlined herein, you will dramatically raise the probability that a useful outcome will occur.

So let us look at some Creative Thinking techniques to generate ideas and solutions to solve the clearly defined problem. Remember that creativity is the thinking process which helps generate ideas and that innovation is the application of these ideas towards doing things better, faster, cheaper, easier, newer, different. Re-inventing, reengineering, restructuring, reorganising.

BRAINSTORMING

Brainstorming is the original problem-solving technique developed by Alex F Osborne in his book *Applied Imagination* in which the group generates a large number of ideas and solutions on a topic before narrowing them down.

There are a number of different variations of this technique. One is where between five and seven people of similar status assemble and give their ideas while one person records these ideas on a notepad or flipchart. Another is to Brainstorm for three minutes, be quiet for three minutes, Brainstorm for another three minutes and so on. Another is to go around the group and get one idea from each person (allowing people to pass if they want). Sometimes, however, quieter people hold back.

To increase the number of ideas expressed, Osborne suggests the following guidelines:

- Suspend judgement or evaluation until later: this is critically important as sometimes people hold back because of low self-esteem and fear of being criticised. When we evaluate we tend to immerse ourselves in old thinking and old approaches. All questions and evaluations should come later. Keeping the process moving with fun. Even shouting the responses is good.
- Freewheel: The wilder the ideas the better. 'Out of the ordinary' ideas flow from creatively freewheeling.
- Quantity: The greater the number of ideas, the greater the likelihood of producing one idea that is innovative and useful.
- Cross-fertilise: Combine and piggyback ideas. You can use trigger ideas to spark still better ideas.

MIND MAPPING

Spray diagrams, ('Spiders webs') are an alternative to linear notes. Mind maps, made famous by Tony Buzan, are a note-taking, note-making and memory device. The principle behind Mind Mapping is that the process of creativity is organic rather than linear. Main categories stretch spoke-like from the centre of the map, with subcategories branching off.

It's a more right brain, free flowing, whole brain approach to gathering and presenting information. Producing successful Mind Maps takes practice and tends to be 'personal' to the writer.

LATERAL THINKING

Dr Edward de Bono divides thinking into two methods. He calls one 'vertical' thinking, that is, using the processes of logic or the traditional historical method. He calls the other 'lateral' thinking – a way of thinking that seeks a solution to a problem through unorthodox methods or elements that would normally be ignored by logical thinking. He says that developing breakthrough ideas does not have to be the result of luck or a shotgun approach.

His lateral thinking methods promote a technique to replace one-dimensional thinking and communication with six-dimensional thinking and communication. His six metaphorical hats separate different types of thinking – emotion from fact, positive from negative, creative from critical. The process allows you to evaluate situations by switching in and out of the six thinking modes (hats) because the main difficulty with thinking is confusion from doing too much at once.

STORYBOARDING

The storyboarding technique involves writing each new idea on a sheet of paper. As ideas pour forth, each is put up on a wall and organised later into categories and/or sequences. A Post-It pad can be useful for recording ideas: the colourful sheets with sticky backs are easy to assemble and stick on a wall.

THE 20 IDEA METHOD

The 20 Idea Method is my favourite technique and one of the best ways to generate a lot of ideas in a short space of time. The key is to re-write the problem in the form of a question and train the group to follow the Brainstorming guidelines. The problem must be written as a SMART (Specific, Measurable, Agreed upon, Realistic, Time bounded) goal. Then use the 'How to' method to develop your problem statement.

For example, you would not write: 'Let's increase sales.' You would write: 'How do we increase our sales by 5% over the next 30 days?' The idea is that the group members brainstorm with energy and enthusiasm 20 ideas to achieve this objective. An appointed facilitator must encourage and cajole them and not let them opt out until they reach 20 ideas. The 20th idea is often the most valuable and productive.

A BETTER SOLUTION

My organisation was engaged by a transport company in the UK to guide them through a change management process. The general manager of the company had a warehouse storage problem. He had spent considerable time and effort seeking additional warehouse space. He eventually sourced the additional space. However, he was given a better solution at a 20 Idea Brainstorming session in which the warehouse staff participated. They saved this manager €30,000 per year by coming up with three ideas to reorganise the current warehouse structure.

The solutions involved a clean out of old stock, the rearrangement of the packing area and a stacking solution that the warehouse staff, 'the experts on the front line' was already aware of. It was a perfect solution. It was creativity in action. It was innovation personified.

BRAIN WRITING

I use the technique of brain writing all the time. The key is automatic writing. Start somewhere, anywhere. Words, phrases, ideas, abbreviations, diagrams – anything goes. Think on paper. This technique works excellently when you have a new project, an open mind and a surge of enthusiasm.

I find I can roller-coaster on this idea for 10 to 15 minutes and then stop. I simply file the relevant page and come back to it over and over again. Inevitably, I can always add to, categorise and sort out a pattern from the initial smorgasboard of ideas. Sometimes I can start a whole project on the back of a business card during a few minutes while waiting for someone, or even in a traffic jam.

Brain writing with a project planning system is creativity and a system working in harmony. I have up to 20 projects in the pipeline at one time. All are under control. I smile wryly when I see people overwhelmed with two or three projects.

PROBLEM GALLERY

Another version of Brainwriting is Problem Gallery where you write each problem on a separate flip chart and display the charts on the wall around the room. People then walk around the gallery and study each problem, write their ideas and solutions on stickers or directly onto the flipchart. Other people can then view what has been written and these suggestions can in turn trigger new ideas.

The physical activity of moving around is different and, of course, stimulates the creative right side of your brain. I encourage people to use diagrams, cartoons and lots of colour.

SORT OUT IDEAS: THE INNOVATION MATRIX

How do you sort out the ideas that originate from creative thinking techniques and position them for innovation?

Ask yourself if they are useful/practical ideas, or if they are original. Using these two parameters you can categorise these creative ideas into four boxes.

ACHIEVING INNOVATION

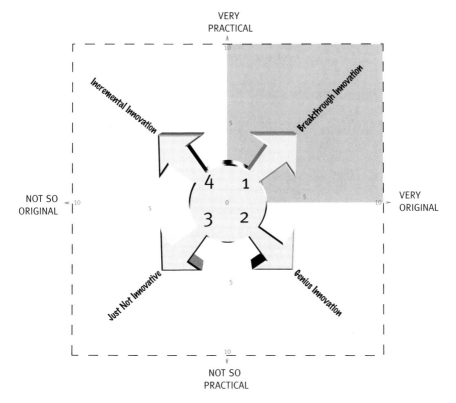

Your ability to creatively originate very practical and very original ideas will lead to breakthrough innovation (Quadrant 1). Breakthrough innovation is critical to creating sustainable strategic advantage.

Quadrant 1 Breakthrough Innovation: This means a total new way of doing things. It involves totally reengineering yourself.

Quadrant 2 Genius Innovation: This often comes from people outside the industry. Every now and then they strike lucky. However, outsiders are turning lots of businesses and industries upside down. Richard Branson, with his Virgin companies, is a genius in this area.

Quadrant 3 Just not Innovation: No apparent application and not so relevant. Well at least it's a home for way-out ideas!

Quadrant 4 Incremental Innovation: This means a series of improvements or modifications are made to an existing product or service. It is Reinvention. These are very practical useful improvements, but not earth-shatteringly novel. Baileys Irish Cream and the musical Riverdance are good examples of reinvention.

STEP IV SELECT THE BEST SOLUTION

Part of the reason why creative problem solving techniques are not used more often is that people confuse the free-for-all roller coaster brainstorming aspects with the need to stick to a disciplined, structured model. After generating lots of valuable ideas and solutions they get side-tracked and lost in the sheer scale of possibilities from their solutions. This is why it is important to sort out and categorise the one best solution. Usually there is a best solution. All the other ideas need not be lost. They could be organised on an ideas board under different themes.

STEP V IMPLEMENT DECISIONS

Many groups put a lot of enthusiasm and energy into generating ideas and solutions. Often times these ideas evaporate because they lack focus or the group simply runs out of energy. This is the advantage of working to a model. The model will help you plan the next step. The purpose of asking the question: 'What action is to be taken?' allows the Leader to set SMART goals. This takes us nicely to the next step which is implementation. Creativity is the start but innovation is implementation. David Ogilvy, the advertising guru says 'It's not creative unless it sells'. Decisiveness. Decisions. Boldness.

STEP VI ASSIGN RESPONSIBILITY FOR THE OUTCOME

You must ensure that someone takes overall responsibility for the implementation of the action steps and plans and their name/or names should be filled in at that time on the chart.

Don't assume or expect that everyone will just execute the actions outlined on the chart. No matter how enthusiastic or how much they swear they will do it, most will not.

One person who commits his or her name to the outcome is better than 20 enthusiastic group members. The reason for this is not malicious. Everyone is busy and everyone assumes too much of one another. Errant assumptions are the core of most failure in this area.

STEP VII AGREE REPORTING AND FEEDBACK PROCEDURE

This is a critical stage to complete the process and to 'lock' in the individuals responsible for taking action to their earlier commitment.

It is important for the upkeep of morale of those group members who contributed to the earlier part of the process. 'What gets measured, gets done' is a good management principle. It is also important to clarify at this point how the outcomes will be communicated back to the main group and when this will take place. Otherwise, a certain cynicism will set in to any future creative thinking technique implemented.

Creating a goal tree chart during the meeting is an effective way to plan out a series of 'next steps' with primary, secondary and tertiary actions outlined. This can be displayed visually and distributed to each member of the team.

It can be useful to evaluate the effectiveness of your creative problem-solving endeavours by asking the group to give you feedback on the effectiveness of using this model.

Simply divide a flipchart down the middle. On one side write:'What went well?' On the other side write:'What we could improve on?' At the end of the meeting, ask for specific feedback from the participants on the effectiveness of the process. Ask for verbal feedback or have them write comments on Post-It pads and stick them on the flipchart as before.

KEEPING MEETINGS PRODUCTIVE

One of the challenges with creative problem-solving techniques is seeing them through to completion – that is, to the innovation stage. How do you keep meetings on track while maintaining maximum energy, involvement and participation to ensure that you get the job done?

Best practice innovation is inevitably a group activity. But it doesn't happen overnight. An innovation culture must seep through the organisation and will be reflected in recruitment policies, manufacturing processes, new product development, the leadership style, project management, and supportive IT systems. Overall, then, innovation is the process that permeates every corner of the business and relies on a range of factors to add value.

Here are some techniques that I have found useful with groups:

Let them talk. Most adults have an insatiable desire to talk. So let them talk by introducing themselves at the outset. A very simple introduction is to have everyone tell the group something they are proud of (their past): something nobody could possibly know about them, a passion, funny incident etc (their present): or an ambition they have (their future). This loosens everyone up and inevitably gets a laugh or two. A combination of humour and relaxation are powerful stimulants for creativity. It sets the atmosphere for a creative flow of ideas and solutions.

Set ground rules. Have participants agree on six to 10 ground rules for the conduct of the meeting. List these on a flipchart. You should also list what should be done if these ground rules are broken. You have to judge when to use some of these ideas. Length of time will be one determinant.

Provide a Parking Lot. To help prevent you from getting side tracked, set aside a 'parking lot', that is, a black/white board, blank sheet or flipchart to list items that are not really on the agenda but have some relevance and may need to be dealt with at a later time.

Force Field Analysis. This is a method that shows both sides of an idea. The best way to deal with an objection (the Naysayers) is to bring it up yourself first. Show the forces that help your idea and those that hinder it.

Keep Time. Appoint a Time Keeper. Ask someone to volunteer to keep track of times and at coffee breaks, lunch etc. This creates involvement. You don't need to do everything – including the thinking.

Present the 'Evening News'. Tell them what you are going to tell them (opening), tell them (middle), and then tell them what you just told them (close). Put extra thought and planning into the Launch (the opening) and the Landing (the close). The middle should concentrate on content (main points), participation and constant review.

Communicate using visuals. A picture is worth a thousand words and people concentrate better and remember much more when you use visual aids. Use charts, overheads, flip charts or any other means of electronic communication to show agenda items, ground rules, discussion questions and exercise instructions.

Use Right Brain techniques. Employ the creative side of the brain by using three or four coloured markers, playing music, having movement and encouraging humour by way of jokes, sketches, drawings and even short video funnies if appropriate. It may seem crazy but crazy is good. We cannot sit around for ten years or even ten hours thinking about a solution. We need it now. Right now.

Take Breaks. It is better to take a 5-10 minute break every 50-70 minutes rather than taking a longer break after, say, two hours. Breaks also allow you to get some informal feedback on the process and talk with individuals who are not as involved or are too involved. Listening and observing skills are the facilitator's temperature checks. By the way, 'facilitation' means 'to make easy'. So make it easy and fun for everyone.

268

MOBILISING BRAINPOWER: Two Minds are better than One

LEFT BRAIN
Logical
Analytical
Linear
Mathematical
Sequential
Conventional

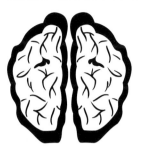

RIGHT BRAIN
Creative
Movement
Humour
Music
Colour
Emotion

Creativity is the starting point of innovation. However, successful creativity depends largely on how you use your brain and your thinking processes. Creativity works best when you integrate the left side and the right side of your brain to turn creative ideas and concepts into practical solutions. 'Integrating' both sides of the brain dramatically increases the quality and quantity of ideas and the overall outcome.

Watch Behavioural Styles. Remember the four different, natural behaviour styles that people tend to display (See Chapter 3). Be aware of these during the meeting. Also try to establish the know-why (the values) of your participants.

Get Kinaesthetic Involvement. One way to keep people involved (especially in a very large group) is to get them writing, drawing or filling in blanks. We learn by listening (auditory), by watching (visual) and by physical involvement (touching, feeling, moving). Be aware that you don't use just one method, ie talking.

Break into Small Groups. Another way to keep involvement and participation is to break the group into smaller groups of two to seven people. Participants can synthesise their ideas and feedback to the main group. Communication is a two way process, even in very large groups.

Set the scene for Creativity Involvement exercises. Tapping into creative teamwork is vitally important in solving complex organisational problems. It is important therefore to create the appropriate atmosphere and prepare the ground for using creative thinking techniques. The 'Nine Dots' exercise is a creative thinking involvement exercise that plugs everybody into realising the limits we impose on ourselves by our traditional formal thinking.

Ask delegates to put nine dots on a sheet of paper and to connect all the dots together using no more than four straight lines and without retracing their steps.

THE NINE DOTS TEST

Put nine dots on a sheet of paper as demonstrated above, or photocopy the above diagram so that you do not mark your book. Your challenge is, within a time-limit of 10 minutes, and without lifting your pencil or retracing your steps, to connect all the dots using no more than four straight lines.

Debrief the exercise by asking, 'What makes it so difficult to think creatively or differently?' 'Why did most people attempt to solve the problem in the traditional way?' 'What are the lessons?' The solution to this problem is given later in this chapter.

Tell two Truths and a Lie. This is another involvement exercise and allows participants to share personal information with other team members. Pair them and ask each person to tell the other person two truths and one lie about themselves. The other person must then guess which of the three statements is a lie. It is a bit of self-revelation and fun and gets the creative juices flowing.

SOURCES OF INSPIRATION FOR CREATIVITY AND INNOVATION

Keep it simple. Organisational creativity is not simply thinking up one brilliant idea and innovation is not simply the implementation of it. Organisational innovation is the process of consistently examining and systematically harnessing ideas emerging from three critical areas:

1 CUSTOMERS
What are they buying from you and why?
What do they like about you?
What improvement would they like to see in your product and service performance?
How are *their* areas changing?
How is their world changing?
Listen carefully to the ordinary questions your customer ask.

2 EMPLOYEES

What core competencies are your employees under-using right now?

What competencies will be needed in three years' time (ie technically)?

What information gathering system is in place to monitor and feedback critical activities and processes?

Do your employees feel 'responsible' to suggest improvements?

3 THE EXTERNAL WORLD

What economic or social tends are occurring? (lifestyles, spending)?

What are your competitors doing? (Market niches etc)

How are some of the best companies encouraging, stimulating and applying creative ideas?

3M's goal is to generate €30 M of its sales from products launched in the previous four years. Employees there are allowed to spend up to 15% of their time experimenting on creative ideas and innovation outside of their main function: it's a cultural thing. They have institutionalised creativity and innovation and everyone is involved. It's Empowerment in action. Their 'Don't kill a project' philosophy allowed Spencer Silver to keep his non-sticking glue idea alive until a colleague was in need of a lightly adhesive book mark for his hymn book. The Post-it pad was born! The rest, as they say, is history.

APPROACHES TO RESEARCH AND DEVELOPMENT

'The enterprise that does not innovate inevitably ages and dies. And in a period of rapid change such as the present, an entrepreneurial period, that demise will be fast' – Peter Drucker.

The key to economic growth is innovation, research and development and the key to innovation, research and development is Creative Thinking. The ever-changing demands of today's consumers means that suppliers must anticipate those demands and attempt to respond immediately to an emerging trend, fad or fashion.

Innovation means making changes and introducing new or novel ways in which your organisation operates or updates the products and services it provides. There are two main approaches to innovation:

1 The first is a market-led innovation process where the starting point is the end-user or consumer demanding new products and services due to new tastes, trends, new fashions or social factors and technology developments.

2 The second innovation is a technology-driven process which arises from the various skills and activities needed to supply them.

The idea of an invention is easily understood by most people. Innovation is the commercial exploitation of an invention. An invention is mainly involved in the technology-driven innovation process. However, market innovation requires a broader range of skills such as market information, management skills, access to finance, legal support in regard to intellectual property rights, copyrights and trademarks and, of course, an understanding of technology.

There is a fundamental difference between the two approaches to innovation. The phases in the technology-driven research are as follows:

1 Basic research, which involves research on topics which have no immediate market relevance but which test theories or concepts. Nobel prizes in Chemistry and Physics are typically awarded in this category.

2 Applied Research, which involves applying the results of basic research to an industrial sector. It is the checkout stage.

3 Technical prototypes are working models which prove that the product will work. Often the technical capability of the product is proven but not the economic viability. The commercial prototype addresses such issues as design for manufacture, quality control, product liability, appearance, documentation, training, economics. This is the crucial phase in the commercialisation of research and development.

The market-led innovation process, on the other hand, starts with the end user in mind and shows that the commercial prototype should only be developed if products do not exist on the market. Technical prototypes and applied research should only be done if commercial prototypes do not exist. This may sound like pure common sense but most R&D development programmes are developed around the technology-driven innovation process rather than the market-led innovation process. The emphasis is changing however and in order to guarantee public funding Universities and research centres are now more inclined to ensure that their work is relevant to the market to guarantee public funding.

Ireland receives up to €25m per year from EU R&D funding but the opportunity for entrepreneurial marketing and R&D people to work together definitely exists.

A typical business could have the following innovation goals:
- Customer Service improvement. Love the customer to death by looking for improvements in the Moments of Impression.
- Product/Service Improvement. Always be asking: How can we improve our present product or service? (Methodology innovation).
- New Products or Services that are needed to attain market objectives.
- New Products or Services that are needed because of technological changes that may make present products obsolete.
- What else does my customer need? (Market innovation).
- New Process and Improvements in old processes (Operational innovation) needed to satisfy market goals ie manufacturing improvements to make possible the attainment of pricing objectives.

INNOVATION IS CONSTANT IMPROVEMENT

Innovations and improvements can be made in all major areas of activity such as accounting or product design, office management or labour relations so as to keep up with advances in knowledge and skill. You need to think what your core competencies will need to be in three years' time.

What are the leaders in your industry doing, and indeed, in other industries? Market leaders are innovators. Their attitude is that the best self-defence is attack. They are always launching new products. They are always seeking new ways to improve. So innovation at its simplest is constant improvement in efficiency and quality.

Innovative capability is an intellectual property and at first it is the only resource that R&D types have. There is a growing awareness that investment needs to increase in developing the creative research and development and innovative process. Because it is filled with risk and uncertainty, small companies tend not to spend on it at all. They occupy themselves copying what the competition does and trying to differentiate it with a different shade or colour.

Few members of the accounting profession, of course, have recognised that such things as brands, research in the pipeline and the know-how of its people have value. The channels of distribution and supply all have a value which is inadequately described as goodwill. Machinery can be easily written down as having value, but how much is talent worth? How much is an idea worth?

Bill Gates of Microsoft has demonstrated that soft technology is worth billions of dollars. In 1988, Philip Morris, the USA Fortune 500 giant, paid $12.9b for Kraft. Less than $2b of that was tangible assets, the rest was intangibles.

Because of an attitude that what is not counted doesn't count, there is a serious worry that there is a built-in bias across all industry sectors against long term R&D. There is, of course, the other school of creativity and innovation that says 'just try it, cut the crap and get on with it'. It is a ready, aim, fire philosophy, a 'constantly re-organise' approach, and there is lots of evidence that this crazy approach works.

Peter Saunders of the Imperial College in London says that there are only two ways to create business ideas. Generate your own or develop someone else's. The latter is more common as virtually every successful business is developed from another business concept. The person who invented the first wheel was probably an idiot. The person who invented the other three wheels was a genius. It's called creative imitation.

CREATIVITY LUBRICATES
Everything outlined in this book is lubricated by creative innovation. Change management *is* creativity and innovation. Change Management is creativity in action. How you deploy your resources requires innovation. Your personality is dead without learning and growth. That's creativity. Strategy *is* creativity, *is* marketing, *is* communication, *is* innovation.

HERE'S THE KEY POINT!
Creative and innovative entrepreneurial managers are constantly talking and thinking about their values, mission, vision and strategic goals. They think about their customers and market opportunities all the time. They use informal, yet system thinking approaches. They cultivate high levels of trust, communication and information flow. They invest in the soft, intangible resources of human capital, knowledge and time. They are entrepreneurial, innovative managers.

APPLICATION STEPS
1 Teach your team some creative techniques, then generate some ideas. That's creativity. Then apply these ideas to improve your current situation. That's innovation. Pick something obvious that will give you an early win, for example sales increase or order processing.

2 You are creative. Accept this. Now build on it. Think on paper. Do it all the time. You are innovative. Just apply those creative ideas. Here's a creative idea for you: Have one creative thinking meeting per month with your team using these techniques.

3 What research and development project could you open a file on right now? Is this a project that only you can do? Would it make a significant difference if you completed it really well? Well then, start with one sheet and a blank file.

4 Genius is 99% hard work. Follow the seven steps process outlined in this chapter to its completion on one project over the next month.

ANSWER TO NINE DOTS TEST

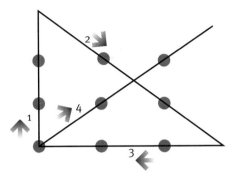

The capacity of most people to originate new ideas is constrained by their pre-existing mental set. They have a self-imposed box on their minds. You must think outside that box. Most people who are trying the nine dots test for the first time, fail the test. The problem may be tackled in different ways. One way may be to fold the paper so that the three lines of dots are aligned. Then a single wide pencil line will touch all the dots.
Another is, as shown in the diagram, to start with the dot on the lower left corner, and drawing to north of the third dot, which is beyond the immediate field of the dots, to continue drawing in the direction of the arrows. It's an outside the box solution!

PITOC™ INNOVATION

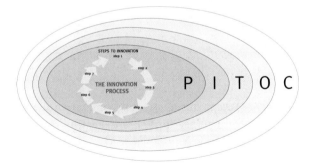

Turning creative thinking and innovative projects into personal and business advantage is the very essence of entrepreneurial management.
Practising this at all five PITOC™ levels is central to your success.

8

REINVENTING PERSONAL

AND

BUSINESS LEARNING

'To know and not to do is not yet to know
To know is to have gained knowledge
To do is to have gained wisdom'

The pure entrepreneur tends to learn by trial and error and from the hard knocks of business. The professional manager tends to learn by taking a business degree, by attending seminars and by reading books. Both methods of learning are expensive. They are also potentially non-productive or even destructive for companies for different reasons.

A more progressive approach to learning is necessary. Your approach as the entrepreneurial manager should be to become a 'continuous learning machine'. This will help you to manage the information explosion, technology development, time compression and the accelerating pace of change. You must keep discovering better, faster, cheaper, easier, newer and different ways to learn.

In the 'old days' it was sufficient to go to school, get a job and career, then throw the schoolbooks away. You would operate on your initial education for a whole lifetime. Today this would be disastrous. In the 21st century, you can expect to totally re-educate yourself at least five to ten times in the average career span because of the explosion of information and the rapid rate of change.

An MBA is virtually obsolete from the minute you qualify. It can be costly, slow and far too traditional in its approach, and virtually useless if not applied in practical ways. There are many not-so-smart business graduates and equally as many clued-in continuous learners. Too many of them do not understand the shocking reality that a lot of learning is unlearning what they have already learned.

As an entrepreneurial manager you make a decision not just to learn from experience. This is reactive learning where the test comes first, and the lessons later. Instead you get the knowledge and the skills ahead of time from the best minds and methods available. However, you don't have the luxury of three or more years to grasp this information in a degree course. You must find a new way to learn – a faster, better, cheaper, easier, newer, different way – such as Accelerated Learning.

RELEARNING TO LEARN

This age of strategic change, knowledge management, reinventing, rethinking and new technology requires managers to be equipped to adapt quickly to new situations and opportunities. You must unlearn the old ways (habits) and relearn the new ways but within a much shorter time frame.

In my experience, the pure entrepreneur rarely takes a proactive learning approach. Professional managers in large organisations tend to have some formal management education. Managers in small and medium-sized businesses have little, if any, formal management training or education. They are expected to somehow understand the science of management because they were good at an operative level, or because of certain personal qualities. This approach is so naïve that it is frightening. Yet it's a fact of life in Ireland today.

The Government tell us that less than 1% of payroll is invested in training and development in Ireland today. In France, more than 3% of payroll is invested. In Germany, it is almost 5%. Moreover, it is the multinationals and the larger organisations here that conduct most of this 1% of training and development. They invest 4% to 8% of their payrolls in training and development. This means that many small and medium organisations invest little in developing their people.

TAKE RESPONSIBILITY FOR YOUR OWN LEARNING, FIRST

As the entrepreneurial manager you realise that this is not only a major problem, but also a major opportunity. You invest your time, energy and money in personal and professional development. You embrace the ideas outlined in this chapter, regardless of the obstacles, time constraints or lack of foresight within your own organisation. You seek out the almost limitless amount of knowledge and information available.

You realise that once your mind is expanded by new ideas, you will never return to your old way of thinking. You realise that the average individual invests about €250 per year on the outside of their heads (shampoos, creams, soaps, toothpastes etc), yet the average manager buys, at most, two or three books for his or her own personal, professional and business development.

You know that you don't need to make all the mistakes yourself, that you can gain the knowledge and skill ahead of time from the experiences of others. You discuss new techniques, attend seminars, read and withdraw to a quiet haven to think, reflect and plan.

As an entrepreneurial manager, you realise that most people have left the formal education system with a dislike for learning or, at least, a reluctance to become self-learners. Somehow the idea has developed that the government or our employers have a responsibility to educate us. This is a self-limiting belief and even dangerous thinking.

Make a decision right now to work on your own personal growth and professional development as a first step towards maximising your performance and unleashing all the potential within you. It's a self-responsibility issue. You must accelerate the pace at which you upgrade your own competencies.

Your next step is to work with other individuals on a one-to-one basis, encouraging them, teaching them, coaching them to become the best people and managers and workers they can possibly be. By doing this, you gain an extra benefit because you, 'the teacher', always learns more than your 'student' does. By teaching these ideas and explaining them to other people, you automatically become better yourself. How you approach this second step will be discussed later in this chapter.

The natural extension of personal development and one-to-one excellence is within the team or small group environment. Can you influence, direct, motivate, or mobilise more than one or two people to embrace the learning and development mentality and apply it for the overall good of the team?

Your ultimate challenge is how to gain a competitive advantage for your organisation through learning and people power. How do you deploy the under-utilised human capital already resident in your organisation? Your objective should be not to be just the best in your field, but to be regarded as so good that you are differentiated as the only one who does what you do in your field. The learning organisation may be the answer in achieving this objective.

I am a personal fanatic on learning and development. I thoroughly read more than 50 books per year. I speed-read another 50. I read executive book summaries (eight page summaries) of another 50. I listen to hours and hours of audiotape as I drive. I view videos all the time. I invest a minimum of 20 days attending conferences or seminars each year. I surf the Internet for

Interactive Computer Based Training (CBT) and to research learning opportunities. I subscribe to about 20 publications and I read newspapers for current maintenance reading.

Continuous learning is an integral part of everything we do in our own organisation. This is our mission statement:

'We partner with our clients to create business advantage by energising individuals, teams and organisations to maximise their full potential'.

Our four core values are:

1 To conduct our business with energy, integrity and professionalism in a client-focused team culture.

2 To be continually improving the effectiveness of our solutions, services and products for the benefit and success of our clients.

3 To be continuously learning and innovating in our personal, interpersonal, team, organisational and client developments.

4 To establish and develop mutually rewarding relationships with all our stakeholders.

Learning, innovation and changing is a central part of everything that we do ourselves and everything we do with our clients. Unfortunately, this idea has been slow to catch on for many managers – it must catch on for you if you are to reach your full potential.

WHY WE NEED TO RETHINK OUR APPROACH TO LEARNING

Before I outline some techniques on how you might embrace the learning and development culture for yourself, it would be useful to clarify why we need to rethink our attitudes to learning.

The major reasons are the social, economic and political changes embracing every aspect of your personal and working lives. Communism has fallen. China is awakening. E-Commerce and worldwide networks mean you can do business in a borderless economy. Brainpower industries are flourishing. New economic powerhouses develop almost overnight and change is not just constant but exponential.

Newer technological miracles drive fiercer competition, and greater customer demands and expectations. This means that flexibility and responsiveness to innovation and change must be rapid. This is why you need to rethink learning–your intellectual capital needs to keep pace with rapid change in other areas.

I spoke with Daniel Goleman, the psychologist and author of *Emotional Intelligence* that has sold more than three million copies. He argues that the human competencies like self-discipline, persistence and empathy are better indicators of life success than IQ and that you ignore the decline in these competencies at your peril. Our view of intelligence and learning is far too narrow. IQ is not destiny.

Following ground breaking research, Goleman shows the factors at work when people of high IQ flounder and those of modest IQ do surprisingly well. These factors add up to a different way of being smart which he calls 'emotional intelligence.' As Goleman demonstrates, the personal costs of deficits in Emotional Intelligence can range from problems in marriage and parenting to poor physical health. New research shows that chronic anger and anxiety creates as great a physical risk as chain smoking.

I have found that business owners 'get mad' and 'personalise' stupidity at work on a regular basis. Outbursts of anger can set things back months, even years, in terms of emotional safety and morale. You must learn this Emotional Intelligence.

What is Emotional Intelligence? Emotional Intelligence is knowing what you are feeling and being able to handle those feelings without having them swamp you. It's performing at your best, being creative and handling relationships effectively.

It has five component parts:

1 Self-Awareness : Knowing your feelings as you have them.
2 Managing Moods: Soothing anxiety, cheering yourself up, handling anger effectively.
3 Motivation: Hope and optimism in the face of setbacks and frustration.
4 Empathy: Reading unstated emotional moods.
5 Social Skills: Managing emotions in relationships.

Work on learning Emotional Intelligence. Your life may depend on it. Your entrepreneurial management competencies certainly will. For Irish men, me included, this is a big challenge I suspect, but we must try to improve it. I believe that Irish women are naturally more emotionally intelligent than Irish men.

The only truly intelligent person of the 21st Century will be the one who learns how to learn, and then relearns. It is 'learning innovation' in practice. In all of human history this same degree of 'relearning' has never been necessary before. Today it is essential. You must relearn or die.

BEWARE THE PEAKS AND VALLEYS OF THE LEARNING JOURNEY

To become a 'born again' learner you need to learn some of the models and techniques that can help accelerate your learning journey. You will have learning peaks and valleys for every new endeavour you undertake. Knowing where you are on this journey can help you progress through it more successfully.

THE PEAKS AND VALLEYS OF LEARNING

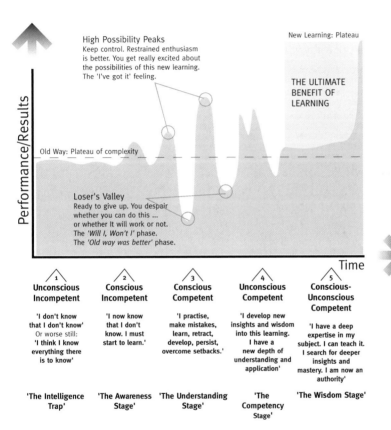

Learning means changing. It's a personal, team or whole organisational change process. However, you must be aware of the traps that await you. Your goal is long term gain. The Peaks and Valleys model will help you understand the journey of learning.

The path to improved performance and long term results takes time and means progressing through ups (Peaks) and downs (Valleys) to ultimately reach a new level in learning (a new Plateau). To reach this new level of improved performance and learning can require you to progress through five stages of Consciousness and Competence. Learning is a never ending journey.

Discipline is doing the things you have to do (Seeing it through) when you have to do it (In the Valley period) whether you like it or not.

281

Learning means changing. Changing means risk. These risks involve being alert to the ups and downs of learning. Let me explain. When you embark on improving your current performance you may get exhilarating highs ('I've got it'), or depressing lows ('It won't work'). My advice is not to get carried away with either state. Just be aware they are natural human feelings as you move from your old habits to a new learning plateau.

Outlined below are the five stages of learning in terms of competency and consciousness:

STAGE 1 UNCONSCIOUS-INCOMPETENT

The Unconscious-Incompetent stage of learning is when you are incompetent in your ability to do something, but you don't know it. Your confidence may even exceed your competence. This is the most deadly of all management traps – the intelligence trap. The mental thought process may be, 'I don't know that I don't know', or 'I don't need to learn, grow or develop' in a particular area, or worse still, 'I already know everything there is to know because of my background or education'.

Before learning to ride a bicycle or drive a car, most of us are unconsciously incompetent. We think it's easy but we quickly realise that, once we get up on the saddle or get behind the wheel, it is actually quite complicated.

STAGE 2 CONSCIOUS-INCOMPETENT

At the Conscious-Incompetent stage you realise that you are incompetent. Your confidence and performance levels drop as you realise that your ability is limited. Your thinking is 'I now know that I don't know.' Or you realise that 'my current knowledge is not relevant to this new situation.'

Awareness of the current situation is the key to moving forward. This is the Loser Trap and many people abandon the learning challenge at this stage and just give up the exercise. 'I'm not good at it anyway', or 'I'm not cut out for this.'

A golf professional explained to me that most golfers have a downturn in performance after getting some lessons from him. Some just return to their old, bad habits of playing and give up on the new way and learn nothing. But some stick with the new way and improve to the next step.

STAGE 3 CONSCIOUS-COMPETENT

At the Conscious-Competent stage you consciously work on improving your competence by practice, drill and repetition. You have to focus on all aspects of becoming excellent at the task in hand. Think about those early days in learning any new skill. You must stick with it. Your attitude keeps you practising, improving and learning. You climb out of the 'learned helplessness' comfort zone – you do not abandon the new journey. You must climb out of the Loser's Trap.

Your mindset is that imperfect practice makes perfect. In your mindset, you love the journey, the mistakes, the struggle – not the destination, the end product. A 29-year-old MBA graduate wrote to me looking for a job in consulting. He felt his education entitled him to advise and demand a starting salary of twice what I would offer him. He forgot the conscious-competent step.

STAGE 4 UNCONSCIOUS-COMPETENT

The Unconscious-Competent stage is where you don't have to think about knowing it. You do it automatically. In your car, you can change the gears and look at passers-by with total ease and no sense of stress or tension. Your ability to co-ordinate a whole series of competencies unconsciously is not difficult for you. Your depth of knowledge, skill levels and mental and physical agility are excellent and fine-tuned. Peak performance comes 'naturally' to you.

STAGE 5 CONSCIOUS-UNCONSCIOUS-COMPETENT

The Conscious-Unconscious-Competent level is the ultimate challenge for the entrepreneurial manager. It's the start of a higher order learning curve when you realise 'the more you know, the more you don't know'. You may have a 'crisis' here as you realise you don't know as much as you thought you knew. However, you quickly regain the lost ground and set off into a new orbit. Not only can you do things automatically, you can transfer that know-how to other individuals, teams and indeed the whole organisation.

Many people who have reached a peak performance level in selling, for instance (Stage 4), have great difficulty in transferring their 'intellectual capital' and know-how to other people. Computer whiz kids are often the same – they forget what it is like to be a beginner and over-talk their subject. They can explain what they do. They can even show you what they do. But somehow, for many, there is a missing link.

Being conscious of your Unconscious-Competence and realising that not everybody can grasp what seems obvious to you is the ultimate step in learning. You are not only unconsciously applying your knowledge, skills and core competencies but you understand the process as it happens and you therefore have a higher understanding of it.

In my public talks and presentations, a lot of spontaneous humour opportunities arise. I am not a comedian but I regularly get a spontaneous roar of laughter from members of my audience because I realise the benefit of humour to connect with and relax everyone. It's a conscious-unconscious - competency. I teach public speaking and presentation skills to managers but usually at Stage 3 (the Conscious-Competent level). If I can get them to Stage 4 during the process, this is exceptional. Therefore as I speak myself, I almost have a dual thinking process operating in parallel: 1) the content of my talk and 2) the process and techniques with which I deliver it.

For most people, being the Unconscious-Competent (Stage 4) will be perfectly adequate but you may want to be aware of an urge within you to explore your areas of excellence at deeper and deeper levels. 'We teach what we most want to learn' is profound psychology and may explain your absorption with a particular subject. To gain wisdom and insight – even enlightenment – truly requires deeper understanding of learning itself and also the subject matter. Abraham Maslow says that the ultimate motivator is the search for truth. This means exploration, discovery and learning.

You must continually explore your subject and the teacher/coach/mentor will develop a more in-depth understanding of the subject. This is indeed higher order thinking where best solutions appear more readily, the right answers pop to mind and generally you are regarded as an expert and an authority on your subject. To become 'the master' is the ultimate challenge for the entrepreneurial manager.

The experience curve is always a factor, of course. A person with little or no experience would take ten hours to do what you could do in one insightful moment. Simplicity beyond knowledge is a gift. Simplicity before you have the experience and knowledge may be dangerous. 'A moment's insight is sometimes worth a life's experience', wrote Oliver Wendell Holmes. Exactly.

KOLB'S LEARNING CYCLE

Here is a process of learning from experience which covers four stages. David Kolb developed this cycle and you can jump on anywhere depending on your own style. Be careful, he suggests, not to stay too long in any one place.

THE ACTION LEARNING PROCESS

The learning process requires action, but concrete experience (1) alone gives divergent knowledge. Reflective observation (2) helps transform and assimilate this knowledge. Further comprehension and conceptualisation (3) leads to convergent knowledge. Finally, active experimentation (4) leads to complete learning and knowing.

ACTION

Learning new practical tasks by just getting stuck in with a hands-on approach can be a powerful process. Just start somewhere. Start anywhere. It's a here-and-now approach. It's practical to learn from mistakes and experiences. If you want to learn how to swim, get in the water. If you want to learn how to brainstorm then get your group together and do it. If you want to learn computers, then sit in front of one, turn it on and start using it. If you want to learn how to learn, well then, use some of the techniques in this chapter. An old Chinese proverb sums it up: 'You will stand for a long time with your mouth open before a duck flies in.'

'I've never been a good reader', a business owner said to me when we were talking about books. 'Well then start' I suggested, 'Buy one book' (his first business book, ever). He did and he's now studying, and learning how to speed-read on audiotape.

Hands-on action is a good starting point but it's often divergent knowledge and needs to be pulled together. Yellow temperament styles love this approach. (See Chapter 3)

REFLECTION

Reflective observation and effective feedback and review of the actions taken are essential to Stage 2. The motivational question 'What did I do well?' and the developmental question 'What could I improve on?' are simple but effective ways to avoid blind spots and get honest learning points for the future. Remember, you are responsible (response-able!) for your own learning.

One of the key roles of the sales manager is to 'shadow' his sales reps on calls – to sit in on customer interviews but not to talk, take over or take away from any significant action. The real learning happens after the call, when he asks the two questions above and gives and receives feedback. By reviewing, you help transform and assimilate the knowledge you gain in the action stage. Green temperament styles tend to reflect more.

THEORY

Stage 3 involves the introduction or formation of theories or concepts to improve future performance. By doing this now, the learner has a practical experience of operating without them and can therefore put them in context and understand how and why they should be applied. They can appreciate the inter-relationship between the experience, the theory and the techniques. The sales manager, for example, can suggest some of his knowledge, even wisdom, and sales techniques to help his sales reps.

'There is no expedient to which man will not go to avoid the real labour of thinking,' wrote Thomas Edison. You must conceptualise and comprehend at a deeper level to really gain the long-term benefit. You bring together all the action and theory into convergent knowledge.

Blue temperament styles exemplify this learning style.

ADAPTATION: LEARNING AND KNOWING

Where acting and reflection have provided the framework for new models for learning, familiar tasks can now be planned and carried through with a new approach, adapting the best of practical experience and theoretical solutions for any given situation. This is pragmatically adapted behaviour change in action.

Red temperament styles love risk, application, practice and role modelling. They love learning and knowing for application purposes.

Your key is to resist taking short cuts with this model. Remember that nature may be stronger than nurture in your personality make-up. Make the time to reflect on and apply the learning model that will make doing a similar task much easier and quicker the second time around. Kolb's learning model allows you to have a system to manage every experience far beyond the experience itself.

THE SELF-DEVELOPMENT REVOLUTION

Self-development or personal development is about you, the entrepreneurial manager, taking the primary responsibility for your own learning and development, and for choosing how to go about doing this. This requires a fundamental paradigm shift from traditional education and the formal management development approach.

The formal management development approach has, unintentionally, de-skilled managers and caused a considerable amount of cynicism and scepticism towards what is, in itself, a good approach. In 1967, Marshall McLuhan, a Canadian professor, wrote a book called *The Medium is the Message.* He suggested that the major impacts of books had more to do with the formal medium and its implications on a psychological and social level than on anything to do with the content or messages within the pages.

Several centuries ago, the printed word made ideas and knowledge mass-produceable so they ceased to be the exclusive province of a well-educated elite who used them to control others. Television can make the distribution of ideas and knowledge instant and conditions us to see the world in a certain way. Today's electronic communication is even more instant and expansive. The potential of the Internet, Intranet and Extranet is only starting.

Ironically, the traditional management development programme solves many of the needs and challenges of today's manager. The curricula, content and message are quite similar. But what is the medium doing? The underlying message seems to be that there is an expert for every type of management situation. Therefore, if you have a management problem, come to the experts. Furthermore, the message seems to be that you don't need to know how to learn because we – the experts – are the fountains of all knowledge and you can always come back to us.

This line of thinking, I believe, has for generations kept managers in a state of paralysis. Worse still, it has probably got them believing that they are incapable of up-skilling their own capabilities and potential. The majority of business owners and managers that I meet on a daily basis just don't believe they have the capability within themselves to solve their own problems. This is 'learned helplessness.' You must avoid it like the plague.

Most of my work as a consultant is helping people learn how to solve their own problems. Most individuals are simply amazed when you give them the key to unlock their own potential for achievement or career development or improve the performance of their organisation. Learning how to define, measure and develop your core competencies is central to 21st century learning.

THE JOHARI WINDOW

The Johari Window is a self-development matrix for analysing interpersonal skills and helping you to carry out a self-appraisal assessment.

THE JOHARI WINDOW

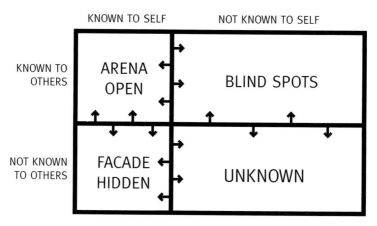

The model gives you a framework to become more aware of areas for development in your behaviour and communications patterns. Joseph Luft, a psychologist and Harry Ingram, a psychiatrist (Joe and Harry, hence the Johari Window) developed the model to show four 'panes' in a window, each area representing an aspect of our behaviour. Each panel can reduce or enlarge in size depending on awareness levels, feedback and learning openness.

The first pane is called Arena which shows aspects known to yourself and known to others, where you have little reason to be defensive. I have often found in a new group that there may not be much free and spontaneous expression in the beginning. As the group members get to know each other, the pane expands in size as people talk and act in a more relaxed way.

The second pane is the Blind Spots (known to others but not to self). These can include mannerisms, annoying phrases that we use, facial gestures or attitudes. Feedback and learning awareness again are important to cure them.

I have a client who had an annoying, fidgeting movement with his head and neck, combined with some flippant throwaway phrases, which became the butt of jokes, wry smiles and nicknames. It affected his credibility. He wasn't even aware of it until I made an audio and video tape of him during an executive mentoring session. Of course, the cure was relatively simple.

The third pane is the Unknown (not known to self or others). Your sub-conscious mind stores virtually every memory and experience and therefore, where there is a willingness to self-disclose some of these deeper mysteries within us, many of these memories surface and free up the mind for learning. We are all prisoners of our experiences and it may help you to 'be all that you can be'. For some, this is very risky learning but it can also be a very powerful release. There is a universal anxiety about this area and this is held in check by social custom, status and diverse fears.

The fourth pane is the Facade (known to self but hidden to others). Fear of failure and fear of rejection are the root causes of this in most cases. 'I'm a fraud', a manager told me once. I asked him what he meant. He replied: 'Well, I'm an empty shell inside. Everybody thinks I'm full of personality, but it's a mask I wear at work. I've crawled my way to this position and everyone thinks I'm doing well but I feel a total imposter.'

So I worked with this person on building a new self-worth and self-respect over a 12-month period. As stress and guilt levels dropped, enjoyment, acceptance and contribution at home and work increased markedly. He took a three-week family holiday for the first time in five years. This was one indicator of major change.

Another client explained to me how he had spent 20 years climbing the ladder of success only to realise when he got to the top, that the ladder was leaning against the wrong wall!

You may also use the Johari Window to pattern the development of your group. The Arena pane may be small at the outset as few people give or seek information. A change in any one pane, of course, affects all the others. It takes energy to hide or deny your thoughts and motives. Interpersonal learning means that a change has taken place in Arena. The smaller the Arena pane is, the poorer the communication.

A LEARNING FRAMEWORK

Your core competencies or your 'collective learning' capability is made up of your character and temperament (see Chapter 3) factors and your actions which are the observable reflection of your competencies. Academics will debate forever what a competency is and what it is not. You and I will just grasp the essence of the concept and get on with its application. You identify your natural competencies and gifts and cultivate them. The three domains of learning are knowledge, skill and attitude, and they provide a simple framework for developing your understanding of your competencies. Use this framework for your own learning and development.

THE DOMAINS OF LEARNING

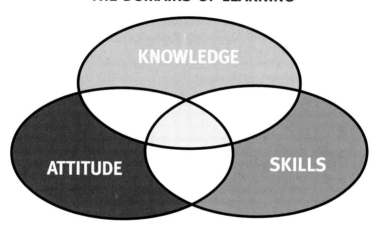

You can decide the level of emphasis that you place on the three domains of learning, whether it is knowledge or attitude or skills or all three domains. You can also decide the time at which to place the emphasis and the factor that needs emphasis now. You may have a strength in one and a weakness in another. What emphasis should you give these three domains of learning? And at what time? Which 'button' needs pushing right now?

KNOWLEDGE

As an entrepreneurial manager, you 'get' the basic knowledge and information you require. You don't wait for such knowledge to be given to you or for some angel or mentor to appear as if by magic and coach you. Self-development is about self-responsibility. You make it your business to know the strategic intentions of your organisation.

You have solid product and technical knowledge.

You realise that individuals, as well as organisations, have core competencies and that these are developed. You realise the importance of 'hard' information such as facts and figures, and the 'soft' information that is about the values and culture and feelings of your staff and colleagues. You develop an insatiable appetite for information that you turn into knowledge. From this comes insight and wisdom.

FROM DATA TO WISDOM

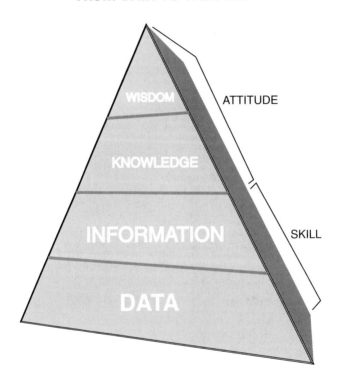

There are four stages in transforming data into wisdom. It's a distillation process. Each stage brings a higher order value to the other.
How you use the store of data and information at your disposal is an operational skill issue. Your intelligence and attitude determines the level of knowledge and wisdom that you achieve from this data and information.

What is knowledge? My reply to that question is: 'Knowledge is information that has been transformed to add value to your organisation and can be used to create more value beyond its original point of entry.' Look at it this way. Every organisation has data. Data is the raw material of information. Procedural systems, computer software tools and IT systems help organise this data to the point where it becomes information. There are lots of well-known automation solutions in organising data and information into business intelligence and knowledge. Experts at IBM say less than 10% of business data is ever analysed.

Your problem starts with the transition from information to its use as value added knowledge. 'In your thirst for knowledge, be sure not to drown in all the information' wrote Anthony D'Angelo. Your mission is to sell this idea to your people.

I was discussing this with a clothing retailer who had difficulty grasping the concept. She wondered at what point does information become knowledge when your customer is buying clothes? Well, think about it. It's the fitting stage, of course. Matching and co-ordinating cloth, accessories and colour schemes meets and adds value to the customer's needs.

The final stage in the Knowledge Triangle is Wisdom – your collective experience, expertise, skill and insight. You will notice that knowledge and wisdom are attitude and people-centred while data and information is system or skill-driven. One great challenge for leaders is to institutionalise ('bottle') their wisdom so that more people can utilise it. The challenge of course is that 'knowledge comes, but wisdom lingers.'

My clothing retailer told me how she advised and sourced special fabrics and outfits for key clients. They appreciated her special insight into buying clothes. More expensive clothes are really cheaper because you get more wear out of them and you have the added value of a sharper image. Many men buy €100 shoes that look cheap, are uncomfortable and wear out quicker. Paying €250 for shoes that look good, that give you six times the wear and are comfortable is obviously a better deal. That's wisdom. How it applies to your business is the question.

A UK survey in 1997 entitled *The Fact Gap Survey* found that, when making decisions, 88% of sales and marketing managers use gut feelings rather than hard facts up to 75% of the time. They do this despite having desktop computers loaded with hard facts. How reliant are you on others for providing information (too little, too late)? How consistent and accessible is your information (a single version of the truth) for decision-making and planning processes? Have you transferred your information into knowledge (Human and Organisational Capital)? How much wisdom is distilled from this intellectual capital? Have you a business strategy to exploit the information age technologies?

You may need to drive data and information integration projects across your organisation. The rise of loyalty and customer profitability analysis as highly effective marketing tools has prompted the widespread desire by sales and marketing teams to segment their prospects by ever-increasing business dimensions to facilitate proactive selection and deselection of customers.

Data warehousing is a process, for example, of replicating, combining, cleaning and transforming data to make it easy to manipulate and access, consistent and understandable. This data becomes useful information and ready to become added value knowledge.

There is a story told of a young man who came to Socrates and said: 'How can I gain more knowledge?' Socrates walked the young man onto the beach and into the sea. When they were both waist high in water, he grabbed him by the neck, pushed him under the water and held him there for several minutes until he struggled violently to catch his breath. Socrates let him up and asked him: 'What did you want more than anything else while you were under the water?' The young man, gasping for breath answered 'Air'. Wise old Socrates replied: 'Well, when you want knowledge with the same passion as you wanted that air, you will receive all the knowledge (and information) you desire.' When the student is ready, the teacher and the opportunities will appear. That's Attitude.

'Prepare! The day will come when Winter will ask what you were doing all Summer', wrote Henry Clay.

The entrepreneurial manager is constantly 'getting ready' by preparing and by learning and is, therefore, alert for the opportunities that will inevitably arise. The ordinary individual is rarely ready and therefore never sees the opportunities that come his way. He constantly bemoans his lack of opportunity and his bad luck. He truly is in the Unconscious-Incompetent intelligence trap, and there are many well-educated Unconscious-Incompetents.

Every good manager should be able to solve problems creatively on an ongoing basis. This is where knowledge, experience and expertise come to the fore. As an entrepreneurial manager you will be asked frequently to make judgement calls. Your ability to make above-average quality decisions will be in proportion to the amount of your background work, and your investment of time in reading, investigating, questioning, and observing your databank of knowledge. It's not luck. LUCK is Labour Under Correct Knowledge.

'Luck' is when preparation meets knowledge and opportunity. Investment in ongoing learning gives you a distinctive edge over those who do not have such learning. An old Chinese proverb says: 'If you want to think for 10 years, you plant a tree. If you want to think for 100 years, you plant education and learning.' Wisdom favours the prepared mind.

SKILL – FROM KNOWING TO KNOW-HOW

An old definition of management is: 'Getting things done through other people.' You, the entrepreneurial manager, will see management in a much broader perspective. This definition zooms in on one key attribute of a manager's skills, which is that of social intelligence. As well as the ability to use your knowledge to read the situation, make sensible value judgements and solve problems, you as an entrepreneurial manager develop skills and expertise on managing change. You also develop skills and expertise in innovation, strategic thinking and planning, delegating, negotiating, resolving conflict, stress management, maximising technology, motivation, lifelong learning, time management, presentation skills, persuading, selling and, of course, communications.

ATTITUDE: FROM KNOWING TO KNOWING-HOW, TO KNOWING HOW TO BE

Everybody is capable of becoming an entrepreneurial manager. The biggest limiting factor is you and your thinking. You can learn thinking and attitude adjustment. How to do this is a mystery for many managers. Sadly, few people grasp the simplicity of how it can be done. Be careful, that you read 'simplicity', not 'easiness'.

The development to become an entrepreneurial manager can occur only through the improvement of the quality of individual thought and the ideals, actions and conditions that arise as a consequence. You can have all the knowledge, education and skill in the world but it is the attitude component of management that gives the other competencies their fire-power. Character is the ability to set a goal and stick to the decision to achieve it, long after the enthusiasm with which that initial decision was made has cooled off. Your old ways of thinking will keep you locked in the land of the pure entrepreneur. The same is true for the professional manager. The master key to entrepreneurial management, therefore, is through self-development and attitude management.

WHICH LEARNING SENSE DO YOU REMEMBER WITH?

Another consideration in your learning is how you prefer to use your five senses – seeing, hearing, touching, tasting and smelling. These senses are controlled from the neo-cortex of your brain. You may be dominant in one learning style and may struggle with the others if you are not aware of your preferred style.

Visual learners tend to memorise things best through pictures, visual demonstrations, illustrations and diagrams by seeing it. Auditory learners tend to retain new information better and longer by talking of it and by listening to the spoken word.

Kinaesthetic learners (who use touching, tasting, smelling) tend to maximise their learning and retention by getting physically involved ('hands-on') in the learning process.

Why not consistently use all three learning styles to more easily retain and memorise knowledge?

For example, when you are reading a book do you:

A Visualise the key messages by exaggeration and by making associations in your mind?

B Read the book aloud to hear the sounds or just listen internally?

C Get actively involved by making notes in the margin, underlining key words, highlighting important sentences or making a mindmap?

You will probably find that you dominate in one style. Do the exercise below to identify your memory and learning styles. Then implement the improvement tips for each style.

HOW DO YOU LEARN AND MEMORISE INFORMATION RIGHT NOW?

For each of the questions below allocate points out of ten to the position that best represents how you do things right now? Then total up the ten answers on a pie chart to get a visual representation of your learning style and what areas to improve on.

QUESTIONS	VISUAL	AUDITORY	KINAESTHETIC
1 When you are in general conversation do you use phrases like:	'I see what you mean' 'I get the picture' 'That looks right' 'Keep your eye on the ball' 'Did you notice the difference?'	'I hear what you say' 'That rings a bell' 'That sounds right' 'Listen carefully' 'In one ear and out the other'	'I can handle that' 'That touched a nerve' 'That feels right' 'It's touch and go' 'Can I kick for touch on that?
2 When you are relaxing, do you prefer to:	Watch a video, go to a play or read a book	Listen to music, an audio tape, or the radio	Play a game, go for a walk or jog
3 When you meet people, do you tend to:	Remember faces and places (How they looked) more easily	Remember names and details of info. (What they said) more easily	Remember body language and actions (What they did) more easily

295

QUESTIONS	VISUAL	AUDITORY	KINAESTHETIC
			Do physical
4 When you are angry do you:	Go silent and visually withdraw	Get verbally loud…phones frequently	actions (clench fists, grit teeth)
5 If you were exploring a new city would you prefer to:	Read the map to get your bearings	Ask for help and be told your destinations	Be shown the way or explore for yourself
6 When praising your staff, would you tend to:	Send a memo or card … responding to dramatic images.	Just say 'Well Done'	Put a hand on their shoulder or give a pat on the back
7 At your meetings do you tend to:	Use illustrations (flipcharts), read or show things	Talk everything out (open forum)	Use samples, demos, get all hands-on
8 When 'reading' people, do you:	Mainly see their clothes and grooming	Mainly hear their tone and pace of talking	Mainly be aware of their body actions and movements
9 When learning which do you prefer:	Video	Audio	Physical activity … to touch, feel and smell products
10 In your creativity, innovation, problem-solving sessions, do you:	Create colourful 'appealing to the eye' results. It looks good.	Go for lots of talk and interruptions to get buy-in and involvement	Have paired and small group workshops with movement and demonstrations etc.

RE-THINKING INTELLIGENCE AND LEARNING

You must change all forms of limitation thinking with regard to your intelligence. You must put into perspective all forms of the 'IQ' way of thinking – you probably have too many comparisons with people and exam systems that tell you how smart you are or are not. This form of aptitude in exams can determine your future, if you let it. Unfortunately, these measures and this thinking permeate society.

IQ tests originated during World War II when more than two million Americans were sorted out for military enrolment through the first mass paper and pencil test. This form of thinking has pervaded the education, economic and social world for decades. In the last few years, however, there are major developments in the area of multiple intelligence.

Howard Gardiner in his influential book *Frames of Mind* (1983) refutes the IQ view. He proposed that there was not just one, monolithic kind of intelligence crucial to life success, but rather a spectrum of intelligences with seven key varieties. You need to become familiar with these seven intelligences and focus your learning on what you are naturally good at – your natural competencies. The seeds of your future successes in learning are already within you.

The first of Gardiner's intelligences is one of two standard academic kinds. The first is verbal or **linguistic intelligence** which includes your ability to express yourself, speak or write well and explain the 'Whys' and 'Wherefores' of what you do. It has dominated traditional education for centuries. If you are strong in this intelligence you probably enjoy language – talking, debating, conversation, listening to lectures, plays, radio, and poetry. You're probably good at explaining things. You even like the tussle of an argument or verbal joust and you are a fluent, expressive talker with a well-developed vocabulary.

The second intelligence is **mathematical/logical**. It's the systematic approach – it makes life easier and it ensures that you get a total grasp of the overall subject. If you are strong in this intelligence, you will like logical explanations of things. You will approach problem solving in a sensible orderly sequence. You will be good at calculating everything from budgets to planning journeys. You analyse assumptions and gather the evidence.

The third intelligence is **spatial/visual** capacity, often seen in artists and architects. You can find lots of ways to explore and learn a subject visually. A picture paints a thousand words. 'Seeing something once is better than learning it 1,000 times.' So use a colour poster or cartoon to make a point. A video uses sight and sound.

Do you engage in visual thinking? Do you naturally use your mind's eye? Do you sketch things to illustrate a point? Do you doodle? Do you use different colours? Have you a good sense of colour, of direction or space? Do you tend to see things that others do not see? If your answer is 'Yes', perhaps you are 'intelligent' in this area.

The fourth intelligence is **kinaesthetic**. This means getting physically involved in the learning. Some people just have to move about to learn better – it helps them to remember the experience much more clearly for later application. Role playing a situation can be a very effective practice ground for making a presentation. Writing is a physical activity and helps visual (reading) interpretation. Do you like to get your hands physically on problems to fix them?

Do you move well – at sport for instance? How's your physical timing? Is your attitude 'Get the experience rather than the theory?' Perhaps you use kinaesthetic Intelligence?

Musical intelligence, the fifth intelligence, is obviously displayed with the gifts of a Mozart. But you may be more musically intelligent than you appreciate! And it may be more useful than you think! Have you a good sense of rhythm or melody? Do you easily remember lyrics? Do you find yourself singing along to a song or an advertising jingle? Do you play a musical instrument? Are you a member of a choir? What is your music collection like?

Even if you are not intelligent in this area, music has now been proven to be an excellent way to help with relaxation and learning. Baroque music, for example, makes your body's rhythms, heartbeat and brainwave activity conducive to maximising retention, memory and learning. You can learn languages quicker by using appropriate music. Perhaps you have more musical intelligence than you think: Check it out.

Gardiner calls the final two intelligences 'the personal intelligences.' He defines **interpersonal intelligence** – the sixth intelligence – as the ability to understand other people. What motivates people? How do they work? How do you work co-operatively with them?

You may be a natural communicator because of your personality style. You may realise that discussing a point helps learning and retention. Do you find that you can 'click' quickly with new acquaintances? Put them at ease? Are sensitive to others moods and responses? Do you enjoy brainstorming, debating and the rough and tumble of teamwork? Influencing? Then you are probably intelligent in this area. Your challenge now is to capitalise on this strength.

Intrapersonal intelligence, the seventh intelligence, is the ability to truly understand yourself. 'Know thyself' said Socrates. It is the ability to tap into your inner self. Do you like peace and quiet and your own company more than others? Do you find yourself reminiscing, reflecting, even daydreaming regularly? Are you conscious of your 'inner eye?' Do you listen to your intuition? Many great geniuses such as Sigmund Freud and Albert Einstein have this intra-psychic capacity to get great insights. Intrapersonal intelligence is the key to self knowledge and wisdom and, if finely tuned, gives access to one's own feelings and the ability to discriminate and draw from them to guide behaviour.

You may like to do things quietly or independently of others. You may like reflecting, daydreaming, fantasising. You are happy with your inner voice and how you are. Then perhaps you are intelligent in this area. Check your hobbies and personal motivators to get an insight into this area.

Howard Gardiner's work continues today. There may be many other different varieties of intelligence. Interpersonal intelligence, for example, could be broken down into four distinct abilities – leadership, the ability to nurture relationships and retain friendships, the ability to resolve conflicts, and general social perceptiveness skills.

Everyone possesses all seven intelligences to some degree. But where are you strong and where are you weak? Can you strengthen the weak ones, because the most effective learning combines all seven. Score yourself on a scale of 1 to 7 on how you measure up on the intelligences (see Diagram). You should also appreciate that your colleagues and team mates all have these intelligences to a greater or lesser degree and are using them consciously or unconsciously to achieve their goals. Perhaps with this insight you can redeploy some of your key people so that they can capitalise on their natural tendencies.

You and I know many people who are apparently not well educated or intelligent by any IQ test methodology. But they are streetwise. They apply this street-wisdom to achieve their objectives.

I have conducted forms of intelligence testing and personality analyses on thousands of entrepreneurs and managers over 10 years. While many of them scored very low on the academic/IQ type of tests, their achievements in business were the opposite. Many would use their lack of formal education as a way of lulling you into thinking you had a 'soft touch' in negotiating business deals. The 'Ah sure, I left school at 13, I'm not as smart as you boys' remark was in direct contradiction to their achievements and to their grasp of reality.

RELATIVE STRENGTHS OF YOUR SEVEN INTELLIGENCES

Circle '7' on the intelligence that you feel is your strongest. Then circle where you rank yourself on the other intelligences compared to your strongest one. For example, if you feel that a particular intelligence is only half as strong as your strongest, circle '4' and so on.

YOUR SEVEN INTELLIGENCES

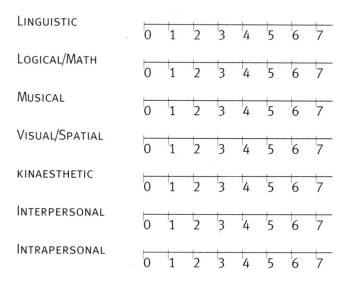

LINGUISTIC

0 1 2 3 4 5 6 7

LOGICAL/MATH

0 1 2 3 4 5 6 7

MUSICAL

0 1 2 3 4 5 6 7

VISUAL/SPATIAL

0 1 2 3 4 5 6 7

KINAESTHETIC

0 1 2 3 4 5 6 7

INTERPERSONAL

0 1 2 3 4 5 6 7

INTRAPERSONAL

0 1 2 3 4 5 6 7

Circle 7 on the intelligence in the list above that you feel is your strongest. Then circle where you rank yourself on the other intelligences compared with your strongest one. For example, if you feel a particular intelligence is only half as strong as your strongest, circle 3 or 4 and so on. Then join up all seven to see your areas of strength and areas for improvement

RELEARNING TO LEARN

Here are some points to help you rethink your learning abilities:

1 The 1:100 words formula

Among my circle of friends is Brian Tracy, who is one of the world's top professional speakers. For every one word that he uses in a speech or presentation to an audience at a seminar, on television or radio he has at least 100 others to back it up. He has such a rich vocabulary to call upon that he doesn't have to stick to his original script. He knows his subject instinctively and can present it with conviction, adapting it as necessary to many different audiences and listeners.

Your goal should be to develop the '1:100 words formula' in your key success area. The way you use words defines you as clearly as your fingerprints. Your words are the musicians in your own orchestra. Now conduct your orchestra. By working on, and regularly using techniques for learning, retention and memorising, you can achieve this kind of expertise.

Research studies prove that a strong command of words is directly linked to greater success. The Johnson O'Connor Research Foundation studies human aptitudes and their link to success. They report:

'An extensive knowledge of the exact meaning of English words accompanies outstanding success more than any other single characteristic.'

In hard times, the same studies show those laid off first tend to be low vocabulary people.

2 Read books by practitioners

Books can give you more than information. They can give you knowledge and wisdom and a condensed insight into the learning of one expert or a team of experts. 'A book is like a garden carried in your pocket', goes the old Chinese proverb.

Read books by practitioners. You can gain more in ten hours reading a book than if you spent 1,000 hours searching out the information and the subject matter yourself. The books which help you most are those which make you think the most.

The hardest way of learning is by easy reading. But a great book that comes from a great thinker is a 'ship of thought' deep-freighted with truth and beauty. Books do change things. They change your perceptions and behaviour. They alter expectations and aspirations. Books make their way around the world shaping the thinking and management of the future. Decide right now to read a minimum of 40 books on your subject within the next year. Read books by practitioners. This book is written by a practitioner. Unless you are interested in theory, limit your reading of books by academics. A good book has more wealth than a bank.

Ireland ranks 17th in the world in terms of book sales per capita, according to The Economist 'World in Figures' survey in 1998. We spend €48 per head, which is low compared to Sweden at €120, Germany at €102 and America at €72 per head. Britons ranked 14th at €54 per head.

3 Listen to audiotapes in your downtime

The development of the audio learning industry has been one of the greatest breakthroughs since the printing press. As time is your greatest asset, you can now listen to the best speakers and thinkers on management development while driving your car. You can listen to them on your home sound system or on a personal audiotape player as you go for a walk. If you drive your car more than 20,000 miles per year at an average of 40 mph, you are spending as much as six weeks working time sitting in your car. What an opportunity! Pack your car with audiotapes and play them over and over again.

Use the spaced repetition technique. Spaced repetition is how you learned your mathematical tables – you picked them up by repetition. It is also the technique used by advertisers to brainwash us into brand awareness. You should use it on yourself to indoctrinate yourself with the best thinking around. Many people make the mistake of playing an audiotape only once or twice. To gain from such a tape, play it ten, 20, or 50 times until you can almost recite the script verbatim.

4 Build a video library

Video learning brings your visual sense into play and means that you can kinaesthetically add to the retention process. You can get actively involved by writing and following instructions from the video. Adults spend so much time watching TV and videos these days that introducing this new way of learning into your team or organisation is often a better, faster, cheaper, easier, newer and different way to spread the Gospel of learning than the traditional classroom approach. Furthermore, build a library of videos on training and education and lease videos and learning materials out to staff.

Most managers have a self-limiting complex about their ability to train or teach. Video-assisted learning, however, bridges the gap perfectly. 'Let the video do the work' was how one business owner described it to me. With a 14' TV set in the canteen, for two hours after work, he achieved more free flowing discussion about 'How things could be improved around here' than in five years of boring staff meetings.

5 Do computer-based learning

Computer-based learning will revolutionise learning and development for the future as new technology and capabilities develop to translate languages and human interactions. You can now complete an MBA degree on the Internet. Interactive web-based workshops, reading rooms and clinics are easy ways to learn.

Intranet technology can help monitor learning and competency levels throughout your organisation on a regular basis.

6 Develop your learning awareness

Your learning capabilities have little to do with your level of IQ. Your lack of attention to learning, or your reluctance to learn, have a lot more to do with

the wrong conditioning, fear of exposing inadequacies, lack of proper methodology, and lack of awareness of your own brain power (how the conscious and
subconscious mind works).

Too many people lack awareness of the importance of learning in the infor-
mation-accelerated change environment of the 21st century.

The good news is that you can make up the ground very quickly over the
next couple of years by taking on board the ideas outlined in this chapter and
this book.

WHAT DO YOU NEED TO LEARN?

You should focus your learning on three critical areas as follows:

1 Personal learning
2 Professional learning
3 Business learning

1 PERSONAL LEARNING

If you have not done so before, you should focus all your initial efforts on
self-mastery. Self-mastery is getting control of the sequence of events in your
life. It is the central message of this book. Getting yourself organised is the first
step. Understand and get feedback on your system of personal mismanagement.

Have you put the emphasis on the wrong things? Are you confusing
activity with progress? Are you confusing efficiency with effectiveness? Are you
clear about the difference between the important and the urgent? Do you
confuse perfection with excellence? Are you prepared to delay gratification –
sacrifice short-term comforts for long term gain? What are your natural
unique abilities?

Self-discipline is at the heart of personal development. Self-discipline is
about integrity. Shakespeare said that integrity means 'to thine own self be
true'. Commitment and integrity go hand in hand. Nobody is born with self-
discipline – you learn it daily. Everything flows outwards from integrity – if
you haven't got it, your performance will suffer. Your sense of achievement will
suffer.

The simple measures always are: 'How far are you along the road to
reaching your goals' and 'What are your stress levels?' Are you enjoying the
journey? It is impossible to be self-disciplined if you have not set clearly
defined goals for your own development and motivation. Everything outlined

in this chapter is really about doing just this – reading, listening, viewing, and using all your intelligence and much, much more.

2 PROFESSIONAL DEVELOPMENT

Professional development means the development of your core competencies to maximise your career/management performance. This book is about professional development. You must understand first the principle of concentration. You must concentrate on the ideas, methodologies, models and strategies outlined here over an extended period of time. You must take the ideas, manipulate them, write the ideas and make them your own.

All the information you could possibly need to be a professional success is freely available in any good library, yet most people fail to avail of this facility. Worse still, they totally ignore it. Mark Twain said: 'The person who does not read a good book has no advantage over a person who can't read.' Be selective about the books that you buy or borrow. Avoid trivia. Spend your time and money only on books that will advance or enhance your business knowledge.

One of the great secrets of advancing your professional career is to do your current job outstandingly well. Do more than you get paid for because you will never get paid or rewarded more than you are today, unless you do more than you are doing today. In order to reap the interest or reward later you must first invest. This is a paradigm shift for many managers who think they are entitled to promotion or development for some totally wrong reason.

The people who can help you most to unlock the blocks to your professional development are your boss, your colleagues and the people who report to you. However, you must ask them in the right way, at the right time and for the right reasons: Then they will tell you all you need to know.

I believe that 50% of managers are misplaced and spend an enormous amount of time moaning and groaning, complaining and bitching about 'what's wrong around here.' They search for the answers in other people, other situations, and factors outside their control.

You, the entrepreneurial manager, must focus all your personal and professional development on the factors within your personal control and get to work on them over time using consistent, proven methodologies. Read this book five, ten, 20 times. Underline the key parts. Use a highlighter pen. Mind-map the whole book onto an A3 page. Be creative. Take action steps. Send me your page of creativity and I will send you a special audiotape for your efforts.

The only thing wrong with business education is its history and method.

I've met so many managers who feel that they need 'the letters' after their name to progress their career today. This is nonsense. What good is all that information if it is not used in practical ways on the job? Getting 'the letters' proves you can pass the exam. That's all! Application means you have learned. I honestly see no difference between high performing managers with MBA degrees and those without MBA degrees. Love learning for the ideas, knowledge and wisdom it gives you – not to massage your ego.

3 BUSINESS DEVELOPMENT

What else do you need to learn? You need to develop business acumen. You need to get an overall sense of what drives a business and what the great thinkers and leaders are doing. What are the trends and opportunities? Put yourself into situations where this is happening. Attend conferences and talk to managers. Use the standards of blue chip companies as a benchmark against which to judge other companies and organisations. Network. Listen and travel to other economies and cultures to see how that benchmark compares with the Irish situation.

I network with more than 500 consultants around the world and I often spend up to seven days in their company. I am convinced that Irish consultants and managers are far more capable, more competent and more productive than those anywhere else in the world, including America. However, the people who believe this the least are Irish consultants and managers themselves. As a nation we have yet to shock ourselves out of our insular 'small island' thinking.

I have worked closely with a very successful sales and marketing manager who played a key role in his senior management team. Yet he had no interest or grasp whatsoever of the financial measures in his business. He argued: 'That's what accountants are for.' I persuaded him to think like a self-employed person and to take the worldview of his business.

Interestingly, in the very same company the financial controller saw the pivotal role of sales management as being of no concern to him whatsoever. We changed his thinking on that also and within three months the financial controller was attending a Professional Sales Management course and the sales and marketing manager was attending a Finance for Non-Financial Managers programme. They became great buddies and teachers for each other and the contribution they made to the strategic management of the company was much more beneficial.

As the entrepreneurial manager, discipline yourself to step out of the rat-race and become a student of leadership and strategy, change and knowledge management, and global and local trends. You must then develop the ability to transfer learning points back to your operational work.

THE LEARNING ORGANISATION

As with every individual and with every great team, the organisation doesn't first start off great. It learns to be great. Your ability to learn faster than your competitors may be the only sustainable competitive advantage for your organisation in the 21st century. But how do you create the learning organisation?

You learn how to see the total picture of organisational development through 'systems-thinking', which is what Peter Senge calls it in his ground-breaking book *The Fifth Discipline*. Senge argues that you will also need to learn how to gain and sustain an advantage by practising in its sister disciplines of personal mastery, mental models, shared vision and team learning. Like excellence and success, these five component technologies are a journey.

Systems-thinking – the fifth discipline – helps us see patterns and learn to reinforce or change them effectively. Unfortunately, we usually focus on isolated parts of the system and wonder why our efforts to solve problems and perpetuate success fail. Systems-thinking also fuses the other four disciplines into a coherent whole that keeps them from turning into fads or gimmicks.

Systems-thinking is a discipline for seeing the total picture and a framework from which you can develop patterns and inter-relationships. Your ability to see the world as a whole is especially important in a time of accelerated change. This book is a Systems-thinking approach to entrepreneurial management. All the ideas, techniques and models blend together over time. This is why you need to read and re-read this book many times.

Systems-thinking is the cornerstone of the learning organisation, and has certain fundamental principles which you must understand:

1 CAUSE SOMETHING TO HAPPEN

The effects of today have their causes in the past. Most of us assume that cause and effect happen close together. Cause and effect may not be closely related in time and space. Today's problems come from yesterday's solutions. Most causes are thoughts and conditions are effects. Therefore the 'rot' in thinking has usually set in before the condition manifests it. So if you want something to happen, you have to cause it to happen. You have a choice. The effects are the consequences.

2 SYNCHRONISE YOUR RESOURCES

Your deployment of resources must be synchronised. You must apply the principles of good strategy to resource deployment. I had a client who invested an enormous amount of time, effort and money into the launch of a new 'pet' product over a 12 month period. He literally 'made it take off' but there were a couple of major downsides in other parts of his marketing and production departments. Quality suffered and the sales of other products decreased. At the end of two years he was critically reviewing the 'success' of his new product. Fortunately he was a learner and didn't make the same mistake in other launches.

3 DROP THE 'BIG HAMMER'

Victims of the 'Big Hammer' syndrome usually try harder without first thinking about trying easier. They see the task ahead and rush in to do it. Just trying harder, investing more energy and more resources in solving a familiar problem may be comforting but it is hardly systems-thinking. Systems-thinking means using creative thinking techniques and innovation. It's seeing the consequences of your choices ahead of time.

4 SOLVE YOUR OWN PROBLEM

A learning organisation learns to solve its own problems, over time. One of the disadvantages of outsourcing is that the internal people become inept at sorting out even the most basic of problems. I listened intently to Peter Senge speaking at a conference recently where he made two key points:

(i) all learning takes place in the context of solving work situations. Where there is no action, there's no learning and

(ii) the best learning is by practice. Sports teams practise all the time. Problems are opportunities to practise. Become a Practitioner.

5 GIVE IT TIME

Don't try to push the river. Learning takes time. Learning is more a gardening process than a production process. You must sow the seeds and allow them time to germinate and grow. You can change a physical resource, overnight. You can't change a culture or a thinking process that quickly.

6 SEE THE BIG PICTURE

Sometimes there are small well-focused leverage points that can produce big results. Unfortunately, it is hard for most people to see these leverage points in the system. Therefore, learning to see the overall structure rather than the events is a good start. See the big picture.

For instance, I was asked recently to sit in on a meeting with a CEO whose main strategic goal was to expand his company from €6m to €12m over the next five years (and €24m over ten years). As the meeting progressed I became aware that our managing consultant and the CEO were spending an enormous amount of time concentrating on two operational nitty-gritty problems. It became apparent to me, as an observer, that this was not systems-thinking. I shouted Stop! I then asked both parties to concentrate on the big picture.

7 THINK PROCESS NOT EVENT

Think in terms of a process, not an event. Sometimes people get caught up in the 'here and now.' They fail to see this dilemma or that problem as part of an overall system. At its simplest, a system has inputs, processes or activities, and outputs.

There is a tendency to become absorbed in sorting out local, smaller problems in the mistaken belief that they will make a big contribution to the achievement of the major purpose. This is flawed thinking. I pointed out to the CEO that even when he reaches his €24m target in ten years' time, he will still have many problems to sort out. Problems do not go away. You have to force yourself to stay in the systems-thinking mode.

Everyone in the organisation should operate in a systems-thinking mode. How does what I am doing right now implicate, add value or contribute to someone else's work at a higher level? How do my present actions contribute to the overall vision? To understand difficult managerial problems or to plot strategy, you will have to be aware of the whole system that generates the issues.

The story of the Three Blind Men who caught a different part of the elephant emphasises the point. Each sees it from a different perspective and a different aspect of the system. Each has great trouble seeing how their per-spective fits into the whole picture.

I repeat: Everyone in the organisation needs to continually ask: 'How does this work fit into the big picture? How can I add further value to it? Who do I need to tell or inform?' From the very simplest operation like answering the telephone, delivering a parcel, posting out correspondence, or closing a one million Euro contract, everyone needs to realise that systems-thinking is the key to the learning organisation.

Henry Ford put it well when he wrote: 'Hunches won't do. Intuition won't do. Simple rules of thumb won't do what it takes to achieve order and steady progress in a system'.

LEARNING ON PURPOSE

Learning is an investment. Learning is growing and changing. Learning on purpose means being proactive in your learning rather than learning informally or by trial and error. Don't let your early schooling experience block your potential. Conversely, don't believe formal education qualifications give you a magic right to be a peak performer. Learning is lifelong, not a once-off. Learn to enjoy the ultimate motivator, learning.

UNLEARN, LEARN, RELEARN

Here are some steps that you can take towards becoming a continuous learning machine for your role as an entrepreneurial manager.

1 Set up a Learning Room at home in which to build your learning library. Use it as a comfortable haven or learning retreat.
2 Learn memory and speed reading techniques to save time and maximise your learning enjoyment.
3 Join a learning network or association in which you take an active part. Attend the meetings and conferences. Learn to network.
4. Turn your car into a 'university on wheels' by listening to audio-tapes/CDs as you drive.
5 Split your reading 70/30 between progress reading (books etc) and maintenance reading (newspapers, magazines etc). Watch less television.
6 Help establish a Learning Resource Library in your company. Actively promote the idea.

PITOC™ LEARNING

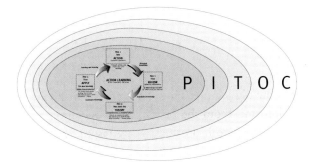

Learning to Learn about yourself, the intricacies of your relationships, the dynamics of the teams you are in, the organisation you work in and the magic of winning customer loyalty and customer retention is the journey of life and business. PITOC™ learning should help guide the way.

EPILOGUE

THE NEVER ENDING JOURNEY

You are in for a surprise. There's a crisis or two coming in your direction. Chances are it will happen within a year and there is a strong possibility that it will happen in the next three months. It could be that the market for your product will shrink or profits will nose-dive. Or you will lose your job. Or key staff will leave. Or a competitor will move in.

Or all of these.

If you have just come through a crisis, you are due another soon. Crisis Handling is the real test of your entrepreneurial management competencies. It's the test of your resource deployment, your communications ability, your strategic intentions, your ability to creatively solve problems, innovate, learn, and hold on to your customers.

But the crisis and the opportunity are just opposite sides of the same coin. Luck is when preparation meets opportunity. The only question is your state of preparedness. Some people bemoan the lack of opportunity. Others are overwhelmed by the potential all around them.

Whether you are a pure entrepreneur, or a professional manager, or an entrepreneurial manager, the ways to achievement are the same. Everything starts with your thinking. Your mind is the control centre of your attitudes, behaviours and actions.

Success is also dependent upon a clear focus over an extended period of time. Your ability to focus on key result areas combined with massive and immediate action will differentiate you from all others.

The realisation that you have more faults and failings than virtues and strengths and your ability to accept your worse mistakes as part of the journey forward, is glued together by the philosophy of entrepreneurial management.

This book is packed with proven systems-thinking formulae. I know they all work because I've personally worked them many times over. Your challenge is to integrate all the parts so that the whole is greater than the sum of the parts.

I have devised the PITOC™ Change Model to help you gain a sense of mastery and control over the ripple effects and increasing complexity of these five factors. The personal, interpersonal, team, organisation and customer variables can be applied to virtually every aspect of the entrepreneurial management journey.

I have devised the Six Link Chain of Resources and you can identify, maximise and deploy them to their best capacity. A resources-based view of the world is critical to creating personal and business advantage for the 21st century. It's a system to help you balance your personal and business journey. Keep a constant vigil on strengthening your weakest link. Don't fix the wrong problem. Fixing something very well that need not be fixed at all is the essence of folly.

The Competency Model is an umbrella formula to create personality and business advantage. You can define, measure and develop your own competencies. This is your first responsibility. And you can do likewise for your team and your business. It takes time and concentration. By itself, it can be the secret code that unlocks your own personality and professional potential and that of your business.

I have devised the LOQVE acronym so that you can maximise all of your personal communications. Everyone is in the communications business. How good you are at it is a test of your professionalism and your discipline to keep learning and risking. If you are not making mistakes in this area, you're probably not extending yourself enough. The balance between going forward at pace, your emotional make-up, and the complexity of human nature and communications guarantees foul-ups. Every organisation has a communications problem at some level. The real challenge is to reduce the detrimental impact to an absolute minimum and continuously work towards achieving profitable communications.

The STP Model gets the twin elements of emotional and analytical strategy flying in formation. Becoming a strategic thinker is like developing an acquired taste. Becoming a strategic planner is relatively easy. But one without the other is what separates the amateur from the professional. Your ability to think, plan and act strategically is the essence of entrepreneurial management. What's your purpose? Your aim? Why do you get up in the morning? Your sense of purpose is the central core of your being. The source of your energy and direction. The sad aspect of life is that most people have never tuned in to their real purpose. This systems-thinking strategy model could do it for you.

Mastering Outstanding Customer Care is the ultimate step to profit … all other basics being equal. There is always a vote going on (like a politician at election time) and the acid test is whether your customers buy enough of what you're selling, and often enough, to keep you in business.

An entrepreneurial manager learns Creativity and Innovation to glue every other element of this book together. Be careful that you are not just being creative because it feels right. Innovation is the critical implementation stage.

Learning *is* changing, *is* resource deployment, *is* a core competency, *is* profitable communication in action, *is* strategy implementation, *is* customer excellence, *is* innovation.

By now, having read this book from page to page or having dipped or dived into it, skimmed or scanned it, you will have realised that you will have to unlearn much of what you have already learned. Adapt or discard your old thinking models, techniques, frameworks, concepts and philosophies and replace them with new creations guided by the demands of 21st century management.

So you have a choice. Stay in your comfort zone where it's easy and safe or discipline yourself to implement these ideas.

'Everyone has a risk muscle. You keep it in shape by trying new things. If you don't, it atrophies and you are no longer able to take chances. How can you exercise your risk muscle today' are the profound words of Roger Von Oech.

You have already learned about thinking processes. In this book I have taken you to the threshold of turning thoughts into deeds. I can do no more. You are now responsible for your own improvement, personal mastery and business success.

Entrepreneurial management is a 21st century concept but it's only as good as your application. Good luck with it!

PLEASE COMMUNICATE WITH ME AND LET ME KNOW HOW YOU ARE PROGRESSING ON THIS JOURNEY.

Write to: John Butler, Managing Director, Century Management Limited, Century House, Newlands Business Park, Dublin 22, Ireland.
Tel: 353 1 4595950. Fax: 353 1 4595949.
e-mail: butlerj@century-management.ie
Website: www@century-management.ie

APPENDIX 1

CENTURY MANAGEMENT

Century Management work as strategic partners in a total, integrated, organisation-wide process to create personal and business advantage for clients.

• A team of professional consultants with a balance of theory, research, innovation, experience, practical know-how and application provides a distinctive capability that is vital to the long-term success of clients' relationships.

• The Century Management business management model and portfolio of solutions integrates the best local and international expertise to maximise and transform the potential of individuals, teams and organisations.

• The company operates within a dynamic, innovative, global network. Affiliation with the world's leading authorities on business development gives the company a global perspective and a 'leading edge' in expertise, competencies, services and resources.

• Century Management specialise in a strategic change management process which enables individuals and organisations (companies) to create business advantage. There are three phases to this process:

1 Research, examination and diagnostics.
2 Organisation development interventions.
3 Long-term follow-up and maintenance of the process.

• Century Management are leaders in the field and are focused on delivery of tangible results that better equip organisations and the people who work in them to meet the twin challenges of competition and change.

Preparing and implementing strategies to successfully adapt to competition and change requires people of the highest calibre. The Century Management team members understand the challenge of change. Their expertise is grounded in experience. They nurture that expertise. They are continually investing in their own knowledge base, refreshing, expanding and adding to their expertise to ensure they deliver solutions that are both relevant and current.

Their focus is on working in partnership at every level in organisations to help individuals and teams to solve their own problems and to equip people with the internal resources that will enable them to improve performances and apply world-class solutions.

APPENDIX 2

APPROACHES TO CREATING ADVANTAGE

There are many approaches to creating personal and business advantage. Picking an *appropriate* approach is critical to a successful outcome and requires professional advice and lots of listening and observing.

Here are just five approaches:

1 THE COMPETENCY APPROACH

The Competency Approach provides an integrated framework for skills, knowledge, behaviours, motivators and learned practices that create and sustain business advantage. It demonstrates how these competencies can be identified, learned, encouraged and improved to drive business performance.

Around the world, competencies are providing an internal, common framework for organisations to clearly understand what values, skills, behaviour benchmarks and learned practices are required to meet their strategic objectives. By defining the competencies, employees, managers and leaders can grasp what is required to reach new levels of excellence and performance.

Once the competencies are defined, competency-based tools and applications are designed and implemented. This is the measuring process. They can, in effect, be incorporated into training and development initiatives. But not just training – they can also be used for performance appraisals, selection, recruitment and interviewing, succession planning, career development, and even remuneration strategies.

2 THE ORGANISATION DEVELOPMENT APPROACH

The Organisation Development (OD) approach is a total, integrated, organisation wide process to create business advantage.

The challenge for most organisations is this:

'How do you bring together world class thinking, systems and strategy to improve individual team and organisational performance?'

The OD approach is very much a hands-on, close partnership type approach and involves every person throughout the organisation. It positions training as a strategic driver of performance improvement and helps to develop an *intangible* competitive advantage which is virtually impossible to copy.

The facts of life are that products can be easily copied and promotional campaigns can be mimicked (quickly). Even technological innovations can be readily imitated. Your only real source of sustainable competitive advantage is to unlock the potential of all your people. People, and people advantages, not only provide credible competitive advantage, they are also difficult to copy, or buy in.

3 Changing the Culture Approach

Every organisation, big or small, has a culture. Culture is your organisation's personality. It may be good, bad or indifferent. Because of its intangibility, it is often quite difficult to measure it and decide how to change it.

Changing your culture, however, may be the driving force for future growth and success. It may also be a catalyst for unlocking the intellectual potential resident in your organisation. Your organisation's culture is an intellectual property. It may well be *the* critical success factor just ready to be primed. Invariably, it's also the characteristic feature that your customers will appreciate most, it saves enormous costs and unlocks marvellous marketing and innovation strategies. How would you develop an Outstanding Customer Care Culture? Do you need a Sales culture? Should you develop an Entrepreneurial culture? An Innovation culture? A Team culture?

4 The Entrepreneurial Management Approach

Twenty-first century management demands a fresh approach to building strategic leadership. Like a financial investment, good deployment of your resources requires a well thought-out system. Like all investments, the down payment and the input are made first and the payback and results come later. The entrepreneurial management approach is outlined in some detail in this book.

5 The Learning Organisation Approach

The Learning Organisation approach should be considered at the outset as to how it might be incorporated in future initiatives. The objective of the learning organisation is to get every person in your organisation taking personal responsibility for their own learning and development and growth.

Traditionally, employees and executives have not been fully responsible for their own learning and development. They may have believed that this is the responsibility of their company. But everything has changed. Greater competition, globalisation and the technology revolution means that everybody must learn and relearn on an ongoing basis.

The installation, implementation and workings of learning libraries and creating the Learning Organisation philosophy is full of danger. It's important to get help and think it out clearly. As you know, third level education and out-sourcing of learning and development can be expensive. Why not develop your own University over time to meet some of your individual, team and organisational learning goals?

APPENDIX 3

JOHN BUTLER – SPEAKER

John Butler is a professional speaker who provides valuable lessons from more than 20 years of leadership and business building experience to each of his speaking, consulting and training assignments. He is a popular public speaker, successful author and business advisor.

His international connections with the world's most progressive consulting and training organisations and his avid readership in management, psychology, business development, personal and organisational development, and history mean that he is up-to-date on business development and management techniques.

However, he is first and foremost an entrepreneurial businessman and is constantly applying these ideas and techniques within his own business and within client organisations.

Careers in management, marketing, publishing, education, sales, distribution, training, consulting and organisational development are the bedrock of the wealth of experience and knowledge that he brings to each speaking, consulting, and organisational development engagement.

As a speaker he can tailor an after-dinner talk, a conference, a seminar, a training event, or motivational speech to your requirements in Strategic Planning, Sales Effectiveness, Management, Communication Skills, Employee and Customer Relations, Team Building and Personal Development – or indeed any of the topics outlined in this book.

His talks and seminars have given thousands of business people around the world the key to survival, profitability and growth.

APPENDIX 4

THE LEARNING RESOURCE CENTRE

The key to the future is your ability to adapt, change and learn. To help with your personal and business development, Century Management provide a wide range of learning materials in audio, book, CD, video, workbook and web-based technologies in the following areas:

TRAINING COURSES

Training courses on Personal Development, Management Effectiveness, Leadership, Professional Selling and Sales Management, Communications and Team Building, Time Management and Presentation Skills.

AUDIO LEARNING

Audio and CD learning allows you to learn, through the medium of your in-car audio player while you drive, or on your personal audio player while you take a walk. Our library of audio materials covers the following subjects:
The Science Of Self Confidence
How To Master Your Time
How Leaders Lead
The Psychology of Success
The Universal Laws of Success and Achievement
How to Raise Happy, Healthy, Self-confident Children
The Psychology of Achievement
The Psychology of Selling
High Performance Management
Master Strategies for Higher Achievement
Strategic Change Management for the 21st Century
Strategic Marketing and Sales Management for the 21st Century
The Excellent Executive and High Profit Strategies
Accelerated Learning Techniques

VIDEO LEARNING

Video learning adds another dimension to personal and professional learning and also provides opportunities for group work and for getting a learning organisation started.

Fully 80% of performance and effectiveness is attitudinal! Positive, optimistic, confident people get more done faster, and with fewer mistakes. The best companies have the best people, and top people. The best people are not born – they are trained.

Maximum Performance Video products available include:

The Seven Secrets of Success	Balancing Your Life
Your 1000% Formula	Making it a Great Life
The Race is On	The Business of Life
Five Steps to Goal Setting	Becoming an Unshakeable Optimist
Setting Your Priorities	The High Road to Achievement
Fast-Tracking Your Career	Negotiation Skills
Seven Steps to Mental Fitness	The Luck Factor
Five Keys to Personal Power	Thinking Big
Developing Personal Power	Character Counts
Programming Yourself for Success	Getting Mentors for Success
Leveraging Your Potential	Designing Your Future
Re-Engineering Your Life	Dream Big Dreams
Being a Better Communicator	The Critical Factors of Success
The Three C's of Success	Effective Decision-Making
Choice and Consequences	Stop Worrying, Start Living

This powerful, practical, video-based training (30 video series), gives you essential skills and techniques that you need to perform at your best. Each session is loaded with proven methods that you can apply immediately to improve the quality of your work and your relationships.

SUCCESSFUL SELLING

To compete in today's marketplace, salespeople must have the key skills necessary to get more and better appointments, make more effective presentations, and close more sales than the competition.

Now there is a powerful series of sales training that you can use and apply to get results fast. Successful selling video products available include:

The Winning Edge	Qualities of Top Negotiators
Prospecting Power	Building Customer Relationships
Mega-Credibility in Selling	Time Management for Sales People
Relationship Selling	Qualities of Top Sales People
How Buyers Buy	Complex Selling

Closing the Sale	Overcoming Price Resistance
Psychology of Selling	Selling Different People
Consultative Selling	Identify Needs, Present Solutions
Asking Your Way to Success	Negotiating The Sale
Personal Sales Planning	Customers for Life
The New Model of Selling	Value-added Selling
Strategic Selling	Selling on Non-Price Issues
Selling Made Simple	Telephone Sales
Service Excellence	Secrets of Success in Selling
Influencing Customers	Overcoming Objections

Each video programme in this series is based on many years of experience in training more than 500,000 salespeople in thousands of companies. Every programme teaches easy-to-use ideas and methods that enable salespeople to increase their sales from the first day.

You learn dozens of tested strategies that have been proven effective by the best salespeople in every industry.

Each programme comes with a complete workbook – a learning tool by itself.

LEARNING MATERIALS FOR LEADERS AND ACHIEVERS

The following two seminars have been devised and researched and presented 'live' in Ireland by Brian Tracy, one of the world's foremost authorities on professional development. Brian's experience and ability in presenting the most up-to-date and valuable material in an exciting, educational and entertaining fashion is central to the effectiveness of these two seminars.

1 HIGH PERFORMANCE LEADERSHIP

High Performance Leadership is a treasure chest of valuable management ideas, methods, and techniques drawn from years of practical experience and research.

2 KEY QUALITIES OF HIGH ACHIEVERS

Your ability to communicate with others will account for 85% of your success and happiness in life. In this exciting seminar you will learn about The Seven Secrets of influencing and the Ten Reasons why some people are more successful than others throughout their working lives.

There are 150 video minutes on each of these top quality seminars which can be used over and over again. You can learn visually, aurally and kinaesthetically. You will also receive a Leader's guide, workbooks and audio tapes to reinforce your video learning.

OTHER VIDEOS

The Great Communicator (2 Video Series)
How To Talk – Secrets of The Great Communicators
How to Listen and Double Your Influence with Others

Superior Customer Service (2 Video Series)
Making Customers Happy
Keeping Customers Coming Back

Sales Management (2 Video Series)
Motivating Sales People
Coaching and Counselling For Sales People

Creating Successful Presentations (2 Video Series)
How to Prepare a Powerful Presentation
How to Deliver a Winning Presentation

Strategic Marketing and Sales Management for the 21st Century
The Excellent Executive and High Profit Strategies
High Performance Leadership (Strategic Change Management for the 21st Century).

Executive Excellence

Since 1984, Executive Excellence has provided business leaders and managers around the world with the best and latest thinking on leadership development, managerial effectiveness, and organisational productivity. Each monthly issue is filled with insights and answers from top business executives, trainers, and consultants – information you won't find in any other publication.

'Excellent! This is one of the finest leadership publications I have seen in the field.'
Tom Peters, co-author of *In Search of Excellence*

'Executive Excellence is the best executive advisory newsletter anywhere in the world – it's just a matter of time before a lot more people find that out.'
Ken Blanchard, co-author of *The One-Minute Manager*

CONTRIBUTING AUTHORS INCLUDE
Stephen R Covey
Ken Blanchard
Tom Peters
Michael Hammer
Peter Senge
Charles Handy
Michael Dell
Warren Bennis
Brian Tracy
Denis Waitley
Peter Drucker
Bill Gates

Irish contributors include: Tony O'Reilly, Feargal Quinn, Gillian Bowler, Chris Horn, Patrick Campbell, and John Butler.

For more information on Executive Excellence, contact: Century Management at 01 4595950